Tax and Benefit Policies in the Enlarged Europe:
Assessing the Impact with Microsimulation Models

Public Policy and Social Welfare
A Series Edited by the European Centre

European Centre Vienna

Volume 35

A substantive part of this book is based on research within the project "Improving the Capacity and Usability of EUROMOD (I-CUE)", Research Infrastructures Design Study 011859.

Orsolya Lelkes / Holly Sutherland (Eds.)

Tax and Benefit Policies in the Enlarged Europe: Assessing the Impact with Microsimulation Models

ASHGATE

Published by

Ashgate Publishing Limited
Wey Court East
Union Road
Farnham
Surrey GU9 7PT
United Kingdom

Ashgate Publishing Company
Suite 420
101 Cherry Street
Burlington, VT 05401-4405
USA

Copy-editing and DTP: Willem Stamatiou
European Centre for Social Welfare Policy and Research
Berggasse 17, 1090 Vienna, Austria

British Library Cataloguing-in-Publication Data. A catalogue record for this book is available from the British Library.

ISBN 978-0-7546-7848-9

Printed by Facultas Verlags- und Buchhandels AG, Vienna, Austria

Acknowledgements

The editors gratefully acknowledge funding for the project "Improving the Capacity and Usability of EUROMOD (I-CUE)" under Framework Programme 6 of the European Commission and the support of the Project Officer, Maria Theofilatou.

We are also indebted to the members of the project partner teams, who all contributed to the construction of the model or its enlargement to the New Member States: Michael Fuchs, Mattia Makovec (European Centre, Vienna), Lenin Ageer, Francesco Figari, Horacio Levy, Alari Paulus, Francesca Zantomio (University of Essex), Christine Lietz (IHS, Vienna), Daniela Mantovani (University of Modena), Andres Võrk (PRAXIS, Tallinn), Silja Kralik (Ministry of Environment, Tallinn), Péter Szivós, Péter Hegedűs (TÁRKI, Budapest), Leszek Morawski (University of Warsaw), Boris Majcen, Mitja Čok and Nataša Kump (IER, Ljubljana).

We also acknowledge the contributions of the other project collaborators, and the members of the EUROMOD User Group established as part of I-CUE: Olivier Bargain, Tim Callan, André Decoster, Herwig Immervoll, Manos Matsaganis, Cathal O'Donoghue, Lucinda Platt, Panos Tsakloglou, Gerlinde Verbist and Heikki Viitamäki.

We also thank the speakers and participants from 25 countries present at the final conference on 3-4 April 2008 in Vienna for a most lively and useful exchange of ideas.

Finally, the editors are grateful for the administrative support received from many people during the project, in particular Eileen Clucas, Lucy Brown and Judith Schreiber.

List of Abbreviations

Country codes

BE	Belgium
BG	Bulgaria
CZ	Czech Republic
DK	Denmark
DE	Germany
EE	Estonia
IE	Ireland
EL	Greece
ES	Spain
FR	France
IT	Italy
CY	Cyprus
LV	Latvia
LT	Lithuania
LU	Luxembourg
HU	Hungary
MT	Malta
NL	Netherlands
AT	Austria
PL	Poland
PT	Portugal
RO	Romania
SI	Slovenia
SK	Slovakia
FI	Finland
SE	Sweden
UK	United Kingdom

Country groupings

EU10: New member states of the EU as from 1 May 2004: CY, CZ, EE, HU, LT, LV, MT, PL, SK, SI

EU15: EU member states prior to the accession of ten candidate countries on 1 May 2004: AT, BE, DK, ES, FI, FR, DE, EL, IE, IT, LU, NL, PT, SE, UK

EU25: EU15 plus EU10

EU27: European Union as of 1 January 2007: see the list of country codes above.

Contents

List of Figures, Tables and Boxes

Figures

Chapter 1: Introduction

Chapter 2: An Enlarged Role for Tax-benefit Models

Chapter 3: Euromod: Past, Present and Future

Chapter 4: The Effects of Taxes and Benefits on Income Distribution in the Enlarged EU

Chapter 5: Flat Tax Reform in Eastern Europe

Chapter 6: Alternative Tax-benefit Strategies to Support Children in Poland

Chapter 7: Reforming Child Allowances in Lithuania

Tables

Chapter 2: An Enlarged Role for Tax-benefit Models

Chapter 4: The Effects of Taxes and Benefits on Income Distribution in the Enlarged EU

Chapter 5: Flat Tax Reform in Eastern Europe

Chapter 6: Alternative Tax-benefit Strategies to Support Children in Poland

Chapter 7: Reforming Child Allowances in Lithuania

Chapter 8: Tax-Free Income vs. In-Work Tax Allowances

Chapter 9: Looking Ahead: What Priorities for Tax-benefit Modelling?

Boxes

Chapter 1

Introduction

Orsolya Lelkes / Holly Sutherland

Ten countries joined the European Union in 2004 and two more in 2007. They added greatly to the diversity of the enlarged EU in terms of income levels, as illustrated in Figure 1.1. GDP per capita in Bulgaria and Romania in 2007 was only 40-45% of the EU-27 average, even when adjusted for price differences across countries. Slovenia and Cyprus had the highest level of incomes of the New Member States, close to the EU average and the level of Greece. The relative levels of GDP, however, are not the whole story. Households are directly affected by the level and changes of their incomes, rather than that of the GDP, which has other components as well (e.g. profits).[1]

The new counties also exhibit different structures of income distribution and pose a variety of economic and social challenges, and brought with them into the EU a wide range of approaches to systems of welfare and redistribution in the form of taxes and benefits (see Ward et al., 2009). On the one hand the ten New Member States from Eastern Europe (Bulgaria, Czech Republic, Estonia, Hungary, Latvia, Lithuania, Poland, Romania, Slovakia and Slovenia) have a common history of transition from communist systems, while at the same time having distinctive histories both before and since the transition. On the other hand, the two countries of Southern Europe (Malta and Cyprus) share more with the Southern countries from the "old" EU-15 while, arguably, being at an earlier stage of development. Such an enlargement poses great challenges both for the analysis of European redistributive systems and for policy development. It also offers opportunities. Not only is there now simply a much larger field of study, but also opportunities are

1 The GDP (Gross Domestic Product) is the sum of the income generated by production in the country in a given period. It can also be measured as total expenditures for final goods and services.

opening up for improving analytical capacity within countries and policy learning between countries.

Figure 1.1: GDP per capita in Purchasing Power Standards (PPS), 2007 (EU-27 = 100)

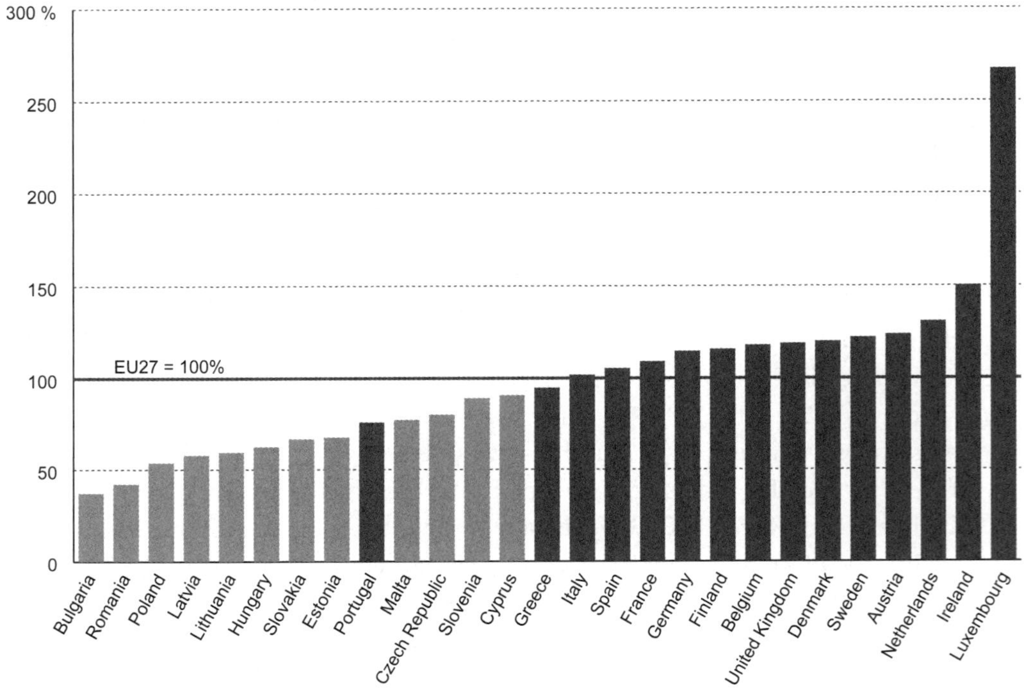

Source: Eurostat on-line database. Date of access: 20 April 2009.

At the same time, the use of comparative evidence based on tax-benefit microsimulation models is in its infancy. While microsimulation models are increasingly used for assessing the impact of policies in individual countries (e.g. Gupta and Harding 2007, Zaidi et al. 2009) and across EU-15 countries using EUROMOD (e.g. Bargain 2006, and see the EUROMOD Working Paper series[2]), there has been only sporadic evidence so far on the New Member States.[3] Such evidence rarely takes a comparative perspective. Nevertheless, with respect to EUROMOD, Atkinson et al. (2002) have emphasized its key role in monitoring and forecasting, and highlighted its virtue in separating the impact of policy parameters from those of changing external

2 http://www.iser.essex.ac.uk/research/euromod/working-papers

3 Exceptions include: Redmond (1999), Bargain, Morawski et al. (2007), Galuščak and Pavel (2007), Benedek and Lelkes (2008), Čok, Majcen et al. (2008).

circumstances (p. 183). Recently, the EU Task-Force on Child Poverty and Child Well-Being has encouraged Member States and the Commission "to invest *inter alia* in microsimulation models to support the assessment of the impact of policy measures on the situation of children and their families" (2008: 134, emphasis in original).

Against this background this book offers an assessment of income redistribution in the New Member States in the context of Europe as a whole. It explores the impact of tax and benefit systems on individuals' incomes and work incentives. The special feature of Part II of this book is that the chapters are based on analysis using the multi-country tax-benefit microsimulation model EUROMOD, which has been extended to cover four of the New Member States, thus allowing a systematic and consistent comparison of these countries (Estonia, Hungary, Poland and Slovenia) with those of the "old" EU-15.

This enlargement of EUROMOD was made possible by a European Commission financed project on "Improving the Capacity and Usability of EUROMOD (I-CUE)". As well as beginning the extension of EUROMOD by adding four new countries, the I-CUE project also paved the way for the addition of the remaining countries by networking with teams of experts, some of whom were already developing their own national tax-benefit models.

Part III of this book presents analysis based on national tax-benefit models for Cyprus and Lithuania, presenting innovative studies that demonstrate the power of the microsimulation method for policy analysis.

An unplanned but most welcome outcome of the I-CUE project was that after identifying potential national experts in the New Member States and explaining the benefits of EUROMOD, some of them have started to develop their own tax-benefit models, tailored to their specific national needs. Similarly, joint work often resulted in research output on issues that had not yet been explored in the specific country. The longer experience of tax-benefit microsimulation in most of the EU-15 could provide important insights for researchers from the New Member States. On the other hand, the policy approaches from the transition countries can have salience in the old Europe. Examples include the lessons drawn from experience of flat tax schemes and the greater reliance on indirect taxes.

One by-product of the I-CUE collaboration was the promotion of the use of tax-benefit microsimulation for informing policy-making and policy-relevant research. This involved serious consideration of the barriers that prevent policy-makers making the most of the tools and expertise on offer. How to maximize the return on the cost of developing models in the future is one of the issues considered in the final chapter of this book.

Another achievement involved making some first steps in using such methods for policy learning across countries. Among the many "What if" questions that EUROMOD can address are those involving implementing common policies in several countries or the import of alternative policies from other countries to test their impact. Here, for example, we explore the introduction of three alternative flat tax schemes in Estonia, Hungary and Slovenia. An experiment with respect to child support in Poland is also implemented, where the potential introduction of Austrian, French and UK systems of support is assessed.

This book is based on selected papers from the final conference of the I-CUE project, which brought together the developers of EUROMOD who had re-designed the model to manage 27 different tax-benefit systems, the teams from Estonia, Hungary, Poland and Slovenia as well as collaborators from many of the other New Member States and from the EU-15 and current and potential users of the enlarged EUROMOD from academia and international organizations, including the European Commission.

As editors we would like to thank all who took part and especially the contributors to this book. An outline of the remaining chapters follows.

The title of *Chapter 2* is a play on words. Tony Atkinson argues for the enlargement of EUROMOD to cover all Member States of the EU. Small countries, such as Luxembourg or Malta, cannot be left out, as EU policies are not simply concerned with the aggregate performance of the whole Union, but also the situation country by country. In addition, he argues for the enlargement of the role for tax-benefit models in the European Union, but also globally. Aggregate level analysis, showing e.g. the relationship between social spending and poverty rates at the country level reveals little of the actual relationship between these two. Instead, a micro-level analysis is necessary at the country level, exploring the most effective way to achieve a target (e.g. to lower the incidence of poverty among individuals). Similarly, the study of GDP or GDP growth alone is inadequate as firstly, there is a conceptual difference between GDP and household incomes, and secondly it is the *distribution* of income of households that also determines living standards. GDP may be on the rise, while household incomes stagnate. Some household incomes may rise but others fall in relative or absolute terms. Thus, "micro-analysis of policy has to move up on the agenda", argues Atkinson.

Models are also necessary for global policy-making, including such key areas as climate change and the financing of development.

In *Chapter 3,* Holly Sutherland provides an overview of EUROMOD, including phases of past development, the recent I-CUE project, which provided the background for this book, and also future possibilities. She openly demonstrates the barriers of use, including the ease of use, data access difficulties, and the policy scope limitations. Luckily, she does not stop there, but discusses the work done to ease these barriers. Sutherland discusses the potential and feasible extentions of the model, including indirect taxes, estimates of non-cash benefits, or a framework for modelling labour supply behaviour. In response to Tony Atkinson's call for global models, she illustrates how EUROMOD can encourage the building of "spin-off" models outside Europe.

Chapter 4 provides an analyis on the redistributive effects of taxes and benefits in the EU-15 countries, extended with 4 East-European countries, including Estonia, Hungary, Poland and Slovenia. The chapter presents how taxes and benefits alter income inequality, poverty, including the aggregate impact of all policies, but also the effect by instrument. The results do not imply that the role of government is larger in *all* former planned economies, and highlight that Estonia has the lowest level of both (direct) taxes and benefits as a share of household disposable income. In Hungary and Poland, inequality of market incomes is one of the highest in the EU. The tax burden on households (more accurately: the share of [direct] personal taxes and [employee] social insurance contributions within the disposable income of households) is relatively high, although below the level of that in Belgium, Denmark and Sweden. Contrary to what could be expected of a flat tax system, the equalizing effect of personal income taxes in Estonia is *not smaller* than that in other countries with more graduated tax schedules.

Flat tax is the theme of *Chapter 5,* comparing the effects of alternative scenarios in Estonia, Hungary and Slovenia. The three alternative proposals considered have actually occurred in the political discussions in one or the other of these countries and in the Estonian case has already been approved by the Parliament to take effect in a few years time. In this chapter, the distributional and fiscal effects of these reforms are estimated, both for the country of "origin" and the other two if the corresponding proposal was "imported". The results suggest that the introduction of flat tax schemes in Hungary and Slovenia would result in a substantial increase of the tax burden for the bottom deciles as well as in increases in inequality and poverty. The impact on inequality and poverty is relative modest in Estonia which already has a functioning flat tax system and a relatively high level of inequality. However, the flat tax schemes would reduce (the median level of) effective marginal tax rates by 4-9% in all three countries which might result in increasing tax compliance or labour market participation. The chapter also demonstrates that the detailed design of such schemes largely determines their impact on fiscal revenues and on the redistribution of individuals' incomes.

Chapter 6 focuses on the problem of child poverty in Poland, by comparing alternative tax-benefit strategies. Child poverty was as high as 29% in Poland in 2005, which is much above elderly poverty in the country (7%), or average child poverty in the EU (19%). Levy, Morawski and Myck assess a recent reform, including a shift from a mainly means-tested family allowance system to one where a non-refundable child tax credit is introduced. Based on analysis with EUROMOD, the authors conclude that the poverty reduction would have been larger if the French or the UK systems were introduced. The Austrian system would have also been more efficient, as it would have resulted in a greater reduction in the poverty gap, with a similar reduction of the poverty rate. For these comparisons, the authors establish budget-neutral solutions, while importing the specific instruments of the countries mentioned, thus providing an insight into fiscally feasible alternative scenarios. This chapter provides an illustration of a policy analysis, which could have been carried out before the implementation of the reform. As the authors note, unfortunately no impact assessment in fact preceded the implementation of the reform.

Similarly, a child support reform is assessed in *Chapter 7*, this time referring to Lithuania. The direction of the changes is similar to those in Poland, representing a shift from means-tested programmes towards a universal system. By using a newly constructed national microsimulation model, Salanauskaite and Verbist are able to test the interaction between new policies and existing cash support programmes (as a result of rising family support some families may lose eligibility to social assistance), and to model the impact of the various stages of the reform's implementation. One of the main findings is that whereas households with three or more children mostly benefit in the first stage of the reform, single-parent households achieve equivalent income gains only upon the full implementation of the reform.

Chapter 8 is also based on a newly constructed national model, for Cyprus. It explores whether replacing in-work "benefits" (tax credits and allowances) linked to family dependants with (revenue equivalent) tax-free labour income can increase the overall labour market participation. In particular, such an increase is expected among older workers without children. Thus, the motivation of the authors, Pashardes and Polycarpou is to describe the heterogeneity of the tax reform effects on the labour market decisions of individuals. The analysis is based on a model where the labour market participation of individuals is influenced by their personal and family characteristics as well as their incomes. Among the demographic variables, the age and the number of children are also considered. This chapter thus mainly focuses on labour market participation decisions rather than distributional effects.

The concluding chapter is "Looking ahead", by exploring future priorities for tax-benefit modelling. What could users and builders of such models do in order to maximize the contribution of these tools towards a more evidence-based policy process? Immervoll and Lelkes set the scene by arguing that although tax-benefit models are powerful and informative, and quickly spreading across the New Member States, they are under-used. Rather than blaming the general political culture and discourse, they focus on the role of users and model constructors. The thematic and geographical scope of the models tends to reflect policy demand. In addition to routine tasks, however, model design needs to anticipate new directions of policy debates. For this, the model architecture needs to be open and flexible to link the models to other analytical tools. Currently, an under-used area with major potentials is the interface between micro- and macro-economic policy analyses. It is particularly so during the current period of economic downturn, where there is a lack of forward-looking assessments of the impact of macroeconomic changes on poverty and income distribution. The authors show how microsimulation models could be utilized for this. Accessibility to the infrastructure and to the underlying datasets are vital for the use of the models, and an institutional "home" of the model may enhance not only access and exchange, but also its long-term survival. Finally, the generous dissemination of the results may play a key role in raising interest and thus creating a greater demand for evidence. In this vein, we publish and recommend this book as well.

References

Atkinson, A.B. / Cantillon, B. / Marlier, E. / Nolan, B. (2002) *Social Indicators: the EU and Social Inclusion*. Oxford: Oxford University Press.

Bargain, O. (ed.) (2006) *Microsimulation in Action: Policy Analysis in Europe using EUROMOD*. Research in Labor Economics Series, Vol. 25. Elsevier, North-Holland.

Bargain, O. / Morawski, L. / Myck, M. / Socha, M. (2007) 'As SIMPL As That: Introducing a Tax-Benefit Microsimulation Model for Poland', IZA Discussion Papers 2988, Institute for the Study of Labor (IZA).

Benedek, D. / Lelkes, O. (2008) 'Assessment of Income Redistribution and a Hypothetical Flat Tax Reform in Hungary', *Journal of Applied Economic Sciences* 3 (5): 173-186.

Čok, M. / Majcen, B. / Verbic, M. / Kosak, M. (2008) 'Use of Simulation Models for the Tax Reform in Slovenia', *Financial Theory and Practice* 32 (1): 29-43.

EU Task-Force on Child Poverty and Child Well-Being (2008) *Child Poverty and Child Well-being in the EU. Current Status and Way Forward*. Brussels: European Commission, Directorate-General for Employment, Social Affairs and Equal Opportunities, Social Protection Committee.

Galuščák, K. / Pavel, J. (2007) 'Unemployment and Inactivity Traps in the Czech Republic: Incentive Effects of Policies', Working Papers 2007/9, Czech National Bank, Research Department.

Gupta A. / Harding A. (eds.) (2007) *Modelling Our Future: Population Ageing, Health and Aged Care*. International Symposia in Economic Theory and Econometrics, Vol. 16. Elsevier.

Joint Report on Social Protection and Social Inclusion (2009) http://ec.europa.eu/employment_social/spsi/joint_reports_en.htm#2009

Redmond, G. (1999) 'Incomes, Incentives and the Growth of Means-testing in Hungary, *Fiscal Studies* 20 (1): 77-99.

Ward, T. / Lelkes, O. / Sutherland, H. / Tóth, I.G. (eds.) (2009, forthcoming) *European Inequalities. Social Inclusion and Income Distribution in the European Union*. Budapest: TARKI.

Zaidi, A. / Harding, A. / Williamson, P. (eds.) (2009, forthcoming) *New Frontiers in Microsimulation Modelling*. Aldershot: Ashgate.

Annex A: EUROMOD: version and data sources

Chapters 4, 5 use EUROMOD *version D25*, while Chapter 6 uses *version D15*.

EUROMOD relies on *micro-data* from 17 different sources for 19 countries. These are the European Community Household Panel (ECHP) User Data Base and the EU Statistics on Income and Living Conditions (EU-SILC) made available by Eurostat (under contract EU-SILC/2007/03); the Austrian version of the ECHP made available by the Interdisciplinary Centre for Comparative Research in the Social Sciences; the Panel Survey on Belgian Households (PSBH) made available by the University of Liège and the University of Antwerp; the Estonian Household Budget Survey (HBS) made available by Statistics Estonia; the Income Distribution Survey made available by Statistics Finland; the Enquête sur les Budgets Familiaux (EBF) made available by INSEE; the public use version of the German Socio Economic Panel Study (GSOEP) made available by the German Institute for Economic Research (DIW), Berlin; the Greek Household Budget Survey (HBS) made available by the National Statistical Service of Greece; the Living in Ireland Survey made available by the Economic and Social Research Institute; the Survey of Household Income and Wealth (SHIW95) made available by the Bank of Italy; the Socio-Economic Panel for Luxembourg (PSELL-2) made available by CEPS/INSTEAD; the Sociaal-economisch panelonderzoek (SEP) made available by Statistics Netherlands through the mediation of the Netherlands Organisation for Scientific Research – Scientific Statistical Agency; the Polish Household Budget Survey (HBS) made available by the Polish Central Statistical Office; a sub-sample of the Population Census merged with Personal income tax database, Pension database and Social transfers database, made available by the Statistical Office of Slovenia; the Income Distribution Survey made available by Statistics Sweden; and the Family Expenditure Survey (FES), made available by the UK Office for National Statistics (ONS) through the Data Archive. Material from the FES is Crown Copyright and is used by permission. Neither the ONS nor the Data Archive bear any responsibility for the analysis or interpretation of the data reported here. An equivalent disclaimer applies for all other data sources and their respective providers cited in this acknowledgement.

Annex B: Tax-benefit systems and input datasets in EUROMOD (version D25)

Country		Policy year	Input dataset source	Date of collection	Reference time period for incomes
BE	Belgium	2003	Panel Survey on Belgian Households	2002	annual 2001
DK	Denmark	2001	European Community Household Panel	1995	annual 1994
DE	Germany	2003	German Socio-Economic Panel Study	2002	annual 2001
EE	Estonia	2005	Household Budget Survey	2005	monthly 2005
EL	Greece	2005	Household Budget Survey	2004/5	monthly 2004
ES	Spain	2005	EU-SILC	2005	annual 2004
FR	France	2001	Enquête sur les Budgets Familiaux	2000/1	annual 2000/1
IE	Ireland	2001	Living in Ireland Survey	1994	monthly 1994
IT	Italy	2001	Survey of Households Income and Wealth	1996	annual 1995
LU	Luxembourg	2003	Socio-Economic Panel (PSELL-2)	2001	annual 2000
HU	Hungary	2005	EU-SILC	2005	annual 2004
NL	Netherlands	2003	Sociaal-economisch panelonderzoek	2000	annual 1999
AT	Austria	2003	Austrian version of European Community Household Panel	1998 + 1999	annual 1998
PL	Poland	2005	Household Budget Survey	2005	monthly 2005
PT	Portugal	2003	European Community Household Panel	2001	annual 2000
SI	Slovenia	2005	A sub-sample of Population Census merged with administrative records	2005 (2002)	annual 2004
SE	Sweden	2001	Income distribution survey	2001	annual 2001
FI	Finland	2003	Income distribution survey	2001	annual 2001
UK	UK	2003	Family Expenditure Survey	2000/1	monthly 2000/1

Annex C: Categorization of income components

1) Public pensions

AUSTRIA
- civil servant's pension
- early retirement pension
- invalidity pension
- old age pension
- other old age related schemes or benefits
- survivor pension
- minimum pension
- minimum pension for civil servants
- child bonus for pensioners
- child bonus for civil service pensioners

BELGIUM
- anticipated pension
- retirement pension
- survivor pension
- other public pension income

DENMARK
- disability pension - basic amount plus supplement
- disability pension - special supplement plus incapacity amount
- disability pension - invalidity amount plus 'augmentation' plus special benefit for disabled with substantial earnings
- old age pension
- supplementary pension
- survivor pension

FINLAND
- gross state pension income
- national (basic) pension increases

FRANCE
- invalidity pension
- pension benefits
- alimony
- minimum old age pension

GERMANY
- own old age pension
- miners' own pension
- civil servants' own pension
- farmers' own pension
- accident own pension
- widow/orphan old-age pension
- miners' widow/orphan pension
- civil servants' widow/orphan pension
- farmers' widow/orphan pension
- accident widow/orphan pension

GREECE
- invalidity pension
- old age pension
- orphans' pension
- widows' benefits
- old age pension
- social solidarity benefit

IRELAND
- deserted wife contributory benefits
- occupational injury contributory pension
- old age contributory benefits
- orphan's contributory benefits retirement contributory benefits
- survivor's contributory benefits

ITALY
- public and private sector contributory old age pensions (including supplements)
- public and private sector contributory disability pensions (including supplements)
- public and private sector contributory survivor's pensions (including supplements)
- foreign pension
- other pension

LUXEMBOURG
- disability pension
- early retirement pension
- pension received from employment in private sector
- pension received from employment in public sector
- private sector reversion pension
- public sector reversion pension
- orphan allowance

NETHERLANDS
- state pension
- survivors' benefit

PORTUGAL
- old-age insurance
- survivors related benefits
- invalidity pension

SPAIN
- old-age (insurance an early retirement)
- survivors (widows or orphans, insurance)
- old age pension supplement
- widow pension supplement

SWEDEN
- non-taxable pension
- other taxable pensions

UK
- retirement pension
- state earnings related pension
- widow benefit

ESTONIA
- disability pension
- old age pension
- old age pension abroad
- survivors' pension

HUNGARY
- disability benefits
- old age income
- survivor benefits

POLAND
- disability insurance pension
- old age pension
- old age pension abroad
- orphan pension
- widow pension
- nursing supplement

SLOVENIA
- disability/invalidity pension
- old age pension
- survivors' pension

2) Means-tested benefits

AUSTRIA
- unemployment benefit
- housing benefits
- maternity allowance supplement
- provincial family bonus
- social assistance

BELGIUM
- in work benefit
- income support
- income support for the elderly

DENMARK
- housing benefits
- day care subsidy
- housing allowance
- social assistance

FINLAND
- pensioners housing benefit
- housing benefits
- home child care benefit
- social assistance benefit

FRANCE
- refundable tax credit
- disabled benefit
- young children allowance
- education related family benefits
- family complement
- housing benefits
- lone parent benefit
- minimum income

GERMANY
- housing benefits
- federal child raising benefit
- direct housing support
- provincial child raising benefit
- social assistance

GREECE
- unemployment assistance for old workers
- social pension
- housing benefit

IRELAND
- housing benefits
- blind persons non-contributory benefits
- carer's non-contributory benefits
- short term disabled contributory benefits
- long term disabled non-contributory benefits
- deserted wives non-contributory benefits
- family income supplement
- home carers tax credit
- long term invalidity contributory benefits
- lone parent non-contributory benefits
- long term unemployed non-contributory benefits
- old age non-contributory benefits
- pre-retirement non-contributory benefits
- short term unemployed non-contributory benefits
- social minimum non-contributory benefits
- widow's non-contributory benefits

ITALY
- education benefits
- housing benefits
- social assistance – national, regional, provincial, municipal, local health centre, other local public administrations and private institutions
- social pension
- family allowances for single persons with no children
- family allowances for single person with children
- family allowances for couples with no children
- family allowances for couples with children

LUXEMBOURG
- education allowance
- housing benefit
- maternity allowance
- social assistance

NETHERLANDS
- general social assistance, self-employed
- general social assistance for families with children
- general social assistance for families without children
- social assistance benefit for unemployed aged 50-64 and disabled unemployed younger than 64 with children
- social assistance benefit for unemployed aged 50-64 and disabled unemployed younger than 64 without children
- housing benefits

PORTUGAL
- social assistance
- child benefits
- income supplement to ensure minimum income
- old-age social pension

SPAIN
- housing benefit
- social assistance benefits
- child social assistance
- old age social assistance
- unemployed social assistance for those with family charges

SWEDEN
- housing benefits
- housing benefit supplement for pensioners
- social assistance

UK
- housing benefits
- council tax benefit
- child tax credit
- income support
- working tax credit (in work benefit)

ESTONIA
- social assistance benefit

HUNGARY
- regular child protection benefit
- social assistance

POLAND
- parental leave allowance
- benefit for unemployed lone parents
- child benefit
- child birth benefit
- supplement for education of disabled child
- supplement for starting school year
- supplement for lone parent (main benefit)

- nursing benefit
- housing benefits
- permanent social assistance
- temporary social assistance

SLOVENIA
- education benefits
- unemployment assistance benefit
- child benefit
- housing benefit
- social assistance

---

3) Non means-tested benefits

AUSTRIA
- caring benefit
- child care benefit
- sickness benefit
- unemployment payment
- maternity benefit (2 months after birth of child)
- education benefits
- child tax credit
- child benefit
- universal long term maternity benefit
- other lump-sum benefits

BELGIUM
- career break allocation
- allocation for handicapped persons
- learning allocation
- long sickness allocation
- professional illness allocation and work accident allocation
- allocation from a special funds
- short-sickness allocation
- unemployment benefit
- young unemployed allocation
- education benefits
- housing benefits
- maternity benefits
- child benefit
- child birth benefit

DENMARK
- education benefits
- maternity benefits
- sickness benefit
- unemployment benefit
- child benefits
- early retirement benefit
- family allowance

FINLAND
- education benefits
- maternity benefits
- basic unemployment benefit
- earnings related unemployment benefit
- labour market support
- military injury compensation
- sickness benefit
- training subsidy for unemployed
- child benefit
- lone parent child benefit
- other lump-sum benefits

FRANCE
- education benefits
- maternity benefits
- social benefit for dependent elderly adults
- social benefit for special education
- social benefit for parental education
- social benefit for lone parents
- social assistance
- war pension
- help for child guard
- unemployment compensation
- pre-retirement pension
- family allowance
- other lump-sum benefits

GERMANY
- education benefits
- unemployment payment
- unemployment benefit
- retraining payment
- old age transition payment
- war victims' own pension
- war victims' widow/orphan pension
- nursing home insurance payment received
- child benefit
- post natal benefit for non-earning mothers
- other lump-sum benefits

GREECE
- education benefits
- maternity benefits
- disability benefit (non-contributory)
- sickness benefits
- unemployment benefit
- child benefit
- large family child benefit
- many–children child benefit
- other family benefits
- third child benefit

IRELAND
- education benefits
- back to work allowance
- constant attendance allowance
- other welfare allowances
- unemployability supplement
- child benefit
- occupational injury disablement contributory benefits
- maternity contributory benefits
- unemployed contributory benefits
- other lump-sum benefits

ITALY
- maternity benefits
- social insurance unemployment compensation
- social insurance unemployment mobility benefit
- disability non contributory pension
- war pension
- other lump-sum benefits

LUXEMBOURG
- education benefits
- maternity benefits
- care benefits
- other public benefits
- permanent accident benefit
- unemployment benefit
- child benefit (family benefit)
- prenatal-, postnatal-, and child birth allowance
- handicapped child benefit
- annual beginning of school allowance
- seriously disabled persons
- other lump-sum benefits

NETHERLANDS
- education benefits
- maternity benefits
- basic disability benefit
- disability insurance (former civil servants)
- disability insurance

- unemployment benefit for civil servants
- unemployment benefit
- sickness insurance
- child benefit
- other lump-sum benefits

PORTUGAL
- education benefits
- housing benefits
- maternity benefits
- unemployment related benefits
- sickness benefits
- family benefits
- other lump-sum benefits

SPAIN
- education benefits
- maternity benefits
- unemployment insurance benefit
- sickness and invalidity benefits
- family benefits
- working mother tax credit
- other lump-sum benefits

SWEDEN
- sickness benefits
- unemployment benefits
- other tax free educational benefits
- other tax-free benefits
- university grants
- study grants for high school
- child benefits
- parental allowance
- other lump-sum benefits

UK
- education benefits
- maternity benefits
- attendance allowance
- disability living allowance
- disability working allowance
- invalid care allowance
- incapacity benefit
- industrial injury
- mobility allowance
- severe disablement allowance
- statutory sick pay
- training allowance
- war pension
- job seekers allowance
- child benefit
- pensioner's annual heating allowance
- other lump-sum benefits

ESTONIA
- sickness benefit
- scholarships and grants
- parental benefit
- parental benefit abroad
- maternity benefit
- other social assistance
- unemployment insurance benefit
- unemployment retraining benefit
- unemployment assistance benefit
- childcare allowance
- large family parent allowance
- single parent child allowance
- child allowance
- child allowance abroad

- childbirth allowance
- school allowance
- large family allowance

HUNGARY
- child care fee
- sickness benefits
- maternity allowance
- unemployment benefits
- child raising support
- child care allowance
- family allowance
- maternity grant

POLAND
- education benefits
- maternity benefits
- social pension
- early retirement pension
- unemployment benefit
- nursing allowance
- other child benefits
- other benefits

SLOVENIA
- compensation for lost income due to care for child with special needs
- attendance supplement
- childcare supplement
- maternity payments
- unemployment insurance benefit
- holiday bonus for pensioners
- disability supplement
- birth grant
- large family supplement
- parental allowance

Part I:
Setting the Scene

Chapter 2

An Enlarged Role for Tax-benefit Models

Sir Anthony B. Atkinson

1 Enlargement of the European Union and EUROMOD

My title is a play on words: I am using the word "enlarged" with two different meanings. The first meaning refers to "enlargement" in the sense of the EU. The aim of I-CUE has been to start the process of expanding EUROMOD to cover new Member States, and considerable progress has been made in this direction. Although not the main focus of this chapter, such an extension is important for both scientific and political reasons.

One of the great strengths of the first version of EUROMOD was that, before May 2004, the model covered the entire European Union (EU). It was an EU-wide tax-benefit model. Since then, the EU has moved on, and EUROMOD has to move too. These moves are costly. The fact that tax and social security policy remain the responsibility of Member States means that the model has, for each new member, to add a new and different policy module. But even in the unlikely event of all policy being harmonized across the EU, the addition of a new Member State would require that EUROMOD be enlarged. It is the essence of EUROMOD that it predicts the impact of tax and benefit changes on real people. It is not concerned with "representative households", or with "average production workers". EUROMOD uses data on actual households, with their actual wages and employment. For each new Member State, EUROMOD has to add data from household surveys or administrative sources. This process may become easier now that EU-SILC is established, but there remain costs of assimilation. (EU-SILC, the European Survey of Income and Living Conditions, provides a common framework for the collection of data, covering all Member States, Iceland and Norway. The first priority is the delivery of comparable cross-sectional data.)

The enlargement of EUROMOD achieved by the I-CUE project has led me to speculate about the cost function for the construction of tax-benefit models. Most of us working in this field began by constructing a national model, and we know just how large an investment this represents. Taking this as the standard, can we say anything about the cost of a multi-country model, like EUROMOD, and how that cost changes with the number of countries covered? It seems possible that a 2-country model costs more than two separate national models, the costs of coordination outweighing the benefits from the exchange of good practice. But a 3-country model does not cost 150% of a 2-country model. The average cost curve is declining, as economies of scale begin to operate. The key question is whether the average cost will continue to decline, or whether there comes a point at which there are diseconomies of scale. It does indeed seem likely, on a priori grounds, that the rising coordination costs will begin to outweigh the economies of scale. (There is a parallel here with the old-style theories of the optimum scale of the firm.)

If costs begin to rise with the number of countries covered, then this has evident implications for the funding of research in this area. A hidden cost of enlargement may be that it will cost disproportionately more to continue funding an EU-wide tax-benefit model. This may lead cost-conscious decision-makers to question whether 100% coverage of Member States is necessary. Surely, we can obtain reasonable results for the EU as a whole without covering all 27 countries? We should concentrate on the largest countries. After all, the overall growth rate of EU national income is not materially affected by what happens in Luxembourg or Malta. In the same way, when measuring the risk of poverty, and how it is affected by policy changes, would it not be wiser to concentrate research resources on a model covering the big countries, and not seek to cover the small countries that do not make much difference to the total figures?

In my view, the continued coverage of all Member States by EUROMOD is essential. While aggregate statistics may not be materially affected by any failure to cover Luxembourg or Malta, use of tax-benefit models is particularly focused on minorities, such as those at risk of poverty and social exclusion. The consequence of omitting a country can only be assessed by reference to the number of people in that country who form part of this minority. (The same, I should add, would apply to any failure to cover the non-household population.) For analytical purposes, it may be quite reasonable to take a subgroup of Member States, but for purposes of evaluation one needs 100% coverage.

Put another way, our concerns are not just with the aggregate performance, but also with how far the experience is being shared by all countries. There is a parallel here with the Millennium Development Goals (MDG). As has been stressed by the UN, it is not good enough for, say, the objective on poverty reduction to be satisfied by reductions in China and India. We have to take account of the fact that conditions in Africa have not improved. The MDG targets are in fact set country by country (or region by region). Analogously, the achievement of the EU social goals requires that all Member States show improvement. (The same applies also to GDP growth; we would be concerned if some countries were growing at a much lower rate, even if they were small.) We need therefore to be able to analyse the impact on people in all Member States. EUROMOD cannot be simply a large-country model.

2 A brief (personal) history of tax-benefit models

The second interpretation of my title – and the one that forms the subject of the rest of this chapter – concerns the enlargement of the role for tax-benefit models. How can we ensure that these models are more widely used and appreciated? There is a contrast between the rapid innovation in terms of developing models and their relatively slow adoption. Tax-benefit modelling has not yet really had sufficient impact on policy analysis outside the academic sphere. We need to look at ways of enlarging the role of tax-benefit models and raising their prominence in policy discussion.

To place this in context, I should like to go back in time. The year 1968 has been a lot in the newspapers, at least in Britain. At the time when the Beatles were in India, and students in Paris were ripping up cobblestones, I was more prosaically spending my evenings cycling from the centre of Cambridge to the Institute of Astronomy, a couple of miles outside Cambridge. I used to cycle out there because at that time they had probably the most powerful computer in Britain, an IBM 360. I wanted access to this powerful computer because I had been given some tabulations of income tax data by the Inland Revenue, which I was using to simulate the effect of tax changes and social security changes for the book that I was writing on *Poverty in Britain and the Reform of Social Security* (Atkinson, 1969). I was using tabulated data but even these were stretching the calculating resources. So I cycled out every evening, punched cards, put them in and then came back the next day to collect the results of an overnight run. (Often, of course, I would discover that I had made a punching error, so it was a slow process.) In this way, I simulated the distributional impact of a basic income and flat tax, and other social security reforms.

In the 40 years since then, much has changed in the field of tax-benefit modelling. First of all, we now have access to micro-data, not just tabulations. Access is in part a technical matter. The bulk of the 1968 storage media, and the special nature of software, did not facilitate information transfer. But access is very much a political matter. The reason why in 1968 we did not have micro-data was not purely technical. The UK Government had in fact released micro-data a few years previously in the form of raw Family Expenditure Survey (FES) questionnaires to Peter Townsend and Brian Abel-Smith. They wrote a very powerful book, one of the classics of British social science, *The Poor of the Poorest* (1965), demonstrating that in post-war Britain there remained poverty, particularly child poverty. This had a major political impact. The political fallout was undoubtedly one of the reasons why the government became unwilling to release micro-data on households. It was not until some 10 years later, around 1978, that Mervyn King, Nick Stern and I were able to secure the release of the FES data for use on the research programme that we ran at University College London and London School of Economics. It was incidentally this research programme that initiated the tax-benefit model, TAXMOD (see Atkinson and Sutherland, 1988), that is the ancestor of the UK part of EUROMOD.

The second important change has been in computer technology. The difference between the IBM 360 and the IBM PC is quite phenomenal. The two dimensions of speed and portability have transformed the role of tax-benefit models. This can have unexpected consequences, as Holly Sutherland and I discovered in 1988. In that year the UK had a major tax-cutting budget; indeed it was the single most important budget of the Conservative government: among other changes the top rate of income tax was cut from 60% to 40%. Holly and I were asked by the Opposition Shadow Cabinet to analyse the tax changes as they were announced in the Budget Speech by the Chancellor of the Exchequer. So we brought a PC to the Shadow Cabinet Room in the House of Commons, and sat typing in the new parameters as the Chancellor was speaking. The tradition is that the details are never pre-announced but the Leader of the Opposition has to respond as soon as the Chancellor stops speaking. Very fortunately there was an interruption in the House of Commons – they had to throw out an MP who was causing a disruption – of about 20 minutes, the time it took to run our tax-benefit programme showing for a sample of some 6,000 households the effects of the budget being announced. This meant that there could be an immediate response by the Opposition. In particular, a young man was able to issue a press release saying that half of the gains would go to the top 10% and only 10% of the gains would go to the bottom 50%. That young man is, at the time of writing, the Prime Minister of Britain. During the 10 years he was himself Chancellor of the Exchequer, the top rate did not move from 40%.

Immediacy is one of the qualities made possible by today's computing technology, and this transforms the potential role of tax-benefit models. It is not just in parliamentary situations. In any situation where people are discussing tax reforms, it is very valuable to be able to have quick feedback. An idea is suggested, but reactions will depend very much on the quantitative implications. What are the revenue costs? What are the implications for different types of family? With high speed models, it is possible for these to be used in the course of such a discussion. Moreover, this has the great merit of forcing people to be precise about the proposal under consideration. One of the lessons from tax-benefit modelling is the importance of writing down the precise details. Such a discipline often reveals latent ambiguities. For example, it is proposed that child benefit is taxed under income tax. Does this mean that it is taxed as the income of the parent, and if so, which one? Does it depend on who receives the child benefit?

A rapid simulation can also reveal unintended consequences. On a number of occasions, certainly in the British context and probably too in other countries, politicians have said "until you ran it through the programme, I had no idea that that could happen". For example, the government can cut taxes but cause some people to be worse off. (This can happen where there are tax reliefs that are worth more than the taxable income.) Policy-makers tend to think in terms of certain household types. These may be reasonably representative of the population as a whole, but fail to pick up special sets of circumstances where the policy may have a quite unintended effect. At the time of the poll tax, another famous moment in British tax history, a Minister said "they did not tell us that could happen".

Given the great potential of tax-benefit simulation, we naively thought in the late 1980s that everyone would start to use this wonderful tool. But in fact there was a very slow rate of adoption. We had, for various reasons, underestimated the barriers:

- First of all, one tends to underestimate the skills required to use the models. It is difficult for people to understand what was going on. This applies not just to non-economists but also to economists working in other fields.
- Secondly, care needs to be used in interpreting the results. Even if you say that it is pure arithmetic, this can be quite hard to grasp. And equally perhaps, on the other hand, the results may be used too enthusiastically without fully appreciating the qualifications.
- Thirdly, at least in the UK context, the public debate about policy options has not advanced. The coverage of things like the annual Budget is very much still in terms of human interest. Four or five families are interviewed on the impact of the Budget on them personally.

I believe that what is needed is to build a community of people who can make effective use of tax-benefit models in the policy arena. This has to involve civil servants, politicians, social partners, NGOs, and journalists. One should not lose sight of the impact of different levels of government; there is increasing interest in local and regional governments in this kind of work. But it probably begins with the academic community, and this is one of the great successes of the EUROMOD project. As this book and the conference it developed from demonstrate, there is a real community.

3 Enlarging the role of tax-benefit modelling in the European Union

I want now to look to the future, first considering how the role of tax-benefit modelling can be enlarged within the EU, and specifically within the Social Inclusion Process. Here too the historical context is important. A decade ago we were not talking about the EU Social Inclusion Process. Ten years ago there was little sign of progress towards a European Social Policy. It was the 2000 Lisbon agenda that led to a step change.

Post-Lisbon, the EU has a set of explicit objectives, symbolized by the structural indicators summarized in Table 2.1. One of the characteristics of the EU that has been rather understated is that, while most national governments do not really state explicitly their objectives, the EU has to be explicit about a lot of things. One feature of this political organization is that it is the mere act of coming together, and forming common policies, that has actually forced us to be much more explicit about our goals. From Table 2.1, we can see that these goals include growth, employment, environmental sustainability, *and* social inclusion. It is here that tax-benefit models have an immediate point of entry. Number 9 on the list of EU structural indicators demonstrates the policy salience of the numbers that we are discussing.

Table 2.1: EU structural indicators

1	GDP per capita	Growth
2	Labour productivity	Growth
3	Employment rate 15-64	Employment
4	Employment rate of older workers	Employment
5	**Youth educational attainment**	**Social Inclusion**
6	R+D spending % GDP	
7	Comparative price levels	
8	Investment spending % GDP	
9	**At-risk-of-poverty rate after social transfers**	**Social Inclusion**
10	**Long-term Unemployment rate**	**Social Inclusion**
11	**Regional cohesion**	**Social Inclusion**
12	Greenhouse gas emissions	Environmental
13	Energy consumption	Environmental
14	Inland freight volume	Environmental

What is more, it is this part of the EU scorecard that gives rise to concern. Despite the general gloom about the Lisbon Agenda, in fact, in terms of the growth rate, the gap with the US has been narrowed, partly because the US has not been growing quite so fast, but also the European growth rates for a number of years in this decade have picked up. Ten years ago, US GDP per capita was 160% of that in EU-27; in 2008 it was 150%. There has been a quite large rise in the EU employment rate. A student of mine, Dirk-Jan Omtzigt, has just written a thesis about early retirement and shown that the previous trend towards early retirement reversed in virtually all Member States around the mid 1990s. Overall, there has been a 5 percentage point increase in the employment rate (for all workers) over the last 10 years. If you want to raise employment, which is the stated objective, then Europe has made substantial progress over the last years.

But where the EU does not seem to have made substantial progress concerns the risk of poverty. The proportion of EU-15 citizens living in households below 60% of the national median was, according to the Eurostat estimates, 16% in 1996 and 16% ten years later. There had been no progress.

Now these estimates are a blend of EU-SILC and results from the earlier European Community Household Panel, and the join is not easy to make. Suppose therefore that one looks at the national studies of relative poverty for two of the largest Member States. Broadly there is some improvement in the UK: from a high level, there has been some reduction in the poverty rates there. But there has been a worsening in Germany, alongside the rise in income inequality (these are the estimates from the Socio-Economic Panel made by DIW – see Grabka and Frick, 2008). In broad terms, we lost on Germany what we gained on the UK. So this is one structural indicator where no progress has been made.

This leads naturally to the analysis of policy alternatives. Such analysis is often conducted in aggregate terms. One diagram that has much currency in European debate is that showing for different countries the risk of poverty rate against social spending as a proportion of GDP. Typically the diagrams show that countries which spend more have lower poverty rates. From this, some policy-makers draw the conclusion that spending more is an answer. As far as policy is concerned, I believe that they are right. However, I do not believe that the aggregate diagram tells us anything about the trade-off. If it did, then the conclusion would be rather pessimistic. The line linking poverty to spending does indeed slope down, but the slope is not very steep. The typical diagram for EU countries has a slope of one for one. So if you want to reduce the 16% overall EU poverty rate to 10%, which is not an unreasonable target, then the apparent cost is 6% of national income. That seems prohibitively expensive.

The aggregate cross-country analysis is the wrong way to do it. The right way is to study each country and examine at the micro-level the relationship between particular fiscal instruments (taxes and spending) and the incidence of poverty among individual households. You need a tax-benefit model. And for European policy-making, you need a tax-benefit model that covers all Member States. Such models allow you to work back from the target to the most effective way by which it can be achieved.

Another way of putting this is to say that we need to integrate micro-level policy-making more closely with macro-economic policy-making. Tax-benefit modelling should be relevant not only to social policy experts but also to macro-economists. But how can this be brought about? I believe that the time is ripe. There is at present a groundswell of dissatisfaction stemming from the fact that improved economic performance (up to 2007) has not been translated into an apparent improvement in individual living standards. As noted above, the EU has narrowed the gap with the US, but people are not basically feeling better off.

We have therefore to investigate the macro-micro linkage. There are two main reasons why aggregate growth is not being translated into improved living standards. The first is the difference between gross national income and the total disposable income of households; the second is the way in which the total income of households is distributed. Considering the first of these, we can see that it is quite possible for gross national income to be growing but for household disposable income to be stagnating. (In both cases, I am referring to amounts at constant prices, although we should note that changes in relative prices are an element that needs to enter the story.) There are substantial sums that form part of national income but which do not enter the disposable income of households. These include the retained profits of the company sector, the net income of non-profit institutions serving households (NPISH), and taxes and other receipts by government. In the opposite direction, there are important elements of household disposable income that have no counterpart in the national accounts, such as transfers received from the government and the NPISH sector (for example, private pensions), and interest paid by the government on the national debt.

In part, the difference between national income and household income is the result of statistical conventions. Where companies retain profits, this may generate capital gains. But conventionally household income is defined to exclude net accrued capital gains. Similarly, the money going into private pension funds, and the implied rise in the value of future pensions is not reflected in the measure of household income. In part, however, there are sources of divergence that cannot be explained away. Where the government is running a budget surplus, there is a net withdrawal from the household sector: the government is raising more in taxes than it is returning in government spending. And even where the government budget is balanced, households may not value the services of government output (such as education or police protection) at an amount equal to their cost.

The second part of the story concerns the distribution of aggregate income. The mean income of households may be rising, but this may not be experienced by the majority of citizens. This is illustrated in Figure 2.1, which comes from the US Census Bureau. In most income distributions, the median is less than the mean. In the US in 1967 the median was 90% of the mean. But since 1967 there has been a dramatic fall in the ratio of median to mean household income. I use the word "dramatic" to highlight both the extent of the fall and the long duration. Nor is the US alone. Grabka and Frick (2008) show that in West Germany the median fell from 91% of the mean in 1992 to 86% in 2006.

Figure 2.1: Median household gross income as % mean gross household income 1967-2006

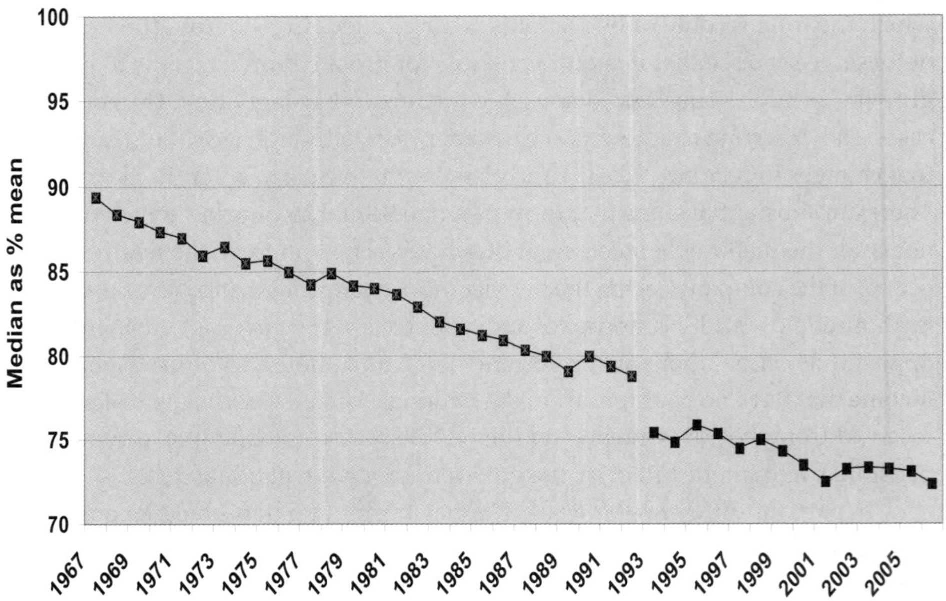

Source: US Census Bureau, 2007, Table A.1

My purpose in highlighting these two departures (household income from national income, and median from mean) is to suggest one way of attracting the attention of macro-economists to tax-benefit modelling. If they wish to address the malaise of the electorate, then they need to supplement the standard national income measures. At the very least, they need to consider the median and not just the mean. That sounds to me a quite reasonable thing to do in a democratic country. It does not sound as threatening as using a Gini coefficient or some other distributional index. Looking at the median is just taking a different central indicator. But this in turn means they have to examine distributional data and the impact of policy on the distribution of income. Micro-analysis of policy has to move up the agenda and the next question is what the effect of policy reform is going to be, requiring the capacity to make policy simulations. So that is my Machiavellian suggestion as to how to raise the salience of tax-benefit modelling.

4 Enlarging the role of tax-benefit modelling globally

EUROMOD can play an enlarged role in another sense. The experience of constructing a multi-country tax-benefit model can be taken outside the European context. It can be applied to countries in the course of development; it can be applied at a global level to public policy issues with a world compass.

The social situation of the EU is undoubtedly very different from that of developing countries, but the EU experience is not without relevance (see Atkinson and Marlier, 2008). In the specific case of tax-benefit models such as EUROMOD, it is true that they have been mainly constructed for developed countries, but the techniques can be applied to developing countries, as the EUROMOD team has demonstrated. The South African tax-benefit model, SAMOD, started from the framework provided by EUROMOD. This model allows the simulation of the effect that different policy reforms would have both on national revenue and expenditure and on individual household budgets, and thus the impact on poverty and inequality.[1] A similar approach is being adopted for certain Latin American countries. At UNU-WIDER, a series of models have been built for African countries, including Uganda.[2] These innovations reflect the swing back to interest in issues of fiscal policy and social policy. The capacity to carry out tax-benefit simulations will become of growing importance as anti-poverty programmes are increasingly funded by domestic fiscal sources.

There is similarly a need to be able to analyse global taxes. In the past few years, I have been involved in two groups studying the prospects for global taxes to finance development, the need for such financing being brought home by the shortfall with respect to the sums believed to be needed to secure the Millennium Development Goals. These led, among other things, to the tax on airline tickets introduced by Presidents Chirac and Lula. One of the issues that struck me in all this discussion was that nobody ever asked who was going to pay these taxes. Questions as to the incidence and the distributional effects of these taxes were never raised. For example, if we assume that the airline ticket tax is fully passed on to consumers, what is the distributional impact? Which countries bear most of the burden? Who within these countries is worse off? Can we follow the input-output effects of this tax? These are all questions that go beyond EUROMOD's capacity

1 See Wilkinson (2009).

2 http://models.wider.unu.edu/africa_web/

in its present form, but illustrate that fiscal issues of this kind are highly relevant to current global policy-making.

These questions enlarge the scope analytically as well as geographically. We need to consider in an integrated way the whole range of policy challenges. Take the debate about policy regarding climate change, which seems to me to be very naturally linked to distributional issues. I was at a recent conference organized by the Anglo-German Foundation, where there were papers on carbon taxes and papers about future social policy design. These two projects needed to be married. There was a wide agreement that we have to take measures on climate change that involve reduction in current standards of living. But there seemed to be little discussion of whose standard of living. This is in part an intertemporal issue. Is the cost to be borne now or in future decades? Here we need models of a different type from EUROMOD. But it also concerns the distribution between those alive at one date. Within the population covered by EUROMOD, there are many different generations, from those of my mother in law, born in 1915, to my own generation born some 30 years later, to my children born in the 1970s, to my grandchildren born in the 21st century. Different forms of energy taxes, and different forms of compensation, have different implications for these generations. Here tax-benefit models of the EUROMOD type, with additional indirect tax elements, can illuminate this global policy issue.

5 Summary of main points

An important strength of the first EUROMOD is that it covered (at the time) all Member States. Even if the costs of model construction rise with Enlargement, this should remain the ambition; it should not become just a large-Member State model.

- Looking back to 1968 allows one to see the extent of progress in tax-benefit modelling; this progress reflects the transformations brought about by access to household micro-data and by powerful, portable computers.
- But much remains to be done to enlarge the use made of tax-benefit modelling in policy-making; to do this one has to build a community of "supporters".

- The need for tax-benefit modelling in EU policy-making is highlighted by the failure to reduce the risk of poverty. The EU Structural Indicators for growth and employment both show progress, but the EU risk of poverty rate remains stubbornly at 16%.
- Anti-poverty policy cannot be designed at an aggregate level; what is needed is an analysis at the level of individual policy instruments and their impact on individual households. A tax-benefit model allows one to work back from the objective to the policy measures that would lead to its achievement.
- We need to integrate tax-benefit models into the mainstream of economic policy-making. I have suggested that an opening is provided by the current concern that macro-economic performance is not leading to perceived improvements in living standards. A focus on median household incomes would force policy-makers to consider the micro-level indicators.
- The role of tax-benefit modelling can be extended geographically and to address new issues. Model construction methods have lessons for developing countries, and models are necessary to understand global policy-making in such key areas as climate change and the financing of development.

References

Abel-Smith, B./Townsend, P. (1965) *The Poor and the Poorest*. London: Bell.

Atkinson, A. B. (1969) *Poverty in Britain and the Reform of Social Security*. Cambridge: Cambridge University Press.

Atkinson, A. B./Marlier, E. (*forthcoming*) 'Analysing and Measuring Social Inclusion in a Global Context', Chapter 2 in UN publication on *Creating an Inclusive Society: Practical Strategies to Promote Social Inclusion* (tentative title).

Atkinson, A. B./Sutherland, H. (eds.) (1988) *Tax-Benefit Models*. STICERD, LSE.

Grabka, M./Frick, J. R. (2008) 'The Shrinking German Middle Class', *DIW Weekly Report*, 26 May 2008.

Sutherland, H. et al. (2008) 'Improving the Capacity and Usability of Euromod – Final Report', Euromod Working Paper EM4/08.

U.S. Census Bureau (2007) *Income, Poverty and Health Insurance Coverage in the United States: 2006*. Washington, D.C.: U.S. Department of Commerce.

Wilkinson, K. (2009) 'Adapting EUROMOD for Use in A Developing Country – The Case of South Africa and SAMOD', EUROMOD Working Paper EM5/09.

Chapter 3

EUROMOD: Past, Present and Future[1]

Holly Sutherland

1 What is EUROMOD? A brief history

EUROMOD is a tax-benefit microsimulation model for the European Union. It enables research on the effects of policies and policy reforms on incomes, poverty, inequality, social inclusion and work incentives. It has been deliberately constructed to be independent of any single theoretical or disciplinary perspective, as a platform on which users can implement their chosen approaches. EUROMOD is not only of relevance to social scientists but also of potential value to policy practitioners, as the model itself embodies a knowledge base about different and changing national policy structures and systems within a comparative framework.

Tax-benefit microsimulation models are based on household microdata representative of populations of interest. They calculate disposable income for each household in the dataset. This calculation is made up of elements of income taken from the survey data (e.g. employee earnings) combined with components that are simulated by the model (taxes and benefits). The basic output from EUROMOD is the micro-level change in household disposable income as a result of changes to direct personal taxes or cash benefits. This provides a basis for the calculation of (a) estimates of aggregate effects on the government budget, (b) the impact on measures of poverty and inequality, (c) differential effects on groups of socio-economic interest, and (d) indicators of work incentives.

EUROMOD uniquely allows such calculations to be made in a comparable way across EU Member States. Use of national tax-benefit models

1 I am grateful to Francesco Figari, Horacio Levy, Christine Lietz and Alari Paulus for their help in writing this chapter.

for comparative purposes has been shown to be highly problematic because national model design and options reflect national priorities, interests and conventions. There have been exceptions (e.g. Callan and Sutherland, 1997; De Lathouwer, 1996) but these tend to be pairwise comparisons. Once three or more countries are involved, difficulties in maintaining comparability tend to multiply. EUROMOD has reduced these difficulties by maximizing flexibility in many dimensions. It enables international comparisons, makes analysis at the EU level of policy reforms a possibility; and provides a framework for analysis exploring the effects of policies from country A on the population of country B.

The current version of EUROMOD represents the accumulation of technical developments and expertise over a number years and involving a large team of people. EUROMOD was first constructed for the then EU-15 by a consortium of academic and research institutes as part of a project funded by the European Commission Fourth Framework Programme (FP4).[2] It was then updated as part of an FP5 project.[3] The FP6 project, known as I-CUE, which sponsored the conference on which this book is based has added four countries (Estonia, Hungary, Poland and Slovenia) and provided a "road-map" for implementing the remaining new Member States and upgrading the EU-15 countries to make them easier to update, maintain and use.[4]

One of the very first activities of the initial project was to design the EUROMOD logo (see Figure 3.1) which was based on a graphical representation of risk of poverty rates for the EU-15 countries, relative to the rate for the EU-15 as a whole.[5] Even though EUROMOD has been enlarged and poverty rates have changed, we have retained the original logo as the symbol of the model and the continuing projects that use it.

Until recently, users of the model were mainly people involved in the original consortium. However, constructing and maintaining EUROMOD is such a huge endeavour that it is important that it is exploited through research applications as much as possible. Training courses have been organized and the number of active users from both academia and policy research is increasing, with a growing number of PhD theses including analysis from EUROMOD, as well as interest in its outputs from such bodies as the Indicators Subgroup of the Social Protection Committee of the EU.

2 EUROMOD: an integrated European benefit-tax model 1998-2000 CT97-3060.

3 Micro Analysis of the European Social Agenda (MICRESA) 2001-2004 HPSE-CT2001-00099.

4 Improving the Capacity and Usability of EUROMOD (I-CUE) RIDS 011859 2005-2008.

5 See Immervoll et al. (1999) for further explanation.

Figure 3.1: The EUROMOD logo

At the present time EUROMOD is in a state of transition between its first version, being used by a limited number of people and a new version which aims to cover all 27 Member States and be used in a wide variety of ways by researchers in many contexts. The next section of this chapter outlines the main challenges that were identified in EUROMOD's first phase, before the I-CUE project. This project helped to identify ways to meet and overcome these challenges, while some aspects remain to be resolved. Section 3 summarizes what was achieved in I-CUE and describes some other EUROMOD-related activities that have taken place in parallel. This is followed in section 4 by a description of some plans for the immediate future, including those that are definite with secured funding as well as some concrete ideas that still need financial support. Finally, section 5 briefly speculates about some more distant future possibilities for coverage of non-EU countries and linkages to other types of model. An annex provides references and links for finding out more about EUROMOD.

2 Challenges from the first phase

The main challenges fall under three headings – barriers for users, relevance for academic research and relevance for policy-making or policy analysis – and these are considered in turn.

2.1 *Barriers for users*

The two main barriers have been the lack of ease of use of EUROMOD and the difficulty in obtaining data access permission for all the EUROMOD input datasets.

2.1.1 Ease of use of EUROMOD

As a multi-country model, EUROMOD was designed to be flexible in order to accommodate a wide range of different tax-benefit systems when it was first constructed for the EU-15 countries. However, EUROMOD's scope and flexibility, together with its current coverage of 19 national populations and sets of institutional rules, make it inherently complex to use. Resolving this problem can be approached in two ways. The first is to offer training and support in using the model and the second is to improve its design so that it is as easy as possible to use, without diminishing its flexibility. Both these approaches have been adopted, as explained in the next section.

2.1.2 Data access permission

EUROMOD currently relies on a large number of national survey datasets from several types of source which not only raises issues of comparability but also and even more importantly, barriers in terms of data access. In order to have full access to the 19-country model a user needs to obtain data access permissions from 17 data providers. Each provider specifies its own conditions for access, meaning that securing such access is a laborious and time-consuming process. Complying with the sum of the conditions can also be arduous. These difficulties would increase further as EUROMOD is extended to new countries. The best solution is considered to be switching to a new dataset, namely the European Union Statistics on Income and Living Conditions (EU-SILC) planned to cover all EU countries.[6] This is discussed further in section 4.

2.2 *Relevance for academic research*

As well as the complexity of using EUROMOD in a hands-on sense, it has also sometimes been difficult to make the case for EUROMOD as a suit-

6 And, at the time of writing, covering all but Malta, Bulgaria and Romania.

able tool to be used in academic research. There are several related reasons for this. First of all, in presenting it as a tool that can be used within many disciplinary or theoretical frameworks for a range of types of purpose, no single group of researchers immediately identifies it as suitable for them and their approach. The solution lies simply in seeing it as a matter of time before individual papers using EUROMOD from each sort of research tradition become published and cited by others. These can act as exemplars, encouraging others to consider use of the model seriously. Relatedly, EUROMOD is a tool that carries out static, arithmetic calculations of the first round effect of policy reform. For many academic and policy evaluation purposes the effects of policy change on behaviour are maybe not only relevant but also, in some contexts, the main points of interest. In section 4 we explain that while there is no plan to hardwire particular behavioural models into EUROMOD, there is instead a plan to provide a framework to facilitate users in incorporating their own model of choice.

The scope of EUROMOD in terms of the types of public policies it simulates (or otherwise accounts for) is also rather limited for some applications. Its coverage of cash benefits and direct taxes excludes non-cash benefits, some benefits that may take the form of either cash or subsidy such as child care support, and indirect taxes, each of which vary in importance and effect across countries. However, adding new policies not only involves effort and resources, it may also present data or conceptual challenges which require specific projects, expertise and funding to explore properly. Current activities related to extension of policy scope are described in section 3 and section 4 considers future plans.

2.3 *Relevance for policy analysis*

Policy scope limitations are obviously also relevant for users from outside an academic setting. In addition, for applications of EUROMOD to be policy-relevant the tax-benefit systems that are modelled need to be current or recent and the input data need to be recent. Updating EUROMOD in these two respects is laborious and requires specific national expertise as well as a full understanding of how EUROMOD works. It has therefore been difficult to keep all the countries covered by EUROMOD up-to-date. Furthermore, for certain purposes it is important to cover all the Member States of the EU. Expanding the model to cover the remaining eight countries is important if analysis using it is properly to represent all the policy systems and populations of the Union. Adding a new country requires not only the expertise needed to update an existing country but also the identification, motivation and training of the new national team. Again, this requires time and financial support. The I-CUE project provided these resources for four countries. Plans for extending the same process and also updating the EU-15 parts of the model are set out in section 4.

3 Current and recent activities

As mentioned above the I-CUE project represented a major step forward in the improvement and development of EUROMOD. The main achievements of this project are summarized below and this is followed by a description of other complementary activities.

Its main objectives were to explore the feasibility of enlargement of the model to cover the whole (then) EU-25, to include four of the new countries, acting as prototypes for a new fully-enlarged model and to design and test ways of re-building EUROMOD to improve usability for users and developers. It is clear that there were very strong interdependencies between the two main parts of the project: enlarging the model and improving its technical foundations. On the one hand, constructing the new country components was greatly facilitated by improvements to the EUROMOD framework, the development of new tools and the discipline offered by defining (a) a common and documented structure of the modules used in building new country components and (b) a powerful yet flexible system for naming variables. On the other hand, these developments were directly informed by an understanding of what was required (in terms of data, information about policy rules and also human capacity and motivation) to build the new EUROMOD components in an effective way. Moreover, when difficult or strategic choices had to be made, consultation with the EUROMOD User Group was invaluable.[7] Again the relationship was a two-way one, with User Group members having hands-on access to new aspects of the model as they developed.

More details about the nature of the achievements of I-CUE can be found in Sutherland et al. (2008) and a list of the major results is available in Box 3.1. Here, we focus on one aspect of the project outcomes: making the model more attractive and easy to use, particularly for the novice user.

7 See Sutherland (2008) for a description of the EUROMOD User Group and the role it has played.

Box 3.1: Key results of the I-CUE project

i. Inclusion of four new countries (Estonia, Hungary, Poland and Slovenia).

ii. Feasibility studies for six of the remaining eight New Member States, providing much of the detail needed to build country components for those countries (Cyprus, Czech Republic, Latvia, Lithuania, Malta and Slovakia).

iii. An established method and process for identifying and cooperating with teams from the remaining countries (Bulgaria and Romania, and others in the future).

iv. A version of EUROMOD that allows for analysis of 19 EU countries, separately or in any combination; baseline EUROMOD statistics for these countries: http://www.iser.essex.ac.uk/research/euromod/statistics

v. Established protocols, guidelines and methods used in the inclusion of the four new countries. These elements also provide a clear blueprint for the re-building of the EU-15 components of the model and a roadmap for the regular updating of the whole of EUROMOD. They include:
   (a) A standardized variable naming convention and input data documentation template.
   (b) A set of revised common modules that act as "building blocks" in programming tax and benefit policies for each country; allowing elements to be swapped across countries and a uniform approach in all countries.
   (c) A template for the documentation of each country component (Country Reports).
   (d) A long-term plan for the use of Eurostat EU-SILC data as the common input database for all countries.

vi. A user interface and operating system that retains the full range of flexibility of choices by the user while requiring no special programming skills nor purchase of special software, but at the same time allowing use and operation of the model to be learned with modest effort.

vii. Some new functions and features of EUROMOD including:
   (a) The ability to calculate effective marginal tax rates using a range of assumptions.
   (b) A mapping of social benefits onto independent and official classifications of these sources of income.

viii. Insights into the feasibility of further technical improvements in the following dimensions:
   (a) Providing web access to EUROMOD in two distinct modes has been established as feasible.
   (b) The choice of underlying software needs further consideration, with a view to improving run speed and long-term sustainability. This review needs to consider the costs as well as benefits of any significant change, given that the existing configuration has proved satisfactory in many dimensions including with respect to user feedback.

3.1 *User-friendliness*

As explained above EUROMOD is a research tool which is extremely flexible and powerful, but which is – inherently and necessarily – complex to use. Making national tax-benefit models user-friendly is relatively straightforward. They usually offer a selection of choices, limited to the ones that the model developers anticipate that users will require. While this has proved appropriate in the context of one country and one tax-benefit system, it is impossible to make a model that aims to cover 27 tax-benefit systems and make use of a variety of datasets accessible in this way without sacrificing flexibility for the sake of user-friendliness. However, as the difficulty of operating EUROMOD was one main obstacle in making the model accessible to a wide user community, there was clearly a need for ways to overcome these difficulties. The approach taken was as follows:

- provide a single surface or entry-point to the model,
- make simple applications easy to accomplish,
- provide some guidance for more complex uses of the model,
- facilitate "navigation" within the EUROMOD parameter files (which store the information about how the tax-benefit systems of the selected countries are implemented, which datasets are used as inputs, plus all the other user options).

Figure 3.2 shows the surface of the so-called operating system that emerged after some trials and design revisions. It contains flags for the implemented countries (and intimations of those which are intended to be implemented in the near future). This not only shows at first sight which countries are available, but also provides, due to its colourfulness, an attractive entry point to the model for the novice user.

The left side of the surface offers some menu points which enable the second and third tasks named above to be accomplished. Clicking "Run EUROMOD" opens the interface shown in Figure 3.3, where users can select the countries and tax-benefit systems they want to run in a straightforward manner. Clicking "Tools" directs users to an overview of the EUROMOD tools collection including, for example a tool that computes a range of commonly used indicators and statistics for analysing EUROMOD micro-output. Clicking "Documentation" directs users to an overview of the comprehensive EUROMOD documentation, which includes Manuals, which describe how to operate the model; Country Reports, which document the way in which each country's tax-benefit system is modelled; Data Descriptions, which describe the datasets, building the EUROMOD database; "Recipes", which provide step-by-step instructions that describe in detail what needs to be done to make EUROMOD produce the output needed for a particular research question; and a link to EUROMOD working papers.

Figure 3.2: EUROMOD operating system

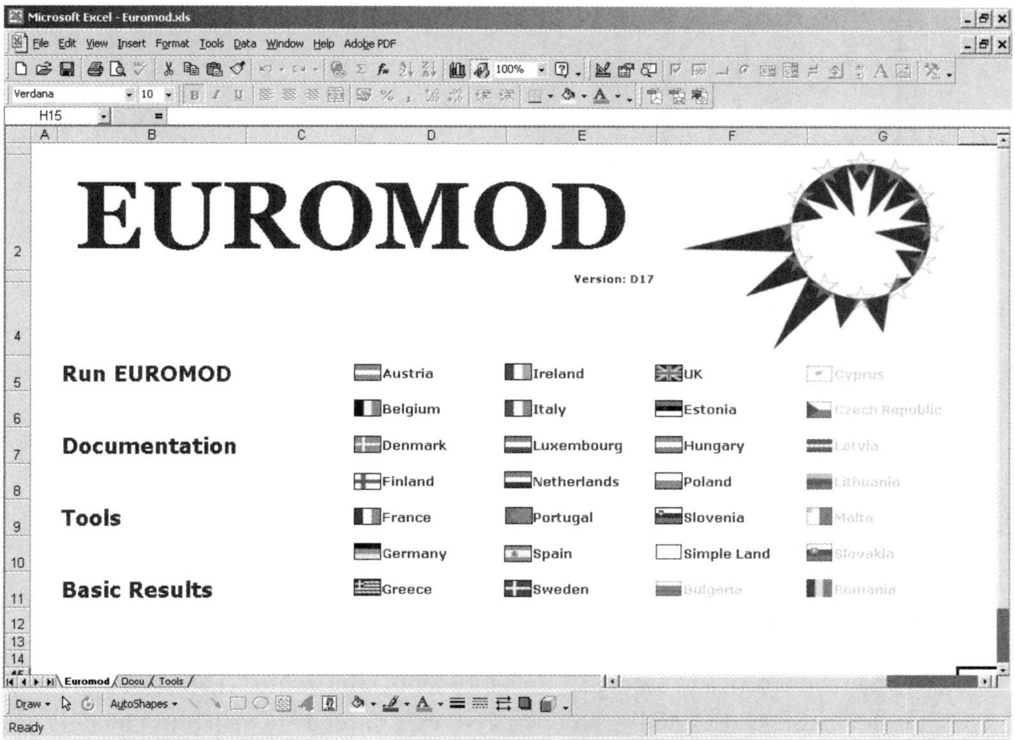

The EUROMOD operating system was put to a comprehensive test by new users (during two EUROMOD training courses within the Essex Summer School, as well as the ECASS visitor programme at ISER in the University of Essex), "old" users and the developer team itself. Indeed, the training courses acted as a test-bed for all the new developments to EUROMOD as well as helping to expand the number of users.

Figure 3.3: Run EUROMOD tool

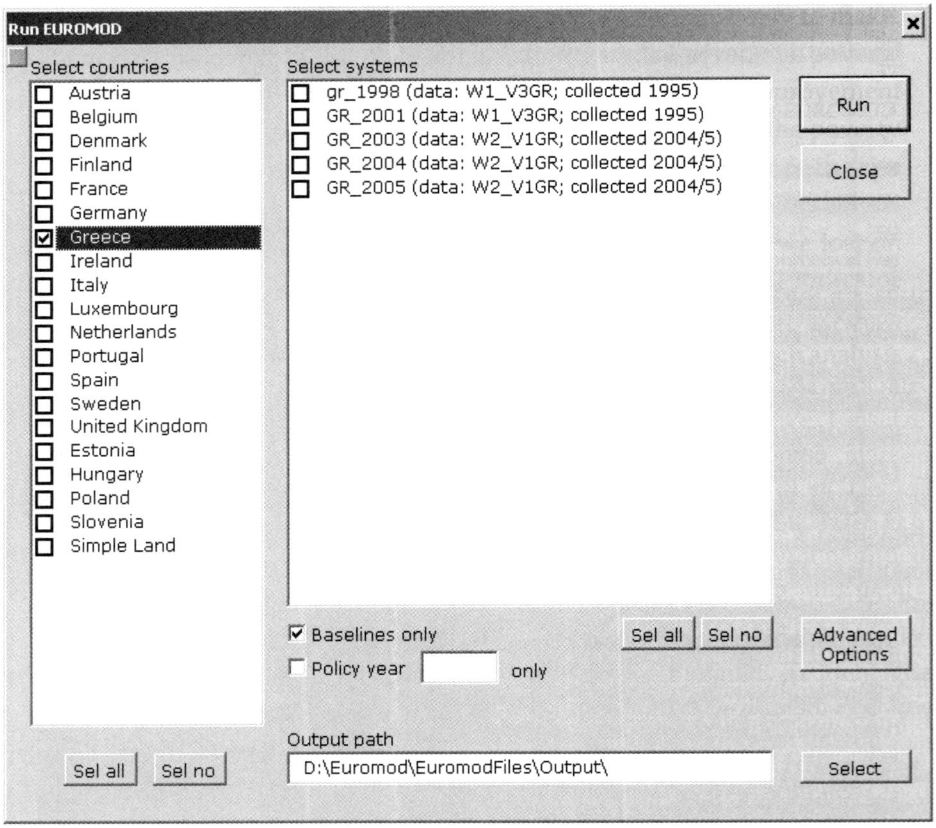

3.2 *Spin-off models*

Other aspects of the technical developments and improvements have resulted in the EUROMOD framework being "adopted" to help build models like EUROMOD for other countries. This is much more cost-effective than starting from scratch and has the added benefit of offering the potential of comparative analysis with the corresponding countries and those in EUROMOD. This technology transfer has been successfully achieved for South Africa and is in progress for Turkey and five Latin American countries (LATINMOD). These spin-off models make use of the generic tax-benefit modelling "language" (or set of building blocks) that has been developed in I-CUE. There is plenty of potential to do more of this and thereby spread the state of the art developed in I-CUE around the world. In each case the provenance of the new model (i.e. its use of the EUROMOD framework and language) will be acknowledged in each model and its applications.

3.3 Extending the scope of EUROMOD

A "sister" project known as AIM-AP (Accurate Income Measurement for the Assessment of Public Policies) has been exploring methods to improve income measurement in various ways that are particularly relevant to microsimulation models such as EUROMOD.[8] This includes sub-projects to explore ways of:

- estimating the incidence and value of non-cash incomes (publicly provided education, health care and rent subsidies as well as imputed rent, employer-provided non-cash benefits and own production),
- modelling non-take-up of benefits and tax evasion,
- inclusion of indirect taxes.

3.4 Policy-relevant monitoring and analysis

It has been demonstrated that policy-relevant EUROMOD analysis, as an input into evidence-based policy-making, is of interest to international organizations such as OECD and DG-EMPL and DG-ECFIN of the European Commission as well as some national agencies. For example, see Dang et al. (2006) and Immervoll and Sutherland (2006) as well as the reports and papers of the Income Distribution and Social Inclusion network within the *European Observatory on Demography and the Social Situation.*[9]

4 Plans for the immediate future

The immediate plans for the period 2009-2011 involve following from the I-CUE results and experience to build a new version of EUROMOD which will

- enlarge the coverage from 19 to 27 countries,
- upgrade the EU-15 parts of the model to conform to the approach developed in I-CUE for the New Member States,
- re-base the model on the Eurostat EU-SILC database (where possible),
- update policies in all upgraded countries to the initial EU-SILC data year and a very recent policy year,

8 http://www.iser.essex.ac.uk/research/euromod/aim-ap-project

9 http://www.socialsituation.eu

- establish a regular programme of updating of both policies (to take account of reforms) and database (to take account of changes in population characteristics and the distribution of market incomes, in particular),
- take on board some post-I-CUE further improvements and additions to the modelling framework.

4.1 *Access*

The existing version of the model, as well as the emerging components of the new version of EUROMOD, are to be made freely available for academic research and non-commercial policy-relevant analysis, subject to some simple conditions. These include the requirement to acknowledge the use of EUROMOD in any publication and offering any paper for publication in the EUROMOD Working Paper series. Users will need to continue secure access permission to the input datasets. However, re-basing the new model on one common dataset – the EU-SILC – can be expected to streamline and make this process more transparent.

Access and use will be encouraged and promoted, and supported where possible. In the medium term, if EUROMOD is to be fully exploited, there is a need for the provision of training courses and access visits and for the exploration of remote web-based access possibilities.

4.2 *Extensions*

Also in the medium term there is significant interest in extending the policy scope and modelling capacity of EUROMOD. The following are examples of relevant and feasible extensions:

- child care policies (in cash and in kind),
- a framework for modelling labour supply behaviour,
- indirect taxes,
- estimates of non-cash benefits,
- options to model non-take-up of benefits and evasion of taxes.

The last three in this list are the subjects of the AIM-AP project (see previous section). In some instances, the case studies and explorations conducted as part of that project are suitable for "rolling out" to all countries within EUROMOD, so extending the type of analysis that is possible and/or improving the measures that are produced.

4.3 *The EUROMOD community*

As expressed by Tony Atkinson in Chapter 2 it is the "community" of people working with, on, and around EUROMOD – its users and developers, as well as "stakeholders" – that is one of the more remarkable and perhaps unusual features of its history. In the future, as this community grows it is important that it is nurtured in various ways. An important component of this includes facilitation of networking among users and dialogue between users and developers so that EUROMOD evolves along a path most useful for leading edge research, and also so that it benefits from developments carried out by users themselves. In practice it means that organization of work-in-progress conferences and workshops, provision of training in new features, and dissemination of development plans need to be part of the work programme.

5 Future possibilities and new challenges

There are many directions in which EUROMOD could be developed in the more distant future, each with its own potential and associated challenges. Here we briefly refer to two possibilities: extending EUROMOD beyond the EU and as the framework for national model development around the world, and linkage with other types of socio-economic model.

5.1 *EUROMOD beyond the EU*

As explained above, EUROMOD is already being used as the modelling framework within which to build models for South Africa, five Latin American countries (LATINMOD) and Turkey. Interest has been expressed in doing something similar in a number of other countries including Russia and Japan. Using the generic features of EUROMOD to encourage the building of similar national (or indeed sub-national or multi-national) policy tools around the world has two consequences. On the one hand it clearly plays a role in encouraging and facilitating evidence-based policy-making across the world. In this sense it can make a very positive contribution.

On the other hand, the fact that these "spin-off" models are built with the same structure and design as each other and as EUROMOD, raises the possibility of a worldwide network of comparable models – and hence the potential for worldwide comparisons of the effects of tax and benefit policies.

One challenge is to develop protocols or methods for allowing countries to develop their own independent model, and then for this to be included back under the EUROMOD umbrella – to make use of new developments or to make comparisons – at a later stage.

5.2 *Linkages to other types of model*

As a flexible tax-benefit model EUROMOD can be used to address many questions of policy and socio-economic interest. However, on its own it is not able to establish the equilibrium effects of policy changes, or the effects on individual behaviour, or to capture their macro-economic or environmental impacts. And at the same time, macro-economic and environmental models do not usually capture the full distributional impacts of change; nor can they or micro-econometric behavioural models be used to design appropriate redistributional policies to mitigate adverse effects of other policy or other change. Instead of trying to design a "supermodel", a potentially fruitful approach is to construct appropriate linkages between existing models. This would have the advantage of making use of the accumulated expertise of the two (or more) modelling communities with the main issue being how to specify the linkage. Such a specification would undoubtedly involve theoretical and conceptual considerations, as well as the purely operational or practical. This would be very challenging to do for general purposes, so an exploratory approach designed to address a particular question may be the best first step for most of these linkages.

One exception is the link between tax-benefit calculations and labour supply responses where there is already a substantial body of experience at the national level. In this case the plan is to construct a framework in which the user can specify his/her own behavioural model (which has been perhaps originally developed for a single country), with EUROMOD providing one part of the toolkit.

Given its complexity and size, once it covers 27 countries, EUROMOD itself can only remain manageable – in all senses of the word – as a static tax-benefit model. Collaborating with experts in other modelling approaches and traditions in order to broaden the range of questions that can be addressed is therefore an exiting – as well as challenging – direction to consider for the future.

References

Callan, T./Sutherland, H. (1997) 'The Impact of Comparable Policies in European Countries: Microsimulation Approaches', *European Economic Review* 41: 3-5, 627-633.

Dang, T-T./Immervoll, H./Mantovani, D./Orsini, K./Sutherland, H. (2006) 'An Age Perspective on Economic Well-being and Social Protection in Nine OECD Countries', OECD Social Employment and Migration Working Papers No. 34. Paris: OECD.

Immervoll, H./Sutherland, H. (2006) 'EUROMOD: An Integrated European Tax-benefit Model and Indicators of Work Incentives', in: Carone, G./Salomäki, A. (eds), *Indicators and Policies to Make Work Pay*. European Economy Special Report No. 2. Office for Official Publications of the EC.

Immervoll, H./O'Donoghue, C./Sutherland, H. (1999) 'An Introduction to EUROMOD', EUROMOD Working Paper EM0/99. Colchester: ISER, University of Essex.

de Lathouwer, L. (1996) 'Microsimulation in Comparative Social Policy Analysis: A Case Study of Unemployment Schemes for Belgium and the Netherlands', in: Harding, A. (ed.), *Microsimulation and Public Policy*. Amsterdam: North Holland.

Sutherland, H./Figari, F./Lelkes, O./Levy, H./Lietz, C./Mantovani, D./Paulus, A. (2008) 'Improving the Capacity and Usability of EUROMOD: Final Report', EUROMOD Working Paper EM4/08. Colchester: ISER, University of Essex.

Annex: How to find out more about EUROMOD

The EUROMOD home page, which includes information on past and current EUROMOD-related projects, is at:
http://www.iser.essex.ac.uk/research/euromod
Statistics on the redistribution of income, using the EU-19 version of EUROMOD can be accessed here:
http://www.iser.essex.ac.uk/research/euromod/statistics
The **EUROMOD Working Paper series**, in which all papers using EUROMOD are published, can be viewed at:
http://www.iser.essex.ac.uk/research/euromod/working-papers

In particular readers interested in **technical aspects** of the model itself might find the following papers useful:
EM0/99, Immervoll, H./O'Donoghue, C./Sutherland, H. (1999) An Introduction to EUROMOD.
EM9/01 Sutherland, H. (ed.) (2001) EUROMOD: An Integrated European Benefit-tax Model.
EM5/06 Lietz, C./Mantovani, D. (2006) Lessons from Building and Using EUROMOD.
and the final report from the **I-CUE project** is available as
EM4/08 Sutherland, H./Figari, F./Lelkes, O./Levy, H./Lietz, C./Mantovani, D./Paulus, A. (2008) Improving the Capacity and Usability of EUROMOD.
For information about **how to download EUROMOD** and what to do about access to the input database follow instructions at:
http://www.iser.essex.ac.uk/research/euromod/downloads
"Recipes" explaining particular uses of EUROMOD in clear steps can be found at:
http://www.iser.essex.ac.uk/research/euromod/documentation/recipes
Country Reports for each of the 19 countries implemented in EUROMOD can be downloaded from:
http://www.iser.essex.ac.uk/research/euromod/documentation/country-reports

Any questions about EUROMOD can be sent to:
euromod-team@essex.ac.uk

Part II:
Comparative Analyses Using the Enlarged EUROMOD

Chapter 4

The Effects of Taxes and Benefits on Income Distribution in the Enlarged EU[1]

Alari Paulus / Mitja Čok / Francesco Figari / Péter Hegedűs / Silja Kralik / Nataša Kump / Orsolya Lelkes / Horacio Levy / Christine Lietz / Daniela Mantovani / Leszek Morawski / Holly Sutherland / Péter Szivós / Andres Võrk

1 Introduction

There is much variety of tax and benefit policies across the European Union, having increased further by the accession of Eastern European countries in 2004 and in 2007. Although this marked the end of transition in some sense for these countries, many of them still face systematic reforms. However, the instruments for preparing and evaluating these reform options are often lacking and government performance tends to be monitored in terms of macro indicators (such as budget deficits) rather than in terms of their impact on individuals or households. Perhaps even less is known about the trade-offs between promoting particular goals and supporting particular social groups. Focusing on the differences between Western and Eastern European countries, this chapter aims to bring novel evidence on the social impact of fiscal policies. In particular, we examine how taxes and benefits affect income distributions in the enlarged EU.

---

1 We are indebted to all past and current members of the EUROMOD consortium. The views expressed as well as any errors are the responsibilities of the authors and do not implicate the institutions to which they are affiliated. In particular, this applies to the interpretation of model results and any errors in its use.
The chapter uses EUROMOD version D25 (August 2008). See Annex A in the Introduction.

A distributional analysis of taxes and benefits requires data at the individual and household level. Most micro-data sources available are collected using surveys and typically focus on benefits, while having little or incomplete information about taxes (if any at all). Taxes are usually better recorded in administrative datasets but these tend to be not widely accessible. Moreover, an international perspective raises comparability issues across national datasets. Given all these difficulties, only few international studies have considered the effect of *both* benefits and taxes on household incomes while relying on micro-data. These have primarily focused on the OECD countries and used two strategies for overcoming comparability issues. On the one hand, studies like Oxley et al. (1999), Förster and Pearson (2002), Förster and Mira d'Ercole (2005), and OECD (2008) rely on a common OECD questionnaire completed by national experts drawing on country-specific analysis of existing data sources. On the other hand, studies such as Atkinson et al. (1995) and Mahler and Jesuit (2006) directly exploit national survey datasets harmonized by the Luxembourg Income Study.[2] Even so, the consistency and comparability of results across countries as well as the level of detail of the analysis have been constrained due to the differences in the underlying national datasets.[3]

We rely on a variety of (partly harmonized) national datasets at the micro-level, but employ microsimulation techniques to calculate benefit entitlements and tax liabilities. In particular we use EUROMOD, the tax-benefit microsimulation model covering the 15 pre-2004 European Union member states plus Estonia, Hungary, Poland and Slovenia. Besides providing more comprehensive and detailed information on personal taxes and benefits, which, among else, facilitates their categorization in a comparable way across countries, this method has other advantages over using recorded taxes and benefits. In particular it allows studying interactions between different tax-benefit instruments and the intended effects of tax-benefit policies under full compliance (i.e. complete benefit take-up and no tax evasion) in addition to their actual performance. Last but not least, applying legal tax-benefit rules across countries in a common framework provides potentially more consistent and comparable results.

2 See http://www.lisproject.org/

3 For example, the results in OECD (2008) are based on micro-data sources where information on taxes (where available) was given by respondents, taken from administrative records or imputed (with microsimulation models).

Nevertheless, our approach shares a number of limitations with previous studies. First, we focus only on the direct impact of existing taxes and benefits on income distributions and ignore possible indirect effects of government policies through changes in relative prices and household behaviour (e.g. labour supply). Second, our analysis is limited with the scope of the model which currently includes cash payments only.[4] Third, as the underlying datasets are cross-sectional we are primarily concerned with redistribution among people rather than across each person's life cycle.

As such it is an updated and extended version of a paper by Immervoll et al. (2006) which, using an earlier version of the same model, analysed redistributive effects of taxes and benefits in the EU15 countries in 1998. In addition to updating these results, we extend the analysis to four Eastern European countries – Estonia, Hungary, Poland and Slovenia – and besides the effect of taxes and benefits on income composition and income inequality also discuss the effects on income poverty.[5] (A similar analysis was also carried out in Figari et al. [2008], but focusing on the changes at the EU level as a whole.) We seek to answer the following questions. Does the scale of redistribution differ between Western and Eastern European countries? Is it larger in the latter given their transition from planned economy where the government had an immense role in society? Are they providing efficient safety nets for those falling behind? Are there any systematic differences in the instruments used by the state for redistributing incomes? In particular, which countries base their welfare systems largely on means-testing, and which ones use a more universalist approach? Do these four Eastern European countries form a homogenous group in some way or another within the European Union?

The chapter is structured as follows. Section 2 gives a short overview of the underlying model and its input datasets, also explaining different income concepts used in the analysis. Section 3 presents and discusses the

4 The inclusion of the main private and public non-cash incomes in the concept of resources available to households in order to implement a more comprehensive income definition is one the aims of the AIM-AP project. The resulting data and method enhancements will be made generally accessible and re-useable by implementing them within EUROMOD. Further information can be found at http://www.iser.essex.ac.uk/research/euromod/aim-ap-project/

5 Less detailed versions of the results presented in this chapter are also available as part of the EUROMOD statistics on the Distribution and Decomposition of Disposable Income.

effect of different types of tax-benefit instruments on the structure of household incomes, income inequality and poverty. The last section summarizes the results.

2 Methodology and data

We use EUROMOD in our analysis. It is a multi-country tax-benefit microsimulation model, which includes tax-benefit systems for 19 European Union countries: EU15 and Estonia, Hungary, Poland and Slovenia, modelled in a common framework. See Box 4.1 for a short overview of the tax-benefit systems for the latter four. All 19 countries are included in the analysis, using the latest tax-benefit policy rules available for each country. This, however, results in a combination of different policy years: 2005 for 6 countries, 2003 for 8 countries and 2001 for 5 countries. Nevertheless, by focusing on relative measures only, we expect to minimize the effect on the results from using different policy years.

The model includes direct taxes and cash benefits but does not cover indirect taxes or non-cash benefits. Most of the tax and benefit instruments can be simulated, except those for which work histories are required (e.g. contributory pensions, unemployment benefits) but usually not available in the cross-sectional survey datasets used as EUROMOD input data. Instruments which are not simulated are taken directly from data (if available). The model focuses on the full potential effect of tax-benefit policies by assuming complete benefit take-up and no tax evasion. For further information, see Sutherland (2001, 2007).

Box 4.1: A summary of the 2005 tax-benefit system in Estonia, Hungary, Poland and Slovenia

- All four *tax-benefit systems* are effectively unified national systems. There are few taxes (mostly on property) set by the local governments in Estonia, Hungary and Poland but the share of these taxes in overall taxation is negligible. Municipalities in the same countries have also some discretion over the (national) social assistance benefits, and provide a few local benefits, such as additional family / child benefits and social assistance benefits, but again the share in overall social expenditures is small.

- In revenue terms, nearly all of personal taxes (i.e. direct taxes paid by individuals) consist of *income taxes* in all of these countries. All of them have individual income tax systems, while married couples in Estonia and Poland can opt to be jointly taxed. Estonia and Slovenia have a comprehensive income tax system where all income sources are pooled and taxed uniformly. Whereas Estonia applies a flat tax (i.e. a single marginal tax rate above a certain threshold), Slovenia has a progressive tax schedule. Hungary and Poland have a dual income tax system, where only non-capital income is consolidated and subject to a progressive tax schedule while capital income (and partly self-employment income in Hungary) is taxed separately at a flat tax rate. The system in Hungary is more complicated as the flat tax rate varies between different types of capital and self-employment income. In Poland, farmers pay separately an agricultural tax that is based on farm size and land area quality, and self-employment income may be taxed in any one of the three mentioned ways (mostly under the general progressive system).
- In all countries, the main components of *social insurance contributions* (SICs) are the same: pension, health and unemployment insurance contributions. In Slovenia, there is additionally a maternity leave contribution. However, the way contributions are shared between the employers and employees varies quite a lot – nearly all of SICs are paid by employers in Estonia, while employees pay only a part of the unemployment insurance contributions and contribute to the funded pension scheme; in Hungary, employers contribute almost 3 to 1 compared to employees; in Poland, SICs are split roughly equally between employers and employees; and in Slovenia, employees pay slightly more (about 10-20%) than employers. Self-employed pay the sum of the rates for employers and employees in all four countries.
- The structure of expenditure on *cash benefits* is rather similar across the countries, especially for Estonia, Hungary and Slovenia – see the table below. About 60% of cash benefits are related to old age, followed by disability (11.2-13.9%), family / child (5.3-16.6%) and sickness / health care benefits (4.4-7.2%). Survivors, unemployment and housing / social exclusion benefits account only for a minor share, except in Poland where the share of survivors' cash benefits is about 10 percentage points higher compared with the other countries. The share of family- and

child-related expenditure, on the other hand, is significantly lower in Poland than in other countries. Estonia, which in relative terms provides the most generous cash support for families and children, has a lower share of expenditure on unemployment and housing and social exclusion. Estonia also differs in only *means-testing* the social assistance benefit, while means-tests also apply to some family benefits in the other countries (especially in Poland) and to an unemployment benefit in Slovenia.

- The relative differences in the structure of expenditure across countries do not change much if *in-kind benefits* are also included. Most notably, the share of old-age related benefits is higher in Poland compared to the other countries, while the share of sickness/health care benefits lags further behind. Also, the share of housing/social exclusion benefits in Hungary is significantly higher when in-kind benefits are included showing that these are substitutes rather than complements to the cash benefits. Overall, in-kind benefits account for 30-37% of total expenditure, except in Poland where the share is 18%, and the share is highest for housing and sickness/health care expenditure.

Social protection expenditure by function (excluding administration costs) in 2005, %

	Cash benefits only				Cash and in-kind benefits			
	EE	HU	PL	SI	EE	HU	PL	SI
Old age	60.6	60.7	58.6	62.5	43.1	41.2	48.3	42.4
Survivors	1.2	1.9	13.3	2.7	0.9	1.3	11.1	2.0
Disability	11.8	13.9	12.8	11.2	9.4	9.9	10.7	8.5
Sickness/ health care	7.2	5.1	4.4	7.0	31.9	29.9	19.8	32.3
Family/children	16.6	13.9	5.3	9.0	12.2	11.8	4.4	8.6
Unemployment	1.3	4.1	3.9	4.1	1.3	2.9	3.3	3.3
Housing/ social exclusion	1.2	0.3	1.7	3.4	1.2	3.1	2.5	2.9
Total	**100**	**100**	**100**	**100**	**100**	**100**	**100**	**100**

Source: Eurostat Database (Living conditions and welfare > Social protection > Social protection expenditure).

- Overall, *public pensions* (old age, survivors', disability) constitute a large part of the benefit systems. All four countries have introduced funded old-age pension schemes in addition to the existing pay-as-you-go systems, however, the first private old-age pensions will be payable earliest in 2009 in Estonia and Poland. The legal retirement age in 2005 was 63 for men and 59.5 for women in Estonia; and respectively, 62 and 60 in Hungary; 65 and 60 in Poland, and 63 and 61 in Slovenia. Both early retirement and postponement are possible (subject to, accordingly, reduced and increased accrual rates) in all countries.

Detailed information on these tax-benefit systems can be found in the EUROMOD Country Reports: see Čok et al. (2008), Hegedűs et al. (2008), Levy and Morawski (2008) and Lüpsik et al. (2008).

There are 17 different data sources used to construct EUROMOD input data for modelling the 19 tax-benefit systems (see Annex A and B in Chapter 1). These are mostly national household budget or income surveys but also register data and European-wide surveys like the European Community Household Panel (ECHP) and the EU Survey on Income and Living Conditions (EU-SILC) are used for some countries. All of these include grossing weights to make samples representative of the whole household population. In most cases the reference time period for income data matches the policy year or precedes it a few years in which case monetary values are uprated according to various price and income indices. Three datasets – those for Denmark, Ireland and Italy – date back to 1994-96.

EUROMOD input databases for each country contain information on household demographic and labour market characteristics, market income generated by household members and non-simulated benefits. (Note that market income does not include lump sum one-off payments nor capital gains.) Based on that, EUROMOD calculates benefit entitlements, social insurance contributions and tax liabilities. The main output is household disposable income which is calculated as the sum of market income and social benefits less social insurance contributions and personal taxes (see Box 4.2 below).

Box 4.2: Main income concepts in EUROMOD

	Market Income *(employment and self-employment income, income from property [rent], investment income, private pensions, private transfers)*
+	Social Benefits *(public pensions, family benefits, health-related benefits, unemployment benefits, social assistance benefits, housing benefits)* Grouped further as: • public pensions • non means-tested benefits • means-tested benefits
–	Social Insurance Contributions *(employee, self-employed)*
–	Personal Taxes *(national and local income taxes, other direct taxes)*
=	Disposable Income

These income concepts will be used throughout the following analysis with social benefits divided into three further groups: public pensions, means-tested benefits and non means-tested benefits. With respect to public pensions we try to distinguish state-enforced savings for retirement from other benefits, as one could argue that these should be excluded from redistribution analysis and be considered along with private pensions which are included in the market income concept. In fact, to address this we provide two alternative starting points on several occasions – market income and market income including public pensions.

As the distinction between retirement and other insurance pensions is often not clear-cut and they might be designed as substitutes, we have also included in the category of public pensions (a) survivors' pensions, (b) invalidity pensions, and (c) means-tested pension top-ups while excluding separate means-tested old-age benefits (even if labelled as social pensions etc.). However, to ensure these are retirement benefits, we have also imposed an age limit of 65 (67 for Denmark, since this was the Danish pension age in 2001). Incomes grouped as public pensions appear as other (non means-tested) benefits for those aged under this limit.

Other benefits are differentiated by whether there are any means-tests applied or not, i.e. whether the benefit entitlement depends on the current amount of other income or capital. These are benefits targeted specifically at those with largest needs or lowest resources and, therefore, explicitly involve redistribution. Whether they achieve more in terms of redistribution than non means-tested benefits – which are usually based on contingencies such as disability, intended for horizontal redistribution (e.g. to children) or earnings replacement (sickness, maternity / paternity or unemployment) – is one of the subjects of this chapter. Detailed information on how individual benefits in each country were categorized can be found in Annex C.

3 Analysis

3.1 *Income composition*

First, we examine the role of tax-benefit systems on the structure of household incomes. Figure 4.1 (and Table A1 in Annex A) show the composition of disposable incomes at the household level in terms of the average size of each income component as a percentage of average household disposable income.

It is important to note that while the graph reflects the composition of incomes that households have available to spend, it does not represent the overall budgetary balance at the government level nor the balance of all the resources available to households. Other taxes (e.g. VAT, excise duties, corporate income tax) and other public expenditures (publicly provided health care, education, housing subsidies and so on) are not included. However, it is still informative to see how much market income is necessary on average to achieve a given level of disposable income; and how much is added as (cash) benefits and deducted as (direct) taxes. Furthermore, the measure of household disposable income that is used corresponds to the income concept commonly used in the calculation of income inequality and poverty (for example, see OECD 2008). It is therefore highly relevant to understand differences in its composition across countries.

Overall, market income equal to 100% of disposable income means that direct taxes and cash benefits balance each other. While there are only few EU15 countries with average household market income below disposable income, it seems more common for the *New Member States* (NMS) – occurring in three out of four and most likely reflecting greater reliance on other taxes and less expenditure on in-kind benefits. On the deduction side, income taxes dominate social insurance contributions, except in Greece, France, the Netherlands and *Slovenia*. Denmark and Sweden tax incomes the most, while *Estonia*, Ireland, Spain, Portugal and Greece tax the least.

Figure 4.1: Income composition, all households

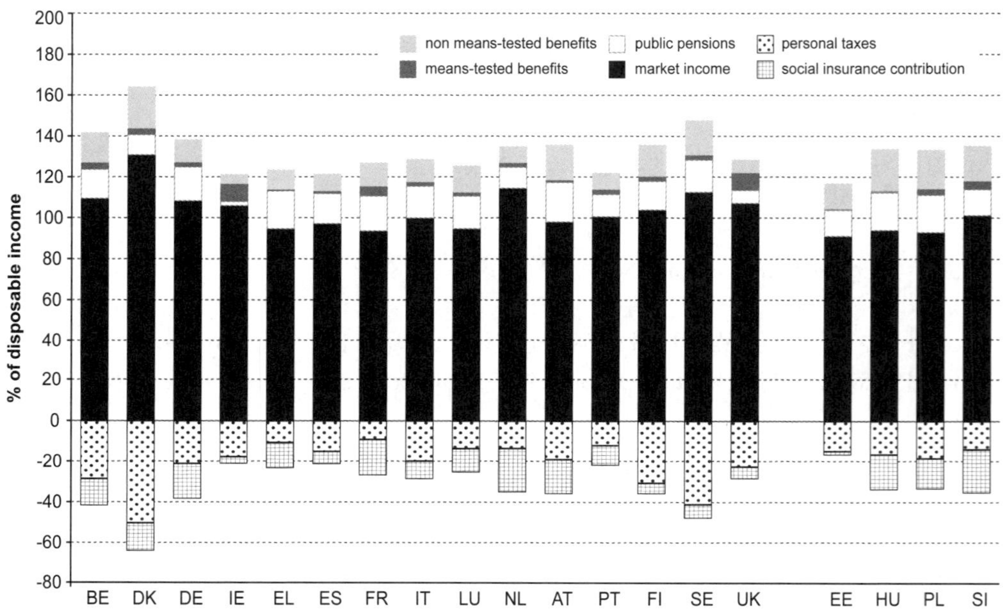

Source: EUROMOD.

In terms of benefits, the bulk is made up of public pensions and non means-tested benefits – contributing from 85% to nearly 100% of *the total expenditure on cash benefits* – except in the UK and Ireland, where means-tested benefits are most important and account for, respectively, 39% and 54% of total cash benefits. Also *the share of disposable income* from means-tested benefits is the highest for these two countries, while they have the lowest shares of disposable income from either public pensions or non means-tested benefits. Besides the UK and Ireland, low public pensions also characterize other countries where most of pensions are flat-rate schemes (e.g. Denmark) or are provided through the private sector (e.g. the Netherlands). Other countries where non means-tested benefits contribute little are the Netherlands and most of the Southern European countries (Portugal, Spain and Greece), while *Hungary*,

Poland, *Slovenia* together with the Nordic countries (Denmark, Finland and Sweden) and Austria have the largest shares. Altogether, the share of disposable income from benefits is the largest in *Poland*, *Hungary* and Austria, and the smallest in Ireland, the Netherlands, the UK and Portugal.

The low share of non-pension benefits may be due to a high level of economic activity as well as to a benefit system that has low coverage and / or small payments. Similarly, a high share may be an indicator of many people needing support, as well as of a system involving relatively generous payments.

Overall, the scale of governments' involvement in altering incomes (as measured by the total length of the bars in Figure 4.1) is significantly higher in Hungary, Poland and Slovenia than in Estonia. The first three show levels above the average and similar to those of the Netherlands, Austria and Finland, while staying behind Denmark and Sweden, countries with the highest levels. Estonia, on the other hand, demonstrates the smallest role of the state in that respect, surpassing even the Southern European countries.

Figure 4.2: Income composition, bottom decile by household equivalized disposable income

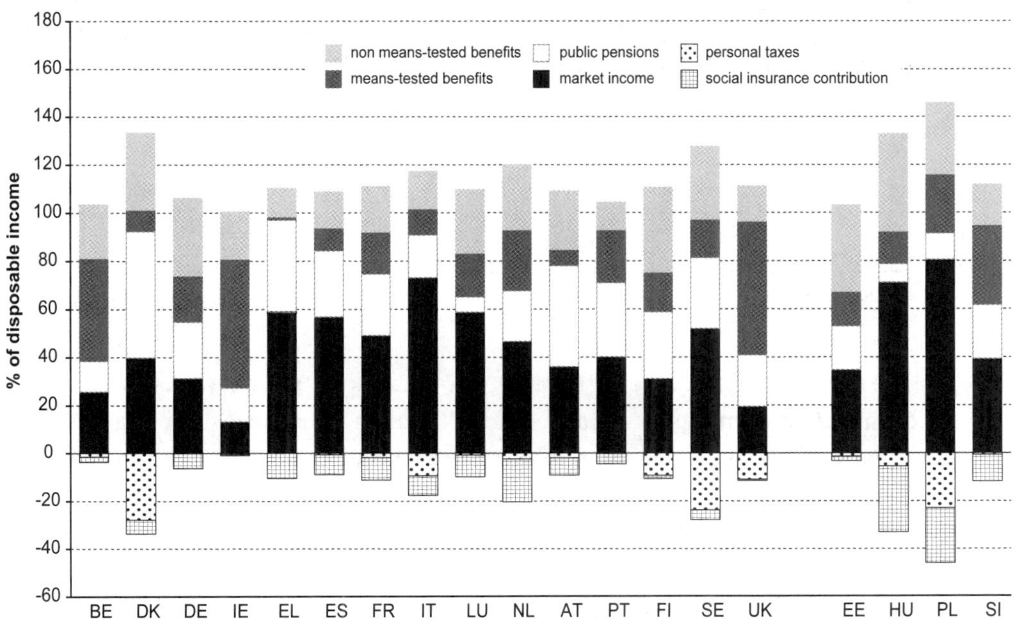

Source: EUROMOD.

As expected, the share of market income is significantly lower and that of all benefits is much higher in the bottom income decile group (see Figure 4.2 and Table A2) – based on household equivalized disposable income using the OECD modified scale.[6] Market income accounts for about 25-60% of disposable income in most countries, its share being lower in countries with high levels of means-tested support (e.g. Ireland, UK) and higher for *Poland*, Italy and *Hungary*.

Figure 4.3: Income composition, top decile by household equivalized disposable income

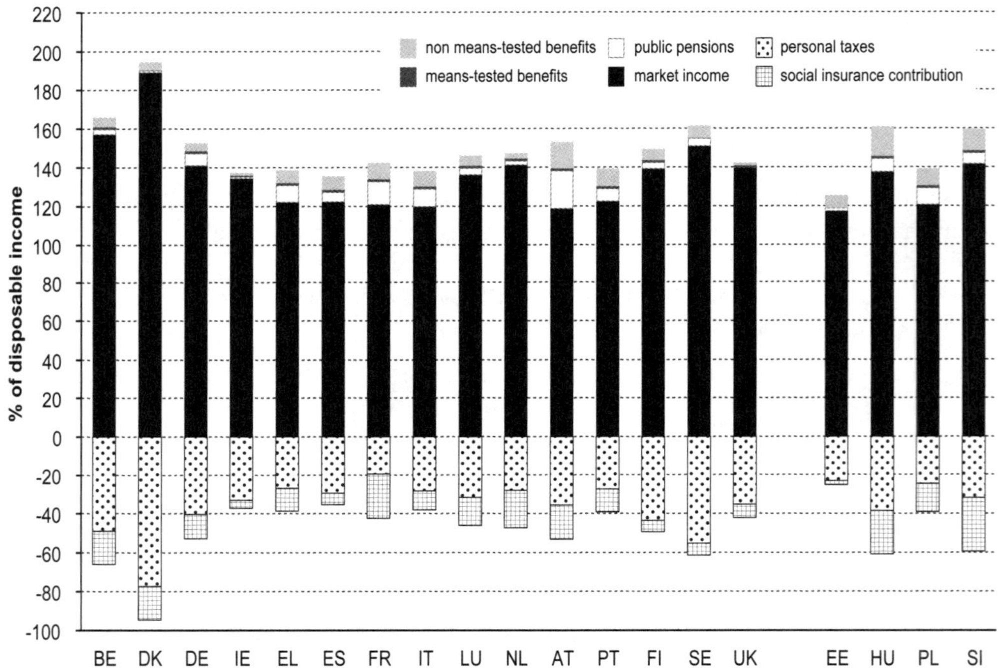

Source: EUROMOD.

The results for *Poland* are partly related to an agricultural tax which is based on imputed earnings from farm land. While we do not consider the latter as part of disposable income in our calculations, the tax is taken into account and, therefore, many of those paying it end up with low disposable income.[7] The high share of market incomes in Italy reflects a situation where most of elderly people receiving pension income are not in the first decile group and the support through other benefits is relatively small. In the case

6 That is weighing the head of household with 1, any other adult with 0.5 and a child (younger than 14 years) with 0.3.

7 Agricultural tax accounts for 10% of total personal taxes and 20% of it is concentrated in the first decile. Excluding it from calculations lowers the share of market income for the bottom decile (after recalculating deciles) from 80% to 67% of disposable income, for personal taxes from 23% to 6% and for contributions from 23% to 20%.

of *Hungary*, the results are influenced by social insurance contributions for self-employed, which are not only relatively high on average but also rather regressive due to a fixed amount component. These factors also explain why there is significant tax liability for the bottom decile group in these three countries. Apart from them, only the Nordic countries and the UK charge the lowest decile with substantial income taxes.[8] The overall tax liability is rather low and mostly comprised of social insurance contributions.

Finally, the composition of disposable income for the top decile (see Figure 4.3 and Table A3) shows that market income exceeds disposable income at least by 20%, meaning that rich households pay significantly more in taxes than they receive back in benefits. While all the benefits are very low, there is almost no support from means-tested benefits as expected. On the other hand, the overall tax liability is much higher compared with the average for all households, mainly due to income taxes as there are often upper limits on social insurance contributions.

3.2 *Income inequality and redistribution*

The equalising effect of tax-benefit systems which varies greatly across the European Union is summarized in Figure 4.4 (and Table A4) depicting the Gini coefficient for market income, market income with public pensions and disposable income.[9]

Countries are ordered by the Gini of disposable income showing low income inequality in the continental countries (Austria, Belgium, France, Germany, Luxembourg and the Netherlands) and the Nordic countries (Denmark, Finland and Sweden) – with a Gini of between 0.22 and 0.27 – and high inequality in the Southern European countries (Greece, Italy, Portugal and Spain) and the Anglo-Saxon countries (the UK and Ireland) with a Gini of between 0.30 and 0.36. *Slovenia* and *Hungary* (0.27 in each) belong to the first group while *Estonia* (0.32) and *Poland* (0.33) to the second.[10] Compared to disposable income, market income inequality seems

8 For the UK the tax mostly comprises Council Tax which is a local property-based tax. A benefit, Council Tax benefit, provides a rebate of up to 100% for those on low income. In contrast with the "static" income decomposition employed here, an "interactive" approach would take account of the net effects of taxes and benefits.

9 In each case, incomes are equivalized using the OECD modified scale. Observations with zero or negative incomes are also included in the calculations of the Gini coefficient.

10 Conditional on non-overlapping confidence intervals around the Gini coefficient of disposable income, we can split each group into further two which statistically differ from each other: the first group into (a) Austria, Denmark, Sweden, Luxembourg, Belgium and the Netherlands, and (b) France, Germany, Finland, *Slovenia* and *Hungary*; the second group into (c) Spain, the UK, Ireland, Greece, *Estonia* and *Poland*, and (d) Italy and Portugal.

to vary somewhat less, with the exceptions of the Netherlands which has remarkably low market income inequality, and *Poland* and *Hungary* with much higher market income inequality.

Tax-benefit systems on the whole reduce income inequality substantially, although to different extents. Apart from the Netherlands, the Southern European countries and the Anglo-Saxon countries together with *Estonia* redistribute incomes the least, also helping to explain their high disposable income inequality. The Netherlands has low redistribution as market income inequality is already much lower than in other countries, most likely due to its labour market institutions. On the other hand, Hungary and Belgium redistribute income to the largest extent, followed by other continental and the Nordic countries. Comparing the effect of public pensions with those of other tax-benefit instruments, the latter dominate by absolute size (except in Greece and Spain). Note, however, that the equalising effect from public pensions is also important for the majority of countries except Ireland, the UK and the Netherlands where, as already said above, private pensions are more common.

Figure 4.4: Income inequality before and after taxes and benefits as measured by the Gini coefficient

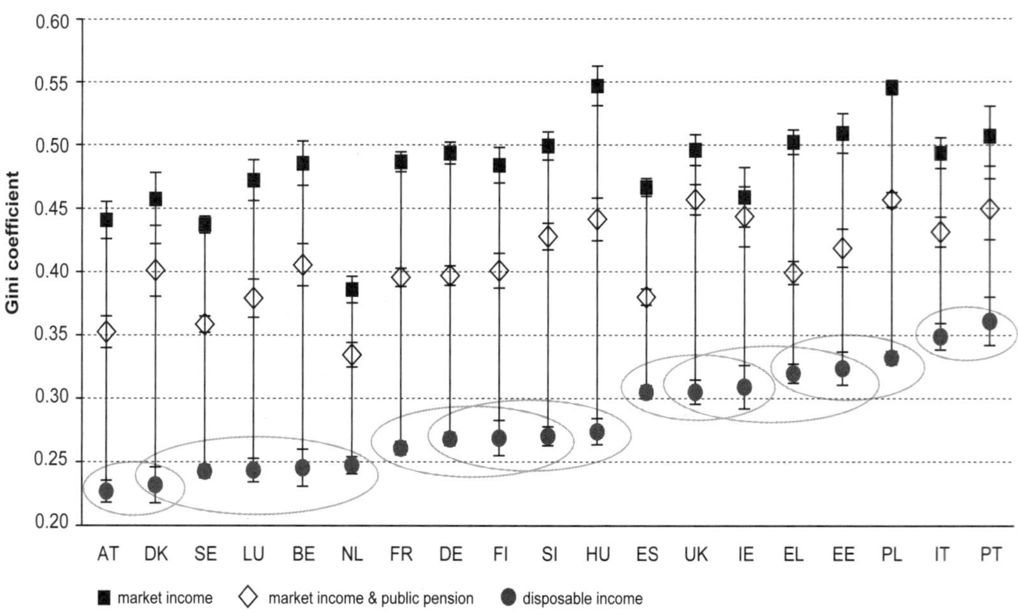

Note: Countries are ranked by the Gini coefficient of equivalized household disposable income; 95% confidence intervals shown are obtained with bootstrapping techniques using 1,000 replications; countries for which the Gini coefficients of disposable income are statistically indifferent are grouped together.

Source: EUROMOD.

In order to see the redistributive effect by the main tax-benefit system components (aside from public pensions), we exclude each group of tax-benefit instruments in turn from the disposable income and compare how much inequality (as measured by the Gini coefficient) would change. Figure 4.5 shows the Gini coefficient of (baseline) disposable income on the right-hand-side scale and the absolute change in Gini coefficient on the left-hand-side scale when each group of tax-benefit instruments is excluded. It is important to note that this is an example of static decomposition as no interactions between instruments are taken into account. For instance, as some benefits might be taxable, excluding benefits would also imply lower taxes, and in the absence of non means-tested benefits, support from means-tested benefits might be higher.

The results in Figure 4.5 (and Table A5) indicate that non means-tested benefits have the largest impact on average and that the extent of their influence varies the most across countries. Excluding these benefits increases the Gini coefficient between 0.02 (Portugal) and 0.15 points (Denmark). The effect is largest for the Nordic countries, *Poland*, and *Hungary;* and smallest in the Southern European countries, Ireland and the UK. The latter two, in turn, show the highest inequality reduction from means-tested benefits: by 0.07 and 0.08 points respectively, while this is at most 0.04 points for the others. Income taxes on average have a larger equalising effect than means-tested benefits, from 0.02 points in Poland to 0.06 points in Belgium; however, without any clear pattern of country groupings. Finally, social insurance contributions have the smallest equalising effect (up to 0.02 points), which is not surprising given that it is not their main purpose.

It is interesting to note that *Estonia* – the only country with a flat income tax among those observed – does not show a drastically smaller equalising effect from personal taxes compared to all other countries using (more) graduated tax schedules, which is contrary to what would be generally expected. Furthermore, a large average tax ratio does not necessarily lead to large reductions in inequality through taxes. As can be seen from Figure 4.2, tax liabilities also exist in the bottom decile in the countries with the highest tax liabilities (see for example Sweden).

Figure 4.5: Redistributive effect of tax-benefit instruments, absolute change in the Gini coefficient

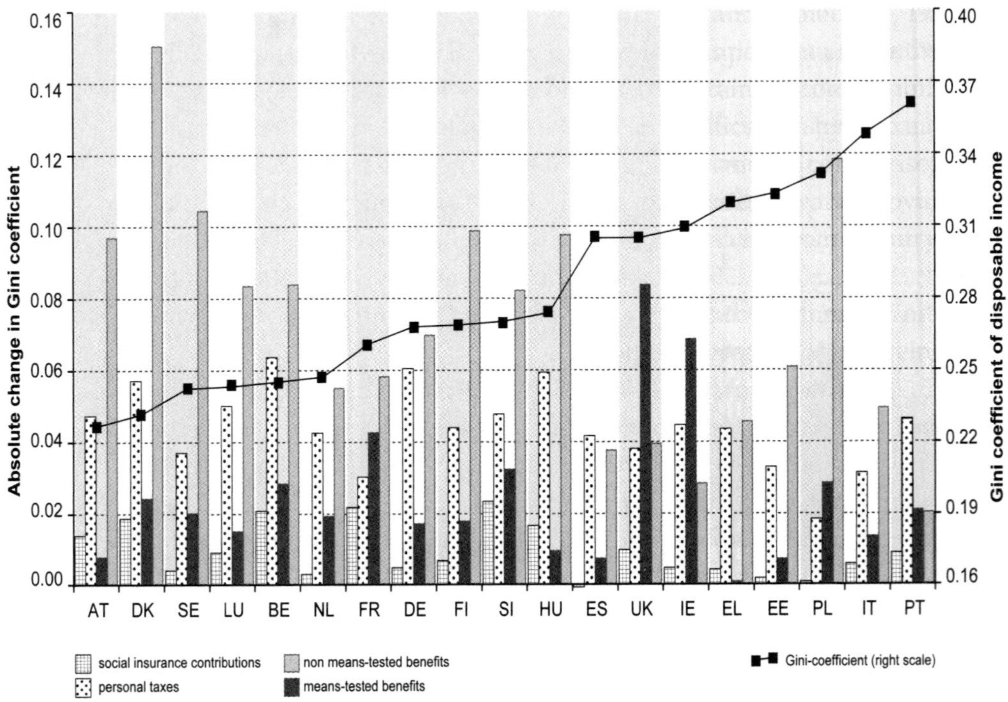

Note: Countries are ranked by the Gini coefficient of equivalized household disposable income.
Source: EUROMOD.

3.3 *Poverty*

Finally, we consider the effect of tax-benefit systems on poverty headcounts. Poverty rates vary from 9.3% in Luxembourg to 21.9% in Ireland, based on the national poverty lines defined as 60% of the median equivalized disposable income (see Figure 4.6 and Table A6). Apart from these countries, the lowest poverty rates are in the Nordic and the continental countries, and the highest in Ireland and the Southern European countries, while *New Member States* are in this case all clustered between these two groups (together with the UK).

We estimate the poverty-reducing effect of different instruments (means-tested benefits, non means-tested benefits and the two together, i.e. all benefits except public pensions) by excluding them from disposable income each in turn and at the same time keeping the poverty lines constant based on the initial disposable income. Similar to the methodology of the inequality decomposition the effects shown are "static" in the sense that they do not take account of any interactions between elements of the system. In practice, however, if non means-tested benefits were abolished, means-tested benefit entitlements would rise to compensate for the loss to some extent.

Overall, means-tested benefits have relatively little effect on poverty rates, except in Denmark, France, the UK and Ireland. It is only in the latter two countries where the effect exceeds that of non means-tested benefits. However, relative to their size overall (see Figure 4.1) means-tested benefits have a larger impact on poverty than non means-tested benefits, as one might expect. While in *Poland* and *Slovenia* means-tested payments have a clear role in reducing the poverty rate, in *Hungary* and even more so in *Estonia* their role in this respect is negligible. All benefits together (without public pensions) reduce poverty rates by between 7 and 26 percentage points and 16 percentage points on average. In *Poland, Hungary* and *Slovenia* the size of the effect is relatively large – between 20 and 22 percentage points, commensurate with that in France or Sweden. In *Estonia,* on the other hand it is lower, equal to 11 percentage points which is similar to that in Italy and Ireland.

Figure 4.6: Income poverty rates before and after benefits

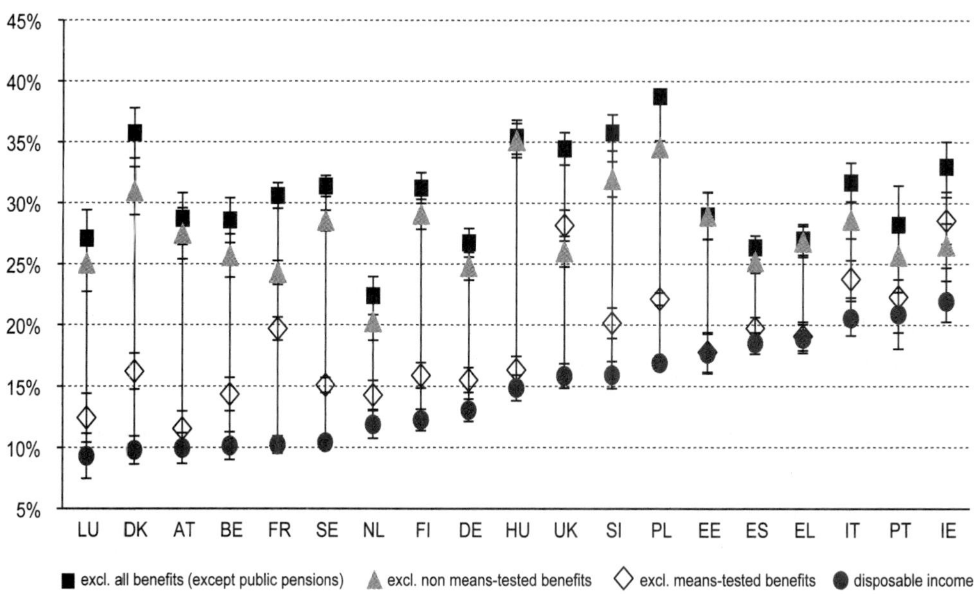

Note: Countries are ranked by the poverty headcount ratio using a poverty line defined as 60% of median equivalized disposable income. 95% confidence intervals shown are obtained with bootstrapping techniques using 1,000 replications.

Source: EUROMOD.

4 Summary

In sum, tax-benefit systems in all the 19 countries considered in this analysis reduce income inequality substantially although to a different extent. There are higher taxes and more support through benefits on average in the Nordic and the continental countries, while lower taxes and smaller benefits characterize the Southern and the Anglo-Saxon countries. The former group is also characterized by a higher degree of redistribution, lower income inequality and lower poverty, whereas the opposite is true for the latter. As a result, inequality of disposable incomes varies more across countries than market income inequality. The redistributive effect of the main tax-benefit system components (while excluding public pensions and considering these together with market income) is on average larger for non means-tested benefits, followed by personal taxes and non means-tested benefits. Social insurance contributions have unsurprisingly the smallest equalising effect, given that it is not their main purpose.

The four *New Member States* are far from forming a unique group together. While *Estonia* is similar to the Southern and the Anglo-Saxon countries, *Hungary* and *Slovenia* are closer to the Nordic and the continental countries. The relative position of *Poland* is less definite with high taxes and benefits along with high inequality. Although redistribution through benefits is large in *Poland*, the effect from taxes is the smallest of all countries. In terms of poverty, however, all four countries are clustered in the middle of the ranking of European countries. Overall, the results do not show that the role of government is necessarily larger in the former planned economies – although Hungary, Poland and Slovenia have a level of taxes and benefits higher than average, Estonia has the lowest level among all the 19 countries.

While benefits account for a much higher share of income for the bottom part of the distribution in all countries, some of them also pay substantial taxes and contributions. From this perspective *Hungary* and *Poland* clearly stand out (along with the Nordic countries), showing also the highest market income inequality among the 19 countries considered. Interestingly, Estonia – the only country with a flat income tax among those observed – does not show a drastically smaller equalising effect from personal taxes compared to all other countries using graduated tax schedules, which is contrary to what would be generally expected.

With this chapter, we aimed to demonstrate that the new infrastructure in the form of an extended EUROMOD can provide further useful evidence in the future, enhancing not only policy-making but also the transfer of knowledge between the West and the East, in both directions. The analysis presented is only one of the numerous potential applications. More specific policy issues or topics in the limelight of political debates could be on the future research agenda of EUROMOD users.

References

Atkinson, Anthony B./Rainwater, Lee/Smeeding, Timothy M. (1995) *Income Distribution in OECD Countries. Evidence from the Luxembourg Income Study*, OECD Social Policy Studies, No. 18.

Čok, Mitja/Kump, Nataša/Majcen, Boris (2008) 'EUROMOD Country Report – Slovenia 2005', EUROMOD Country Reports, http://www.iser.essex.ac.uk/research/euromod/documentation/country-reports/

EUROMOD statistics on Distribution and Decomposition of Disposable Income, http://www.iser.essex.ac.uk/research/euromod/statistics/

Eurostat Database, Living Conditions and Welfare, Social Protection, Social Protection Expenditure. Retrieved 3 November 2008 from the World Wide Web: http://ec.europa.eu/eurostat/

Figari, Francesco/Paulus, Alari/Sutherland, Holly (2008) 'Income Inequality and the Effect of Public Policies in the European Union: What Happens with Enlargement?', Presentation at the 30th General Conference of the International Association for Research in Income and Wealth (IARIW), Portoroz, Slovenia, 24-30 August, 2008.

Förster, Michael/Mira d'Ercole, Marco (2005) 'Income Distribution and Poverty in OECD Countries in the Second Half of the 1990s', OECD Social, Employment and Migration Working Papers, No. 22.

Förster, Michael/Pearson, Mark (2002) 'Income Distribution and Poverty in the OECD Area: Trends and Driving Forces', *OECD Economic Studies* 34: 7-39.

Hegedűs, Péter/Lietz, Christine/Szivós, Péter (2008) 'EUROMOD Country Report – Hungary 2005', EUROMOD Country Reports, http://www.iser.essex.ac.uk/research/euromod/documentation/country-reports/

Immervoll, Herwig/Levy, Horacio/Lietz, Christine/Mantovani, Daniela/O'Donoghue, Cathal/Sutherland, Holly/Verbist, Gerlinde (2006) 'Household Incomes and Redistribution in the European Union: Quantifying the Equalizing Properties of Taxes and Benefits', pp. 135-165 in: Papadimitriou, Dimitri B. (ed.), *The Distributional Effects of Government Spending and Taxation.*

Levy, Horacio/Morawski, Leszek (2008) 'EUROMOD Country Report – Poland 2005', EUROMOD Country Reports, http://www.iser.essex.ac.uk/research/euromod/documentation/country-reports/

Lüpsik, Silja/Paulus, Alari/Võrk, Andres (2008) 'EUROMOD Country Report – Estonia 2005', EUROMOD Country Reports, http://www.iser.essex.ac.uk/research/euromod/documentation/country-reports/

Mahler, Vincent A./Jesuit, David K. (2006) 'Fiscal Redistribution in the Developed Countries: New Insights from the Luxembourg Income Study', *Socio-Economic Review* 4 (3): 483-511.

OECD (2008) *Growing Unequal? Income Distribution and Poverty in OECD Countries.*

Oxley, Howard/Burniaux, Jean-Marc/Dang, Thai-Thanh/Mira d'Ercole, Marco (1999) 'Income Distribution and Poverty in 13 OECD Countries', *OECD Economic Studies* 29: 55-94.

Sutherland, Holly (2001) 'EUROMOD: An Integrated European Benefit-Tax Model, Final Report', EUROMOD Working Paper EM9/01. Microsimulation Unit, ISER, University of Essex.

Sutherland, Holly (2007) 'EUROMOD: The Tax-benefit Microsimulation Model for the European Union', pp. 483-488 in: Gupta, Anil/Harding, Ann (eds.), *Modelling Our Future: Population Ageing, Health and Aged Care*, International Symposia in Economic Theory and Econometrics, Vol 16. Elsevier.

Annex A: Statistics on income distribution

Table A1: Income composition (% of disposable income), all households

Country	Market income	Personal taxes	Social insurance contribu-tions	Benefits	Public pensions	Means-tested benefits	Non means-tested benefits
BE	109.2	-28.7	-13.1	32.6	14.6	3.1	14.9
DK	130.7	-50.3	-13.9	33.5	10.1	2.9	20.5
DE	108.1	-21.2	-17.2	30.3	16.9	2.1	11.3
IE	105.7	-17.7	-3.5	15.6	2.3	8.5	4.8
EL	94.4	-10.6	-13.0	29.1	19.1	0.1	9.8
ES	96.9	-15.1	-6.4	24.6	15.0	1.1	8.5
FR	93.4	-9.0	-18.0	33.6	17.4	4.5	11.7
IT	99.7	-19.9	-8.9	29.1	15.9	1.9	11.4
LU	94.5	-13.6	-11.9	31.1	16.2	1.6	13.2
NL	114.3	-13.6	-21.5	20.8	10.6	1.9	8.2
AT	97.8	-19.2	-16.7	38.1	19.6	1.0	17.5
PT	100.4	-12.1	-10.1	21.7	11.2	2.2	8.3
FI	103.7	-30.6	-5.3	32.2	14.3	2.2	15.7
SE	112.3	-41.1	-6.8	35.5	16.2	2.2	17.1
UK	107.0	-22.7	-5.8	21.6	6.7	8.4	6.6
EE	90.9	-15.0	-1.9	26.0	13.0	0.6	12.5
HU	93.8	-16.7	-17.1	40.0	18.7	0.8	20.6
PL	92.7	-18.6	-14.8	40.7	18.5	2.8	19.3
SI	101.0	-14.2	-21.2	34.3	13.0	3.9	17.4

Source: Own calculations with EUROMOD (version D25).

Table A2: Income composition (% of disposable income), bottom decile

Country	Market income	Personal taxes	Social insurance contributions	Benefits	Public pensions	Means-tested benefits	Non means-tested benefits
BE	25.5	-1.5	-2.2	78.1	13.1	42.5	22.6
DK	39.7	-27.8	-5.8	93.9	52.8	8.6	32.5
DE	31.1	-0.1	-6.2	75.2	23.8	18.9	32.6
IE	13.1	-0.4	-0.2	87.6	14.4	53.2	19.9
EL	58.7	0.3	-10.5	51.5	38.2	1.0	12.3
ES	56.7	-0.6	-8.3	52.2	27.8	9.2	15.3
FR	49.0	-1.8	-9.3	62.2	25.8	17.1	19.3
IT	72.9	-9.4	-8.1	44.6	18.1	10.5	16.0
LU	58.6	-0.8	-9.1	51.3	6.6	17.9	26.7
NL	46.4	-2.4	-17.9	73.9	21.3	25.0	27.5
AT	35.9	-2.0	-7.2	73.3	42.2	6.4	24.6
PT	40.0	-0.2	-4.3	64.5	31.0	21.7	11.8
FI	30.9	-9.3	-1.4	79.9	28.1	16.1	35.7
SE	51.7	-23.7	-4.1	76.1	29.7	15.6	30.8
UK	19.3	-11.0	-0.3	92.0	21.8	55.1	15.1
EE	34.5	-1.4	-1.9	68.8	18.5	13.9	36.4
HU	70.8	-5.5	-27.5	62.2	8.0	13.1	41.0
PL	80.3	-22.9	-23.1	65.7	11.2	24.2	30.3
SI	39.1	-0.7	-11.1	72.8	22.7	32.8	17.3

Note: Deciles based on household equivalized disposable income.

Source: Own calculations with EUROMOD (version D25).

Table A3: Income composition (% of disposable income), top decile

Country	Market income	Personal taxes	Social insurance contribu-tions	Benefits	Public pensions	Means-tested benefits	Non means-tested benefits
BE	157.0	-48.9	-17.1	9.0	3.9	0.2	5.0
DK	190.0	-77.3	-17.4	4.6	0.4	0.0	4.3
DE	140.9	-40.4	-12.4	11.9	7.2	0.5	4.2
IE	135.5	-33.2	-4.1	1.9	0.3	0.8	0.8
EL	122.0	-26.9	-11.8	16.8	10.1	0.0	6.7
ES	122.2	-29.5	-6.0	13.4	5.5	0.9	7.0
FR	120.7	-19.5	-22.9	21.8	13.1	0.2	8.5
IT	119.6	-28.5	-9.8	18.6	10.1	0.4	8.1
LU	135.9	-31.9	-14.2	10.1	4.7	0.2	5.2
NL	141.0	-28.2	-19.1	6.3	3.5	0.0	2.8
AT	118.5	-35.7	-17.4	34.6	20.8	0.1	13.7
PT	122.3	-27.6	-11.7	17.0	7.6	0.3	9.1
FI	139.0	-43.6	-5.8	10.4	4.2	0.4	5.8
SE	150.7	-55.2	-6.2	10.7	4.4	0.0	6.4
UK	139.9	-35.4	-6.8	2.3	1.0	0.2	1.0
EE	117.2	-23.3	-2.1	8.2	1.6	0.0	6.6
HU	137.3	-38.6	-22.3	23.6	8.2	0.0	15.3
PL	120.4	-24.7	-14.4	18.8	9.9	0.1	8.8
SI	141.4	-32.1	-27.4	18.1	6.6	0.5	11.0

Note: Deciles based on household equivalized disposable income.

Source: Own calculations with EUROMOD (version D25).

Table A4: Income inequality before and after taxes and benefits as measured by the Gini coefficient

Country	Market income			Market income & public pensions			Disposable income		
	point estimate	confidence interval		point estimate	confidence interval		point estimate	confidence interval	
		min	max		min	max		min	max
BE	0.486	0.468	0.503	0.405	0.389	0.422	0.245	0.231	0.260
DK	0.457	0.436	0.478	0.401	0.380	0.422	0.232	0.218	0.246
DE	0.494	0.485	0.502	0.397	0.389	0.405	0.268	0.263	0.273
EL	0.502	0.493	0.512	0.399	0.390	0.408	0.320	0.312	0.327
ES	0.467	0.460	0.474	0.380	0.374	0.386	0.305	0.300	0.310
FR	0.487	0.479	0.495	0.396	0.388	0.403	0.261	0.256	0.266
IE	0.459	0.435	0.483	0.444	0.420	0.467	0.309	0.292	0.326
IT	0.494	0.482	0.506	0.431	0.420	0.443	0.349	0.339	0.359
LU	0.472	0.456	0.488	0.379	0.364	0.394	0.243	0.234	0.253
NL	0.386	0.375	0.396	0.335	0.325	0.344	0.247	0.241	0.254
AT	0.441	0.426	0.455	0.353	0.340	0.365	0.227	0.218	0.235
PT	0.507	0.484	0.530	0.450	0.425	0.474	0.361	0.342	0.380
SE	0.437	0.430	0.444	0.359	0.352	0.365	0.243	0.237	0.248
FI	0.484	0.470	0.498	0.401	0.387	0.415	0.269	0.255	0.283
UK	0.496	0.484	0.508	0.457	0.445	0.469	0.305	0.296	0.315
EE	0.509	0.494	0.524	0.419	0.404	0.434	0.324	0.311	0.337
HU	0.547	0.531	0.563	0.441	0.425	0.458	0.274	0.264	0.284
PL	0.545	0.540	0.551	0.457	0.451	0.463	0.332	0.327	0.337
SI	0.499	0.488	0.510	0.428	0.417	0.438	0.270	0.263	0.278

Note: 95% confidence intervals shown are obtained with bootstrapping techniques using 1,000 replications. All income concepts are equivalized using the OECD modified scale.

Source: Own calculations with EUROMOD (version D25).

Table A5: Redistributive effect of tax-benefit instruments, Gini coefficient

Country	Disposable income	Absolute change in Gini coefficient of disposable income, excluding ...			
		social insurance contributions	personal taxes	means-tested benefits	non means-tested benefits
BE	0.245	0.021	0.064	0.029	0.084
DK	0.232	0.019	0.057	0.025	0.151
DE	0.268	0.005	0.061	0.017	0.070
EL	0.320	0.004	0.044	0.001	0.046
ES	0.305	0.000	0.042	0.007	0.038
FR	0.261	0.022	0.030	0.043	0.058
IE	0.309	0.005	0.045	0.069	0.029
IT	0.349	0.006	0.031	0.014	0.050
LU	0.243	0.009	0.050	0.015	0.084
NL	0.247	0.003	0.043	0.020	0.055
AT	0.227	0.014	0.047	0.008	0.097
PT	0.361	0.009	0.046	0.021	0.021
SE	0.243	0.004	0.037	0.020	0.105
FI	0.269	0.007	0.044	0.018	0.099
UK	0.305	0.010	0.038	0.084	0.040
EE	0.324	0.002	0.033	0.007	0.061
HU	0.274	0.017	0.059	0.010	0.098
PL	0.332	0.001	0.019	0.029	0.119
SI	0.270	0.024	0.048	0.033	0.082

Note: All income concepts are equivalized using the OECD modified scale.

Source: Own calculations with EUROMOD (version D25).

Table A6: Income poverty rates before and after benefits

Countries	Disposable income			Disposable income excluding … means-tested benefits			non means-tested benefits			all benefits (except public pensions)		
	Poverty rates	conf. interval min	conf. interval max	Poverty rates	conf. interval min	conf. interval max	Poverty rates	conf. interval min	conf. interval max	Poverty rates	conf. interval min	conf. interval max
BE	0.101	0.090	0.113	0.144	0.130	0.157	0.257	0.239	0.274	0.286	0.267	0.304
DK	0.098	0.087	0.109	0.162	0.148	0.177	0.310	0.290	0.330	0.357	0.337	0.378
DE	0.130	0.121	0.140	0.155	0.145	0.165	0.248	0.237	0.260	0.267	0.256	0.279
EL	0.189	0.177	0.201	0.191	0.179	0.203	0.268	0.256	0.281	0.270	0.257	0.283
ES	0.185	0.176	0.194	0.197	0.188	0.206	0.252	0.243	0.262	0.264	0.254	0.273
FR	0.102	0.095	0.109	0.197	0.187	0.206	0.243	0.233	0.253	0.306	0.295	0.317
IE	0.220	0.203	0.236	0.286	0.267	0.305	0.265	0.247	0.284	0.330	0.309	0.350
IT	0.206	0.191	0.220	0.238	0.223	0.253	0.286	0.271	0.302	0.317	0.301	0.333
LU	0.093	0.075	0.112	0.124	0.104	0.144	0.251	0.227	0.274	0.271	0.248	0.294
NL	0.119	0.107	0.130	0.143	0.131	0.155	0.203	0.187	0.218	0.224	0.208	0.240
AT	0.100	0.087	0.112	0.115	0.101	0.130	0.275	0.254	0.296	0.287	0.266	0.308
PT	0.209	0.180	0.237	0.223	0.194	0.253	0.257	0.227	0.287	0.282	0.250	0.314
SE	0.104	0.099	0.109	0.151	0.145	0.157	0.285	0.277	0.294	0.314	0.305	0.323
FI	0.122	0.114	0.131	0.159	0.149	0.169	0.291	0.278	0.303	0.312	0.300	0.325
UK	0.159	0.149	0.168	0.282	0.269	0.294	0.260	0.248	0.273	0.345	0.331	0.358
EE	0.177	0.161	0.193	0.178	0.162	0.194	0.290	0.270	0.309	0.290	0.271	0.309
HU	0.149	0.138	0.159	0.163	0.152	0.174	0.351	0.337	0.365	0.354	0.340	0.368
PL	0.169	0.164	0.173	0.222	0.216	0.227	0.346	0.340	0.351	0.388	0.382	0.393
SI	0.159	0.148	0.170	0.202	0.189	0.214	0.320	0.305	0.334	0.358	0.343	0.373

Note: Poverty line defined as 60% of the national median equivalized disposable income. 95% confidence intervals shown are obtained with bootstrapping techniques using 1,000 replications.

Source: Own calculations with EUROMOD (version D25).

Chapter 5

Flat Tax Reform in Eastern Europe: A Comparative Analysis of Alternative Scenarios in Estonia, Hungary and Slovenia, Using EUROMOD

Alari Paulus / Orsolya Lelkes / Mitja Čok / Nataša Kump / Péter Hegedűs / Andres Võrk / Péter Szivós / Silja Kralik

1 Introduction

Flat tax schemes are popular in Eastern Europe, with an ever-increasing number of countries where they are introduced, and yet many other where they are recurrently discussed. The majority of Eastern European countries seems to have introduced such a scheme, starting with the Baltic States in the mid-1990s, followed by Russia, Ukraine, the Slovak Republic, Serbia, Romania, Macedonia, Montenegro, and then most recently by Albania, Bulgaria, the Czech Republic (2008), Belarus and Bosnia and Herzegovina (2009). Poland and Greece are also considering such a move. In many of the countries it meant simplifying the tax scheme (e.g. eliminating tax allowances and tax deductions), but also lowering the average tax burden. Not in all countries, though, as Lithuania, for example, set the flat tax rate at the highest bracket of the existing regime: 33% (Keen et al., 2008).

What is actually meant by "flat (income) tax" varies a great deal by country. Very few countries have a flat rate tax scheme where all types of incomes are taxed with the same rate, including earnings, capital income and corporate income. In its "pure" form flat tax would impose one single rate on the whole population, irrespective of their income levels (and their abilities to conceal incomes, e.g. via transfers to foreign countries), thus giving up the role of the state in redistributing incomes via the tax system. This may save administrative costs, as all redistribution is costly. In all the flat tax countries but Georgia and Bulgaria, there is a basic allowance for people with low incomes, which is often supplemented by an allowance for families. Flat tax reform may have its appeal as an opportunity for simplifying the tax scheme, primarily from numerous tax allowances accumulated over long years due to interest groups' rent-seeking. Simplicity in turn is likely to save administration costs and increase compliance. On the other hand, flat tax rates required to attain budget neutrality tend to benefit mainly those with high incomes at the expense of low and middle income households (Lelkes and Benedek, 2007; Paulus and Peichl, 2008). As Paulus and Peichl note, this may explain why flat taxes have not been politically successful in Western Europe.

Albeit the international popularity of the scheme, little is yet known on its impact on macro-performance and tax compliance. One of the success stories is Russia, where tax revenues increased by 25% following the 2001 introduction of the scheme. However, according to Ivanova et al. (2005) it is not clear to what extent this is attributable to the parametric reform or to increased law enforcement. The authors also highlight that oil revenues increased massively in this period, resulting in fast economic growth and thus producing greater tax revenues. Nevertheless, the reform itself was associated with increased tax compliance rather than improved law enforcement as shown by Gorodnichenko et al. (2007). Another example, Slovakia, introduced flat taxes as part of an overall structural reform, including pensions, social transfers, education, health care and the tax system. They implemented a uniform 19% tax rate (replacing 18 different rates), widened the tax base, and decreased the progressivity of the tax system.[1] The reception of the reform by the international financial market was positive, reflected in the improved country credit rating. On the other hand, there is no empirical evidence on the behavioural impact of the reform. The Slovakian reform was also an inspiration for the Slovenian debate on the flat tax idea in 2005,

1 Note that the employee social security contribution remained, thus the all-in tax rate (calculated as the combined central and sub-central government income tax plus employee social security contribution, as a percentage of gross wage earnings) equals 30%, which is not different from the pre-reform rate for those with average incomes. It was the distribution of the tax burden that has changed, increasing from 21.5% to 30% for those with low incomes (67% of average wage) and decreasing from 36.5% to 29% for those with high incomes (167% of average wage meaning the average annual gross wage earnings of adult, full-time manual and non-manual workers in the industry) (OECD Tax Database, www.oecd.org/ctp/taxdatabase).

which was however finally rejected and instead their progressive personal income tax system was modified to some extent.[2]

Our aim with this chapter is to contribute to the empirical literature on flat taxes by focusing on recent flat tax proposals in three Eastern European countries – Estonia, Hungary and Slovenia. Using microsimulation techniques we estimate the potential impact of these proposals on household incomes. We simulate each alternative scenario not only for the country of origin but also for the two other countries, thereby three in total for each country. These scenarios are compared to the existing tax system in 2005, focusing on the redistributive impact of the reforms. All scenarios assume full compliance, and as such, do not estimate potential changes in tax evasion. Also, these policy scenarios are not designed to be revenue-neutral on the national level, and therefore, the total fiscal cost varies both across countries and scenarios.

We find that the most radical scenario with a flat tax rate of 20% and no tax concessions (apart from exempting pensions from tax) would have a dramatic effect on inequality and poverty, and most of the cost of the reform would be borne by lower income groups. In this case, the government budget and the richest fifth of the population appear to be the only beneficiaries. A less radical proposal, with a 20% tax rate, a basic allowance and a family allowance still has a negative impact on the majority of the population, albeit to a much smaller extent, although the total budgetary effect is slightly negative. Another scenario with a slightly lower tax rate and an additional allowance for pensions (corresponding to the future Estonian flat tax scheme) would cost between 0.9-1.2% of the GDP, while having rather diverse effects on households across countries, depending on the original tax system.

In the following section we present methodology and data. This will be followed by the description of the existing tax and benefit schemes and the three alternative scenarios in section 3. Section 4 describes how these hypothetical flat tax schemes would affect inequality and poverty of the total population and that of specific age groups. We will then show in section 5 how the change of tax burden affects the budgetary balance and households at various income levels. Finally, section 6 concludes.

2 The proposition of a tax system similar to the Slovakian one, was included among government reform proposals (*Odbor za reforme*, 2005). However, this concept triggered a sharp response from labour unions in Slovenia, mainly due to the idea of a replacement of the existing double VAT rate system (with a reduced 8.5% and standard 20% rate) with a single VAT rate and thus ultimately was not regarded to be politically feasible.

2 Methodology and data

The analysis is based on EUROMOD, the European tax-benefit microsimulation model, which covers all 15 pre-May 2004 Member States of the European Union and Estonia, Hungary, Poland and Slovenia, of which we focus on Estonia, Hungary and Slovenia. The model is designed to answer "what if" questions about different policy reforms at European level. EUROMOD is unique in being a research tool that is relevant both at the national and European level, offering infrastructure for comparing complex and often very different tax and benefit systems across countries.

EUROMOD, as other tax-benefit models, is a computer programme which operates on household micro-data from representative sources (Immervoll et al., 1999). It calculates disposable income for each household in the dataset. This calculation is made up of elements of income taken from the survey data combined with components that are simulated by the model (i.e. taxes and benefits). An evident advantage of such models is the possibility of evaluating the effects of hypothetical changes to tax- or benefit rules. As Lietz and Mantovani (2007) note, it is a tool, which allows " 'laboratory experiments' concerning tax-benefit systems, as by simulating reforms their potential effects can be studied before their actual implementation".

EUROMOD focuses on cash benefits, social insurance contributions and personal direct taxes. It can simulate most of these instruments except where the underlying datasets lack the necessary background information, most notably benefits which entitlement is based on previous contribution history (e.g. pensions). EUROMOD calculations are carried out under the assumption of full benefit take-up and no tax evasion, therefore focusing on the intended effects of tax-benefit systems. EUROMOD's concept of disposable income includes monetary incomes without capital gains and other lump-sum incomes, net of income tax and social insurance contributions. (For further information on EUROMOD, see Chapter 3 in this volume and Sutherland 2001, 2007.)

Databases for all three countries studied here are derived from administrative sources or from household budget surveys (see the details in Table 5.1). There are two main modifications to the original datasets: (a) net-to-gross imputations and (b) income uprating. First, as tax-benefit calculations are applied to gross incomes, these were imputed where the original dataset only recorded incomes net of (withholding) taxes. Secondly, in order to match the baseline tax-benefit policy year and income data reference period, incomes which refer to the year 2004 were uprated to 2005 using different uprating factors based on available statistics.

Table 5.1: Features of EUROMOD datasets: Estonia, Hungary, and Slovenia

Country	Base Dataset	Year of collection	Income reference period	Sample size: individuals (households)
Estonia	Household Budget Survey	2005	2005	9,201 (3,432)
Hungary	EU-SILC	2005	2004	17,958 (6,924)
Slovenia	A sub-sample of the Population Census merged with the Personal income tax database, Pension database and Social transfers database	2005 (2002)	2004	13,798 (4,777)

3 Description of existing and alternative policy scenarios

This section summarizes the key parameters of the existing personal income tax (PIT) systems as of 2005 in the three countries as well as three alternative flat tax proposals and highlights the main changes.

The existing income tax systems in 2005 vary to a large extent (see Table A1 in the Appendix for the main tax parameters, also indicating the scope of simulation of the income tax systems in EUROMOD). All three countries have effectively progressive tax systems, although the structure of tax schedules (i.e. the number and level of tax brackets) varies widely and countries operate with rather different kinds of tax allowances (or tax credits). One of the main differences across the three countries concerns the unit of assessment: while married couples can choose to be jointly taxed in Estonia, the income tax is solely levied on individuals in Hungary and Slovenia. Finally, there are also differences in the underlying tax bases. It is broader in Estonia and Slovenia, where it includes capital gains, interests and dividends and pensions, in contrast to Hungary, where the personal income tax base excludes capital income and (part of) self-employment income, which are taxed under different schemes, not as part of the PIT system.

Estonia was the first Eastern-European country to introduce a flat income tax system in 1994, applying a single marginal tax rate (above a certain income threshold) initially at the level of 26%. In 2005, the income tax rate was reduced to 24%, and it is expected to be gradually reduced to 18% by 2011.[3] The basic allowance component (1,303 EUR[4] annually per person) effectively induces progressivity in the personal income tax system in the sense that the average tax rate increases with the income level, even though the marginal tax rate remains constant. An additional allowance of the same amount is granted for every dependent child, starting from the third, and another allowance applies to pension incomes (2,300 EUR per year in 2005). Some expenses are also deductible (e.g. mortgage interests), but usually are of less importance.

The actual (2005) Hungarian personal income tax system comprises of two tax brackets for all taxpayers, supplemented with a tax credit on wages and salaries and with numerous other tax credits. The tax rates applied are 18% on the first 6,086 EUR (in annual terms) and 38% on the part of incomes exceeding that. There is a "targeted" basic allowance to employees, with a maximum amount of tax credit on wages and salaries of 438 EUR per year. Among other tax credits, family and disability tax credits can be simulated in EUROMOD (see Table A1). Other allowances, which relate to tuition fees and voluntary pension insurance and a large number of other expenditures cannot be simulated due to missing information in the income survey.

The Slovenian system may be called a "standard progressive" PIT scheme, which includes five tax brackets and marginal tax rates between 16% and 50%, the latter being rather high by international comparison. Pensioners benefit from an additional tax credit, which reduces their tax bill to the extent that only a few of them effectively pay income tax. Similarly to Estonia and Hungary, there is a basic tax-free threshold (2,355 EUR per year), and a tax concession for individuals with children. Simulations in EUROMOD cover a large number of special tax allowances, including those for disabled, self-employed journalists, student work, payments on voluntary private insurance etc., made possible by the rich original dataset, which includes a vast array of information from administrative data sources.

The actual tax systems (referred to as baselines) will be compared with three alternative scenarios reflecting flat tax policy proposals in these

3 This was the situation in 2008. However, rapidly deteriorating economic conditions and declining tax revenues forced the government to postpone the final target by one year (i.e. to 2012) in the beginning of 2009.

4 The currency exchange rates as of the 1st of July 2005 were used to convert values to euros: 1 EEK = 1 / 15.6466 EUR, 1 HUF = 1 / 246.485 EUR, 1 SIT = 1 / 239.64 EUR.

countries. In order to apply different scenarios in a consistent way across countries, we define the value of tax allowances relative to the average gross wage. All other tax-benefit policies in the reform scenarios remain the same as in the baseline, e.g. the eligibility and entitlement *rules* for cash benefits. Note that this does not imply that other taxes and benefits remain necessarily constant as their value might depend on some concept of net income which in turn is affected by the changes in income tax liability. For instance, in case of means-tested benefits, provided only if the personal or household net income is below a certain threshold, we consider the potential change of incomes due to the changes in the tax parameters. Therefore, some households may become eligible to benefits, others might lose eligibility and those who retain eligibility might see their entitlement change. The microsimulation technique used here allows us to take into account such interactions between taxes and benefits.

The simplest hypothetical scenario (referred to as *Flat1*) represents the flat tax in its purest and "most radical" form, with a single 20% tax rate and no tax concessions (apart from exempting pension incomes from tax). Note that although this scenario is motivated by the general flat tax discussion in Hungary, we do not consider it as a realistic policy proposal (partly also due to its budgetary costs), but rather as a test and a further base of comparison for alternatives.

The second scenario (*Flat2*) applies also a 20% flat tax rate but additionally introduces two allowances that are expected to benefit low-income households. A basic tax allowance which is equal to 20% of the average gross annual wage and an additional family allowance, equal to 15% of the average gross annual wage for the first child and increased by further 5 percentage points for each subsequent child. On the other hand, pension incomes in this scenario are fully taxable. This scenario follows the flat tax proposal which was seriously considered in Slovenia but eventually abandoned.

The third scenario (*Flat3*) represents the future actual PIT system in Estonia, taking effect in 2011 (according to the legislation as of 2008). This scenario includes a 18% tax rate and a basic allowance equal to 17% of the average gross annual wage, both being lower compared to the second alternative. A child allowance is available for families with children and compared to the 2005 system in Estonia, the allowance is extended also to the first two children.[5] An additional allowance applies to pension incomes; however,

5 In 2005 it was available for each child except for the first two (so only families with at least 3 children benefited) (see Table A1 in the Annex). With the reform it was intended to grant it for every child.

given that the future level of this allowance is not agreed in Estonia yet, we assume in our calculations that it will be increased in proportion to income growth by 2011 and, therefore, remains equal to 37% of the average gross annual wage (as it was in 2005).

Table 5.2: Flat tax scenarios

	Flat1	Flat2	Flat3
Income tax rate	20%	20%	18%
Basic allowance (annual)	No	20% of AGAW[1]	17% of AGAW[2]
Additional allowance per child (annual)	No	15% AGAW for the first, increasing by 5 pct. points for each subsequent child	17% of AGAW [2]
Additional pension allowance (annual)	Pensions untaxed (i.e. effectively 100%)	No	37% of AGAW[3]
Tax base	Pensions excluded	Pensions included	Pensions included

Notes: 1) AGAW = average gross annual wage. Its amount in 2005: Estonia: 6,192 EUR, Hungary: 7,709 EUR, Slovenia: 13,885 EUR.
2) Ratio to the average gross annual wage in 2011 (13,742 EUR, estimated figure by the Estonian Ministry of Finance).
3) Ratio to the average gross annual wage in 2005 (i.e. assuming that the pension allowance will be increased in proportion to income growth).

The tax bases vary for the baseline systems (see Table A1 in the Annex) and since we retain these differences across countries (with the exception of pensions) this affects the outcome of the alternative scenarios. The reason for adjusting tax bases with respect to pensions is that these are excluded from the tax base in Hungary, but taxable in Estonia and Slovenia while both have specific tax allowances for that. Therefore, in order to make these pension-related tax concessions comparable, pensions were added to the Hungarian tax base in the *Flat2* and *Flat3* scenarios[6] and removed from the tax base for Estonia and Slovenia under *Flat1*.

6 Note that this was done without any compensation, e.g. grossing up of the pension benefits. The calibration of such compensation packages could be part of further, in-depth studies on this subject.

Tables 5.3 to 5.5 summarize the main changes compared to the existing tax systems. In all countries the marginal tax rate decreases in each alternative scenario. In case of the *Flat1* scenario all the allowances are eliminated (while exempting pensions from tax), which makes it much different from the baselines. The *Flat2* policy increases the value of family allowance for all countries, especially in case of households with a larger number of children, while at the same time removing the allowance on pensions. The third scenario is somewhat less generous than the second one (in terms of general and family allowances) but includes an allowance for pension incomes.

Table 5.3: Estonia: Main changes in the tax system compared to the baseline

	Flat1	Flat2	Flat3
Marginal tax rate	Decreases	Decreases	Decreases
Basic tax allowance	Disappears (i.e. significant decrease)	Decreases (slightly)	Decreases (though increase in nominal terms)
Pension allowance	Pensions not taxable (i.e. significant increase)	Disappears (i.e. significant decrease)	No change (i.e. allowance retained)
Allowance for self-employment income from agriculture	Disappears (i.e. significant decrease)	Disappears (i.e. significant decrease)	No change (i.e. allowance retained)
Family allowance per child	Disappears (i.e. significant decrease)	Extends the coverage, increases the value for households with more than three children	Extends the coverage but decreases in real value (per child)

Notes: Flat1: flat rate of 20%, no tax concessions (apart from exempting pensions from tax).
Flat2: flat rate of 20%, basic allowance and child allowance.
Flat3: flat rate of 18%, basic allowance, child allowance and pension allowance.

Table 5.4: Hungary: Main changes in the tax system compared to the baseline

	Flat1	Flat2	Flat3
Marginal tax rate	Decreases	Decreases	Decreases
Basic tax allowance	Disappears	Decreases	Decreases
Pension allowance	Pensions not taxable (i.e. no change)	All taxable without allowance (i.e. significant decrease)	All taxable with allowance (i.e. decrease)
Family allowance for children	Disappears (i.e. significant decrease)	Increases the value in all households with dependent child/ren	Increases in households with 1 or 2 dependent child/ren, decreases for those with 3+ children
Tax credit for serious disability	Disappears	Disappears	Disappears

Notes: See Table 5.3.

Table 5.5: Slovenia: Main changes in the tax system compared to the baseline

	Flat1	Flat2	Flat3
Marginal tax rate	Decreases	Decreases	Decreases
Basic tax allowance	Disappears	Increases	Increases
Pension allowance	Pensions not taxable (i.e. significant increase)	Disappears	Decreases
Family allowance for children	Disappears (i.e. significant decrease)	Increases the value, especially for households with more than 3 children	Decreases the value, especially for households with more children
Family allowance for other dependent family members	Disappears	Increases	Disappears
Other tax allowances (disabled person's allowance, seniority allowance, self-employed professionals' allowance, allowance for selected expenses)	Disappear	Disappear	Disappear

Notes: See Table 5.3.

4 Effects of alternative scenarios on income distribution[7]

The introduction of a flat tax scheme (including all its alternative versions examined here) would have a substantial effect on inequality in Hungary and Slovenia, while less so in Estonia (see Figure 5.1). This is due to the fact that Estonia already has a functioning flat tax system as well as the highest income inequality in the baseline. The *Flat1* scenario would increase the Gini coefficient from 0.27 to 0.32 in Hungary and from 0.27 to 0.3 in Slovenia.

The current level of inequality in Hungary and Slovenia is below that of Estonia, as shown by the Gini coefficient and quintile ratio (S80/S20).[8] The introduction of the 2011 Estonian scheme (*Flat3*) would retain inequality as the highest in Estonia. Note that under the current assumptions, inequality in Estonia would increase with the 2011 system (adjusted to 2005 prices) compared to the 2005 one, holding demographic characteristics and incomes constant. This is not particularly surprising, given that the distributional considerations were not on the agenda at the formulation of the tax changes.

The alternative flat tax scenarios have a more profound effect on poverty. The risk of poverty, using a constant poverty line at 60% of the median baseline equivalized income, increases significantly under *Flat1*, due to the abolition of tax allowances. The relative effect is the greatest in Hungary, a country with substantial tax concessions in the baseline system. Overall poverty somewhat increases in *Flat2* and *Flat3* compared to the baseline in all three countries, although the magnitude of change is much smaller than under *Flat1*. A marked difference is Estonia, where poverty under *Flat2* remains high. This is mainly due to the large increase in the poverty risk of the elderly (see further below). Note that the estimated poverty rate in Estonia is smaller in *Flat3* (the future scenario) compared to the baseline, suggesting that the reform is likely to have a beneficial effect on low-income groups.[9]

Next, we explore whether the changes affect any specific age group in particular. The flat tax scenarios have the largest impact on the poverty risk of the elderly in Estonia. In contrast, the working age population and especially children are affected more in Hungary and Slovenia. In particular, we

7 All the following results for income distribution are computed for individuals according to their household disposable income equivalized by the modified OECD equivalence scale, i.e. weighing the first adult with 1, additional persons aged 14+ with 0.5 and persons under 14 with 0.3.

8 The ratio of the share in total income of those in the top quintile to those in the bottom quintile of the distribution.

9 The incomes of the affluent groups have increased to a larger extent in monetary terms, which explains why inequality rises and poverty declines at the same time.

found three main features: (1) elderly are strongly hit by the *Flat2* scenario in Estonia (7.8 percentage points increase in the poverty rate), while in the other two countries this effect is moderate (2.2-3.3 percentage points), (2) children suffer the most in Hungary under *Flat1* (poverty increases by 8.9 percentage points), (3) poverty increases among the working age population in all three countries under *Flat1*, although the magnitude is greater in Hungary and Slovenia.

Figure 5.1: Income inequality under different policy scenarios in Estonia, Hungary and Slovenia

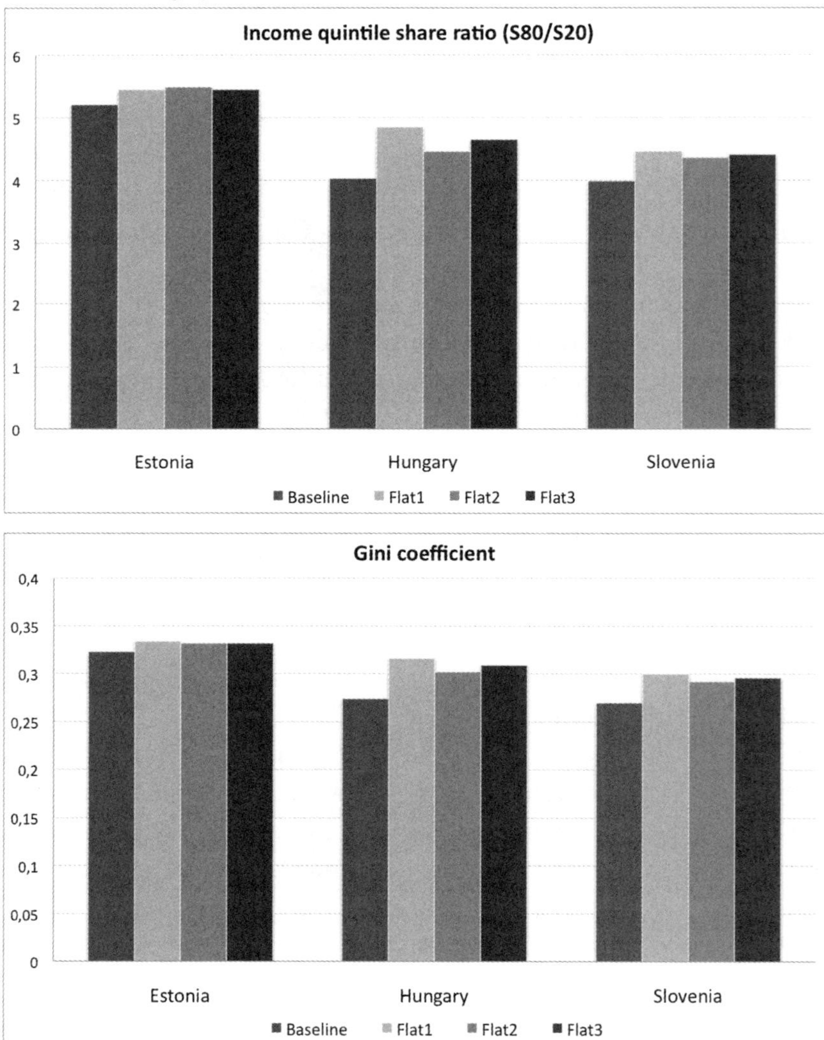

Source: Own calculations using EUROMOD version D25.
For more details, see Tables A11-A13 in the Annex.

Figure 5.2: Poverty rates under different policy scenarios in Estonia, Hungary and Slovenia, in percentages

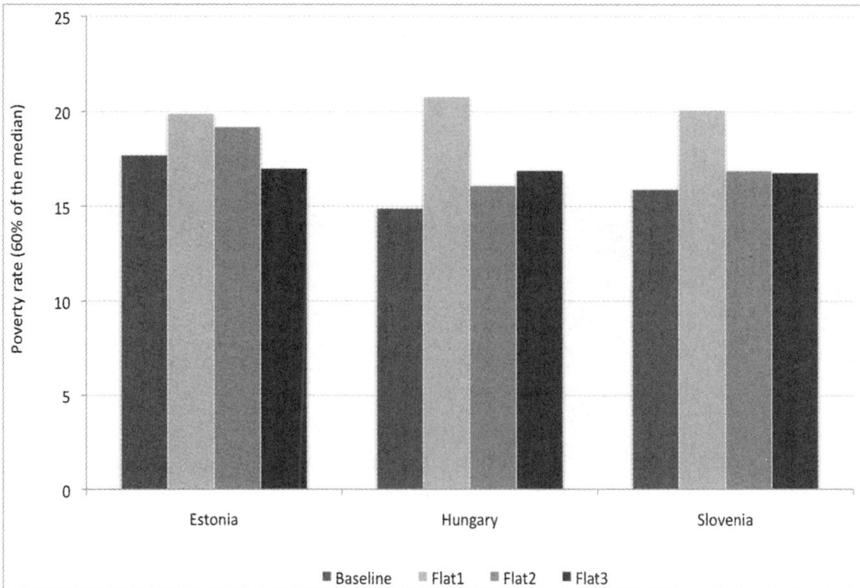

Note: Poverty thresholds are kept constant at 60% of the (national) baseline median equivalized income.
Source: Own calculations using EUROMOD version D25.
For more details, see Tables A3, A6 and A9 in the Annex.

The reason for the elderly being so profoundly affected in Estonia under *Flat2* is that they would lose their current tax allowance which increases their tax burden significantly, and given that many of them are concentrated around the poverty line, this can change the poverty measure quite considerably. The poverty risk of the elderly would decline in the *Flat1* scenario, as the whole pension income becomes tax-free. However, given that the existing pension allowance combined with the basic allowance makes the effective tax burden on pensions rather low already, the decline in poverty risk is marginal. Surprisingly, for Slovenia the poverty risk of the elderly increases slightly under *Flat1*, in spite of the fact that their pension incomes would be entirely tax-exempt (which are partly taxed in the baseline system). In other scenarios, *Flat2* and *Flat3*, where pensioner incomes would be partly taxed, the poverty risk of the elderly, respectively, increases and remains unchanged. Pensioner incomes are not affected by *Flat1* in Hungary because pensions remain untaxed. The increase of the poverty rate of the elderly in *Flat2* reflects that pensions become fully taxable, although the magnitude of change (2.2 percentage points) is modest.

Figure 5.3: Poverty rates in different age groups

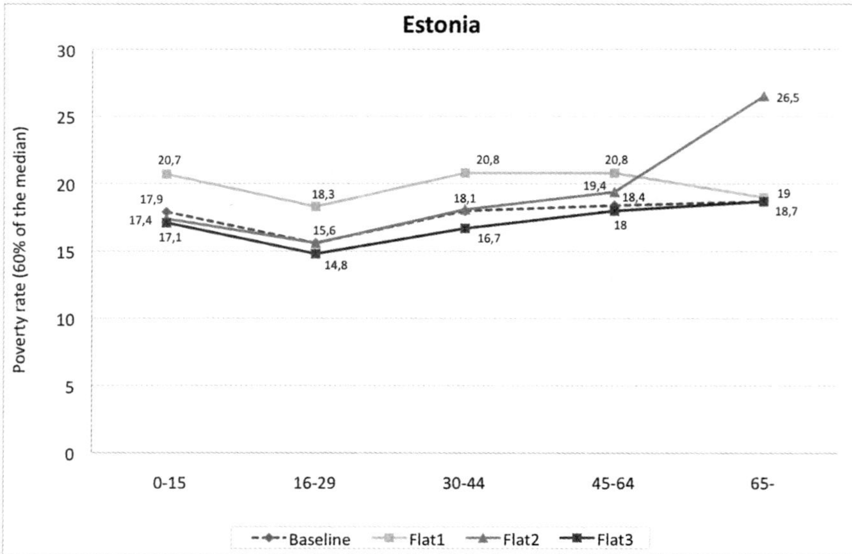

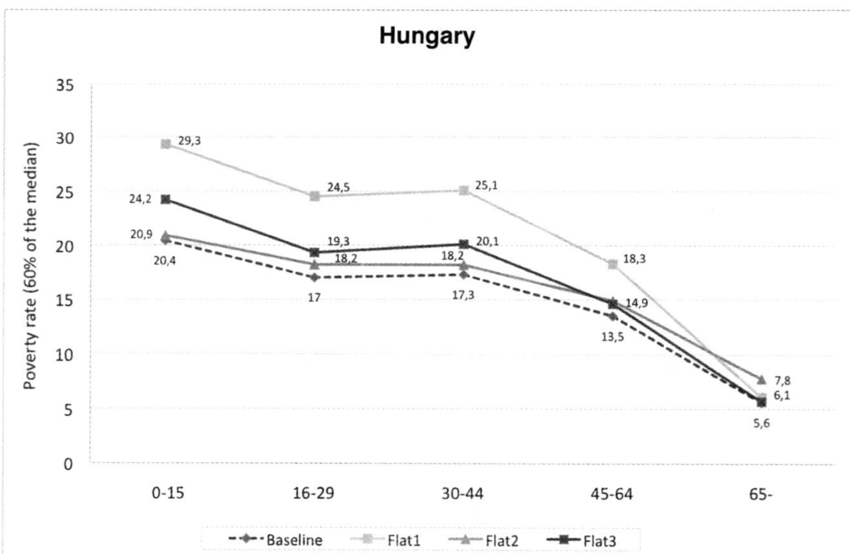

Figure 5.3: Poverty rates in different age groups (continued)

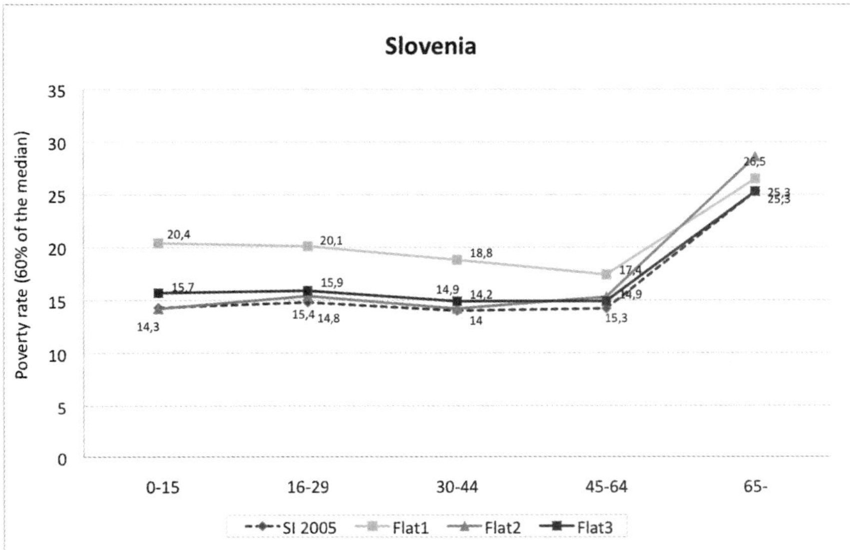

Note: Poverty thresholds are kept constant at 60% of the (national) baseline median equivalized income.
Source: Own calculations using EUROMOD version D25.
For more details, see Tables A3, A6 and A9 in the Annex.

Why are children and working age households affected in Hungary? *Flat1* would increase poverty as it eliminates the general tax allowance for employees and the tax allowance for families with children, which do benefit households substantially in the baseline system (for an overview of major changes, see Table 5.4). The introduction of *Flat2* would increase both of these major tax allowances compared to the baseline, but at the same time would make pensions taxable. This latter might also affect some households with dependent children. As a result of these two contrasting effects, poverty among children (up to the age of 15) would remain largely at the same level as in the baseline.

5 Fiscal cost and change of the total tax burden

The fiscal effect of the flat tax scenarios simulated here largely depends on the actual tax system. While the introduction of a 20% PIT with no tax exemptions (*Flat1*) is expected to raise extra budget revenues in all the countries, a scheme with a basic and a child allowance and pensions fully taxed (*Flat2*) would generate a moderate loss for the budget (see Figure 5.4), assuming no changes in tax compliance and labour force participation. The third scenario, with a lower tax rate and an additional allowance for pensions (*Flat3*) would cost more in all countries. The cost of this, probably most feasible, scenario ranges between 16 and 26% as a share of total personal income tax revenues, although it remains below 1.3% of the GDP in all three countries. The fiscal cost is the highest in Estonia, compared to the baseline system.

Figure 5.4: Total fiscal cost of alternative scenarios in Estonia, Hungary and Slovenia

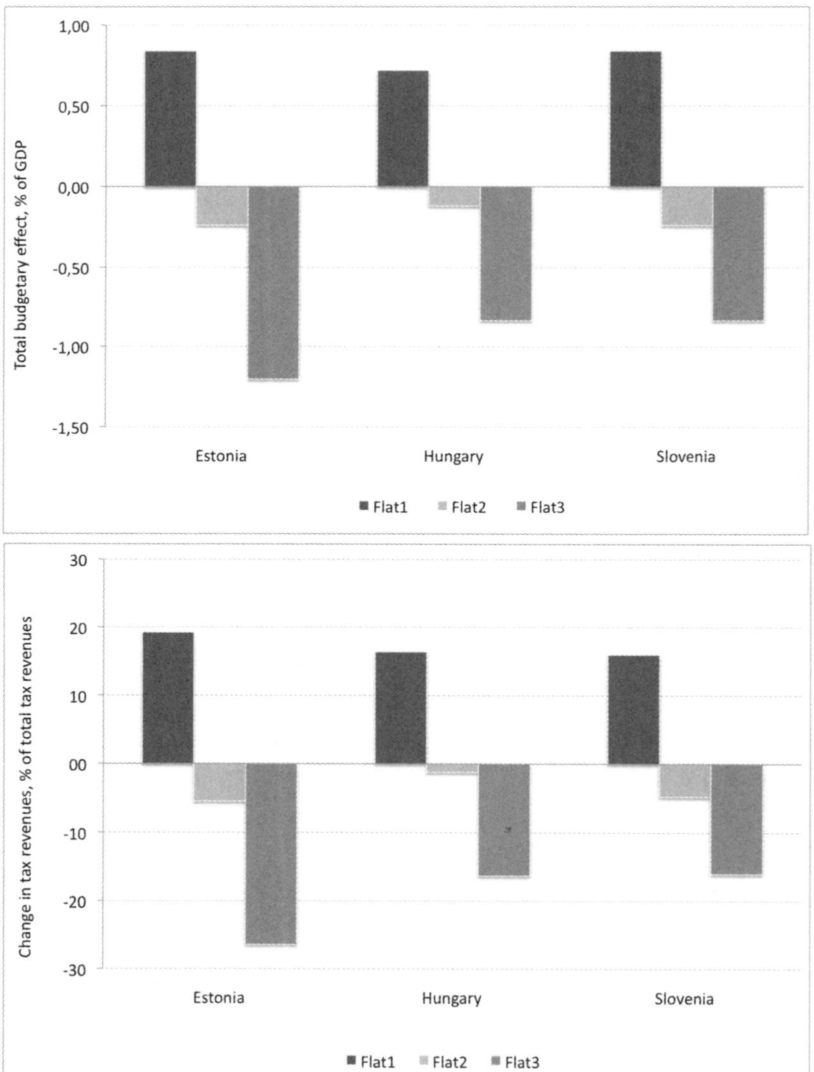

Note: The total fiscal effect is measured in terms of the change in personal income taxes, social security contributions and cash benefits. Only "day-after" effects are considered (neglecting longer-term effects or effects due to change of behaviour).

Source: Own calculation using EUROMOD version D25.

Parallel to the falling tax revenues, the work incentives for individuals improve with the introduction of all three alternative scenarios (see Figure 5.5). The indicator used here is the effective marginal tax rate (EMTR), which measures the extent to which the combined effects of taxes and benefits reduce the financial gain from additional work effort. In other words, it measures which part of any additional earnings is "taxed away".

Figure 5.5: Effective marginal tax rates (for working age population) – median value

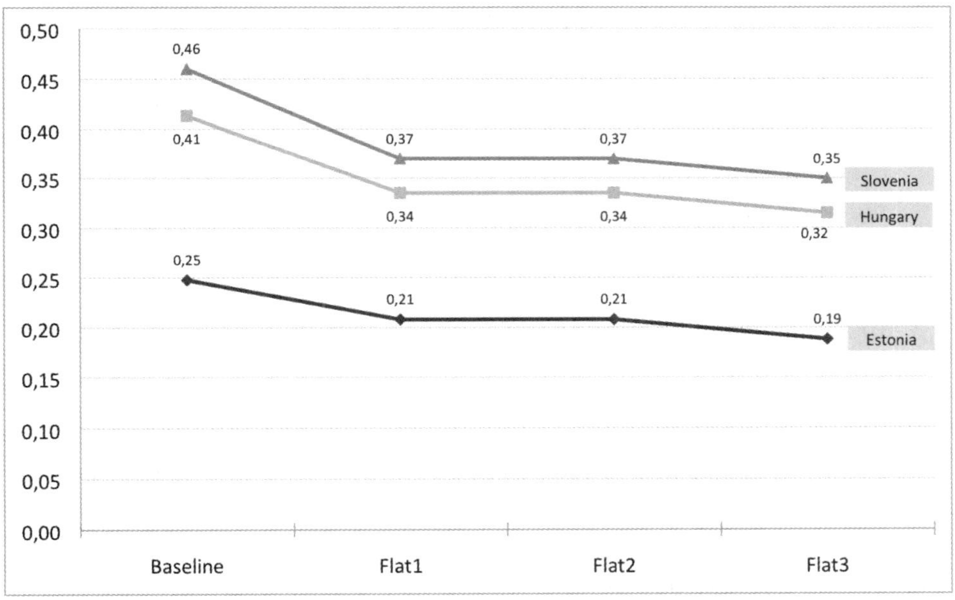

Note: EMTRs are calculated for the working age population (those aged 18-64) with positive employment or self-employment income, increasing earnings of each individual in the household in turn by 3% while the change in all benefits and taxes (including social insurance contributions) is observed at the household level.

Source: Own calculation using EUROMOD version D25.

There are large differences in the baseline level of effective marginal tax rates, mostly due to the differences in the level of employee social insurance contributions. Estonia has the lowest rate, 25% in contrast to 41% and 46% in Hungary and Slovenia, respectively. The change in EMTRs across the various scenarios has the same pattern for all three countries, but the decline is greater in Hungary and Slovenia which have higher baseline values. Tax rates are the lowest under *Flat3*: compared to the 2005 baseline system, the reduction of the median EMTR is 6-9 percentage points. In sum, the reduction of tax rates as a result of a flat tax reform would be greatest in Hungary and Slovenia, countries with relatively progressive tax systems.

We also assessed the impact on incomes at the household level to determine who are the winners and losers of these alternative reforms. In most cases, households with lower incomes are likely to be losers, while those at the top would gain. As shown by Figure 5.6, the tax burden would increase the most under the flat tax rate with no tax exceptions (apart from exempting pensions from tax) (*Flat1*), and in particular the bottom deciles would be adversely affected. This is not surprising, as the low-income groups tend to be beneficiaries of the existing zero-income tax brackets.

In Estonia, the *Flat1* scenario would increase the tax burden of low income earners over 400% for the bottom decile. The extra tax burden decreases with income, and for the top decile there is effectively no change compared to the baseline scenario. The *Flat2* scenario will also increase the tax burden for the low-income earners, although considerably less than the *Flat1* scenario. This is again due to lower tax allowances and eliminated pension allowance. High-income earners, starting from the 6th decile, will benefit from the decrease in the marginal tax, albeit modestly. Overall the tax burden is about 6% less compared to the baseline. The *Flat3* scenario will decrease the marginal tax rate and extend the allowance for families with children and this will decrease the overall tax burden by one quarter on average. The changes will benefit all income deciles through the reduction of the income burden, compared to the baseline. There is no significant difference across deciles when measuring the percentage changes of the tax burden. In terms of total tax paid, top income groups would benefit more, which results in a modest increase in total inequality, as shown before (Figure 5.1).

The overall majority of Hungarian households would suffer from the introduction of any of the three flat tax systems examined here. The tax burden increases by over 100% for the bottom half of the population in the "most radical" *Flat1* scenario. The income loss remains also substantial, over 50% for this group (except the bottom decile) under *Flat2* and *Flat3*. The main reason for this is the taxation of pensions (pensioners are concentrated between the second and the sixth deciles), which are tax-exempt in the baseline scenario. The increase of tax payments in the second decile surpasses that of the bottom decile, due to the withdrawal of tax allowances which affect the working poor the most (but not the poorest tenth, where many people are out of work). The top tenth of the income distribution gains under all scenarios, with the tax burden decreasing by around 30-40%.

Figure 5.6: Change of tax burden per income decile in Estonia, Hungary and Slovenia (comparing alternative flat tax scenarios to the baseline)

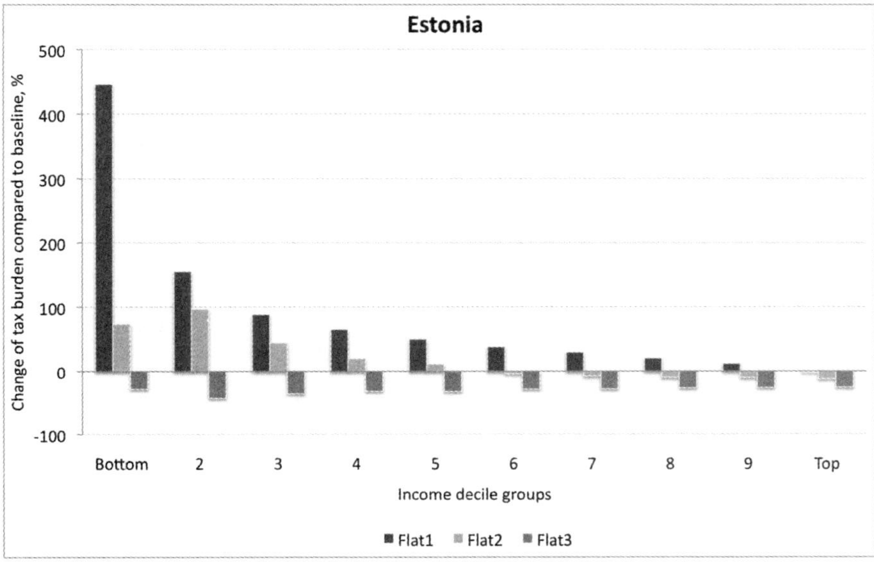

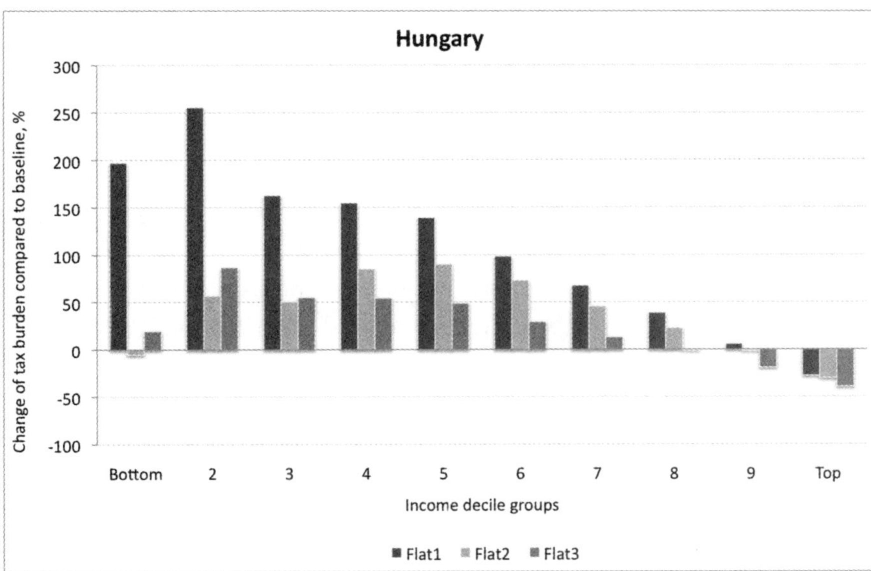

Figure 5.6: Change of tax burden per income decile in Estonia, Hungary and Slovenia (comparing alternative flat tax scenarios to the baseline) (continued)

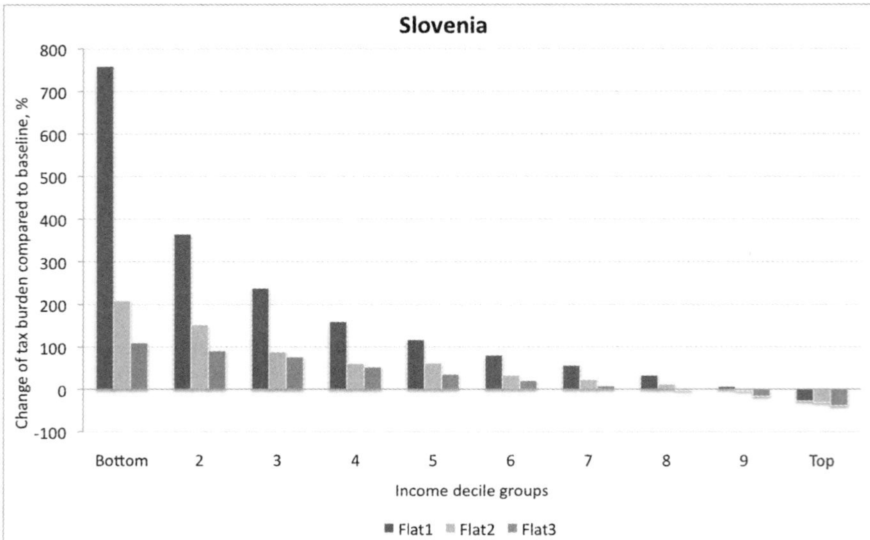

Note: The decile groups are defined based on the baseline equivalized disposable income, i.e. kept unchanged also in the alternative scenarios (in order to show the income change for the same group of people)

Source: Own calculation using EUROMOD version D25.

For more details, see Tables A15-A17 in the Annex.

Most Slovenian households would be hit by an increase of the tax burden under all three scenarios, especially *Flat1*. The increase is enormous for the first decile, by over 700% compared to the baseline scenario. This is due to the disappearance of all tax allowances. The tax burden will be 150-200% higher under the *Flat2* scenario for the bottom two deciles compared to the baseline. Subsequent deciles would suffer gradually less, and only the two highest deciles will benefit. The overall tax burden is 5% less compared to the baseline scenario. The social impact of the tax reform in Slovenia is mildest in the case of the *Flat3* system. However, this version will still increase the tax burden for individuals in low-income households, yet to a considerably less extent than either *Flat1* or *Flat2*. In this "future Estonian" scenario, the upper third of the income distribution would benefit from the decrease in marginal tax.

6 Conclusions

Flat income tax schemes bring simplification in the tax rates, but more importantly, in the system of tax allowances and the calculation of the tax base. This might explain their popularity in Eastern Europe, where this pursuit of transparency in the tax system is hoped to increase tax compliance and economic growth and thus ultimately tax revenues.

The purpose of this chapter was to illustrate the "day-after effects" of the introduction of alternative flat tax schemes in Estonia, Hungary and Slovenia in a comparable manner. The analysis is based on EUROMOD, the European tax-benefit microsimulation model, which now includes these countries, enabling cross-country comparisons. These reform scenarios keep all other tax-benefit policy *rules* unchanged, but not necessary the value of these taxes and benefits. For instance, in case of means-tested benefits, provided only if the personal or household net income is below a certain threshold, entitlements might change as a result of the tax reform. With EUROMOD, we are able to take into account such interactions between taxes and benefits.

The three alternative proposals considered have actually occurred in the political discussions in these countries and in the case of Estonia, it has been already approved by the parliament to take effect in a few years' time. In this chapter, we estimate the distributional and fiscal effects of these reforms, both for the country of origin and the other two if the corresponding proposal was "imported". These scenarios may be thought of as illustrations of the possibly many alternative approaches.

The results suggest that the most radical scenario considered here, with a flat tax rate of 20% and no tax concessions (apart from exempting pensions from tax) would have a dramatic effect on inequality and poverty. For instance, the Gini coefficient would increase from 0.27 to 0.32 in Hungary and from 0.27 to 0.30 in Slovenia. Also, most of the cost of the reform would be borne by lower-income groups, while the "taxman" (the government budget) and the richest fifth of the population appear to be the only beneficiaries. This scenario, which has appeared in Hungarian politics, would increase the poverty of children by 9 percentage points and poverty among the working age population by 7-8 percentage points if implemented there, highlighting the drawbacks of *ad hoc* policy ideas without thorough impact assessment.

A less radical proposal, originated in Slovenia, with a 20% tax rate and certain allowances (but without any special concession for pensions) still has a negative impact on the majority of the population in all three countries, albeit to a much smaller extent, although the total budgetary impact is slightly negative. Implementation of the Slovenian flat tax proposal in their own country would result in rising inequality (from 0.27 to 0.29 in case of the Gini coefficient) and an increasing tax burden on the bottom eight deciles of the population. At the same time, the median level of effective marginal tax rates would decline from 46% to 37%.

The reform taking effect in Estonia by 2011 will cost the country 1.2% of the GDP while being somewhat less for the other two countries. The impact on households in all three countries is rather varied, depending on the original tax system. In Estonia, the inequality will increase, but the tax burden would decline almost uniformly in all income groups, compared to the tax system of 2005. In Hungary, the middle of the income distribution would lose the most, because of the novel tax burden on pension incomes, while the effect on the bottom decile would be more modest (but still negative). The richest fifth of the population would benefit from the uniform income tax rate of 18% (keeping social security contributions unchanged), both in Hungary and Slovenia, countries with relatively progressive tax systems.

In sum, in Hungary and Slovenia, the introduction of the flat tax schemes as considered here would result in a substantial increase of the tax burden for the bottom deciles as well as an increase in inequality and poverty. The impact on inequality and poverty is relative modest in Estonia which already has a functioning flat tax system and a relatively high level of inequality. However, these flat tax schemes would reduce (the median level of) the effective marginal tax rates by 4-9 percentage points which might result in increasing tax compliance or labour market participation.

Overall, the analysis on these three countries shows that the specific design of flat tax schemes largely determines their impact on fiscal revenues and income distribution. Radical and simple solutions, such as introducing a single rate and abolishing all benefits appear to have detrimental effects on lower-income groups. The combination of a flat tax rate with a basic allowance and some other benefits seems to offer a more viable strategy. Note, however, that this also implies a certain degree of progressivity in the system. These solutions thus may ultimately not differ fundamentally from the simplification of the tax systems as they are. The charm of "flat tax" may ultimately lie in its simplicity and transparency, but not necessary in its feature of having a single rate.

References

Gorodnichenko, Y. / Martinez-Vazquez, J. / Peter, K. (2007) 'Myth and Reality of Flat Tax Reform: Micro Estimates of Tax Evasion Response and Welfare Effects in Russia', IZA Discussion Papers 3267.

Immervoll, H. / O'Donoghue, C. / Sutherland, H. (1999) 'An Introduction to EUROMOD', EUROMOD Working Paper No. EM0/99.

Ivanova, A. / Keen, M. / Klemm, A. (2005) 'The Russian "Flat Tax" Reform', *Economic Policy* 20 (43): 397-444.

Keen, M. / Kim, Y. / Varsano, R. (2008) 'The "Flat Tax(es)": Principles and Experience', *International Tax and Public Finance* 15 (6): 712-751.

Lelkes, O. / Benedek, D. (2007) 'Assessment of Income Distribution and a Hypothetical Flat Tax Reform in Hungary', Paper presented at the Conference of the International Microsimulation Association, 20-22 August 2007, Vienna.

Lietz, C. / Mantovani, D. (2007) 'A Short Introduction to EUROMOD: An Integrated European Tax-Benefit Model', pp. 1-26 in: Bargain, O. (ed.), *Micro-Simulation in Action: Policy Analysis in Europe Using EUROMOD,* Elsevier Ltd. Research in Labor Economics, 25.

Odbor za reforme (Committee for Reforms) (2005) 'The Framework of Economic and Social Reforms for Increasing the Welfare in Slovenia'. Ljubljana: Government of the Republic of Slovenia.

Paulus, A. / Peichl, A. (2008) 'Effects of Flat Tax Reforms in Western Europe on Equity and Efficiency', ISER Working Paper Series 2008-06. University of Essex. (Downloadable at: http://www.iser.essex.ac.uk/publications/working-papers/iser/2008-06).

Sutherland, H. (2001) 'EUROMOD: An Integrated European Benefit-Tax Model, Final Report', EUROMOD Working Paper EM9/01.

Sutherland, H. (2007) 'Euromod: The Tax-Benefit Microsimulation Model for the European Union', pp. 483-488 in Gupta, A. / Harding, A. (eds.), *Modelling Our Future: Population Ageing, Health and Aged Care,* Vol. 16 of International Symposia in Economic Theory and Econometrics, Elsevier.

Annex

Table A1: Personal income tax parameters for 2005 in Estonia, Hungary and Slovenia, as simulated in EUROMOD

	Estonia	Hungary	Slovenia
Tax schedule			
number of tax brackets	1	2	5
marginal tax rates (%)	24	18/38	16/33/38/42/50
type	comprehensive (applied on all sources of incomes)	schedular (capital and partly self-employment income are taxed separately)	comprehensive
Tax allowances and credits			
general	allowance of 1,303 EUR (20,400 EEK) per year	tax credit on wages/ salaries with the maximum amount of 438 EUR (108,000 HUF) per year	allowance of 2,355 EUR (564,400 SIT) per year
child-related	yearly allowance of 1,303 EUR (20,400 EEK) per child, starting from the third	tax credit of 146 EUR (per year) if 1 child, 195 EUR per child if 2 children, 487 EUR per child if 3+ children	yearly allowance of 1,982 EUR for the first child, 2,154 for the second, 2,872 for the third and increasing further by 718 EUR for each additional child (e.g. 3,590 EUR for the 4th, 4,309 EUR for the 5th etc.)
old age/ pensions-related	yearly allowance of 2,300 EUR (36,000 EEK), applied to pension incomes	pensions not taxed	yearly allowance of 1,149 EUR and a tax credit equal to 14.5% of individual pensions
invalidity-related	none	tax credit of 97 EUR per year in case of serious disability	yearly allowance of 14,361 EUR
other	none	not simulated	yearly allowance for self-employed journalists and culture professionals (up to 15% of income or 2,441 EUR per year); yearly allowance of 5,007 EUR on student work (not simulated)

	Estonia	Hungary	Slovenia
Deductible expenses			
compulsory social insurance contributions	yes	no	yes
voluntary pension insurance	up to 15% of taxable income	not simulated	up to 5.844% of gross wage or 2,293 EUR per year
other	housing loan interest payments, education and training expenses (altogether up to 50% of taxable income or 3,196 EUR per year)	not simulated	other selected expenses (up to 2% of intermediary tax base)
Standardized costs	none	none	10% of contractual work (including student work) and royalties, 40% of rents, 35% of dividends
Unit of assessment	individual or married couples (optional)	individual	individual
Tax base	Earnings, self-employment income, royalties, rent, pensions, contributory benefits (unemployment, maternity, sickness) – *after deducting employee and self-employed SICs*	Earnings, (part of) self-employment income, property income, contributory benefits (unemployment, maternity, sickness, child care) – *without deducting any SICs*	Earnings, self-employment income, royalties, interests, dividends, rent, imputed rent from land, pensions, contributory benefits (unemployment, maternity, child care) – *after deducting employee and self-employed SICs*

Table A2: Estonia: poverty rates under the alternative scenarios using alternative thresholds (40, 50, 60, 70% of the baseline median), 2005

percentage of individuals below:	EE 2005	Flat1	Flat2	Flat3
40% of median equivalent income	5.7	6.7	6.0	5.7
Males	5.7	6.9	6.0	5.6
Females	5.8	6.5	6.1	5.7
50% of median equivalent income	10.6	12.3	11.1	10.3
Males	10.9	12.5	11.2	10.5
Females	10.4	12.2	11.1	10.1
60% of median equivalent income	17.7	19.9	19.2	17.0
Males	16.9	19.2	17.7	16.2
Females	18.3	20.5	20.5	17.8
70% of median equivalent income	25.2	28.5	26.0	24.2
Males	23.1	26.5	23.5	22.1
Females	27.0	30.1	28.1	25.9

Notes: Computed for individuals according to their household disposable income (HDI) equivalized by the modified OECD equivalence scale. HDI are calculated as the sum of all income sources of all household members net of income tax and social insurance contributions. Poverty thresholds are kept constant at the baseline levels (see Table A14).

Source: Own calculation using EUROMOD version D25.

Table A3: Estonia: poverty rates under the alternative scenarios by age and gender groups, 2005

	EE 2005	Flat1	Flat2	Flat3
Population	17.7	19.9	19.2	17.0
0-15	17.9	20.7	17.4	17.1
16-29	15.6	18.3	15.6	14.8
30-44	18.0	20.8	18.1	16.7
45-64	18.4	20.8	19.4	18.0
65-	18.7	19.0	26.5	18.7
Men	16.9	19.2	17.7	16.2
Women	18.3	20.5	20.5	17.8

Notes: Poverty threshold: 60% of the baseline median (i.e. constant across scenarios).

Source: Own calculation using EUROMOD version D25.

Table A4: Estonia: percentage of winners and losers in comparison to baseline scenario

percentage of individuals by deciles	Flat1		Flat2		Flat3	
	winners	losers	winners	losers	winners	losers
1	0.0	47.2	14.6	33.6	18.3	8.8
2	0.0	52.5	26.8	60.0	34.5	7.0
3	0.0	61.9	43.2	49.6	47.7	5.8
4	0.1	70.9	48.2	47.5	59.2	6.2
5	0.0	77.7	54.9	42.4	64.5	6.3
6	0.2	95.2	69.5	30.5	83.8	6.8
7	0.8	98.1	72.5	27.5	90.9	6.4
8	3.7	96.0	77.2	22.8	96.9	2.8
9	11.4	87.9	76.5	23.4	98.4	0.9
10	47.7	52.3	84.8	15.2	99.9	0.0
Total	6.4	74.0	56.8	35.3	69.4	5.1

Notes: Winners are individuals with higher equivalized standard disposable income comparing to baseline scenario; losers are individuals with lower equivalized standard disposable income comparing to baseline scenario. Deciles refer to baseline scenario.

Source: Own calculation using EUROMOD version D25.

Table A5: Hungary: poverty rates under the alternative scenarios using alternative thresholds (40, 50, 60, 70% of the baseline median), 2005

percentage of individuals below:	HU 2005	Flat1	Flat2	Flat3
40% of median equivalent income	4.1	6.0	3.9	4.4
males	4.6	6.8	4.4	4.9
females	3.7	5.3	3.6	3.9
50% of median equivalent income	8.4	12.0	8.7	9.2
males	9.1	13.0	9.5	9.9
females	7.7	11.0	8.0	8.5
60% of median equivalent income	14.9	20.8	16.1	16.9
males	15.5	21.6	16.5	17.4
females	14.3	20.1	15.8	16.4
70% of median equivalent income	22.5	30.0	25.2	25.6
males	23.0	30.8	25.3	25.9
females	22.1	29.4	25.1	25.3

Notes: Computed for individuals according to their household disposable income (HDI) equivalized by the modified OECD equivalence scale. HDI are calculated as the sum of all income sources of all household members net of income tax and social insurance contributions. Poverty thresholds are kept constant at the baseline levels (see Table A14).

Source: Own calculation using EUROMOD version D25.

Table A6 Hungary: poverty rates (60% of the baseline median) by age and gender groups, 2005

	HU 2005	Flat1	Flat2	Flat3
Population	14.9	20.8	16.1	16.9
0-15	20.4	29.3	20.9	24.2
16-29	17.0	24.5	18.2	19.3
30-44	17.3	25.1	18.2	20.1
45-64	13.5	18.3	14.9	14.6
65-	5.6	6.1	7.8	5.7
Men	15.5	21.6	16.5	17.4
Women	14.3	20.1	15.8	16.4

Notes: Poverty threshold: 60% of the baseline median (i.e. constant across scenarios).
Source: Own calculation using EUROMOD version D25.

Table A7: Hungary: percentage of winners and losers in comparison to baseline scenario

percentage of individuals by deciles	Flat1		Flat2		Flat3	
	winners	losers	winners	losers	winners	losers
1	2.0	80.7	20.5	28.5	16.7	43.9
2	2.4	83.2	14.8	61.6	15.4	63.2
3	4.6	79.8	16.9	73.4	14.6	66.4
4	4.6	72.1	18.4	77.5	15.0	59.5
5	4.7	72.3	16.4	82.1	15.7	60.4
6	5.7	69.6	21.9	77.7	19.8	55.6
7	10.7	70.2	22.1	77.5	22.2	66.4
8	14.3	70.0	31.6	68.3	33.1	61.9
9	33.8	55.0	47.4	52.6	51.4	48.1
10	70.2	25.0	73.9	26.0	80.1	19.8
Total	15.3	67.8	28.4	62.5	28.4	54.5

Notes: Winners are individuals with higher equivalized standard disposable income comparing to baseline scenario; losers are individuals with lower equivalized standard disposable income comparing to baseline scenario. Deciles refer to baseline scenario.
Source: Own calculation using EUROMOD version D25.

Table A8: Slovenia: poverty rates under the alternative scenarios using alternative thresholds (40, 50, 60, 70% of the baseline median), 2005

percentage of individuals below:	SI 2005	Flat1	Flat2	Flat3
40% of median equivalent income	3.5	4.1	3.7	3.6
males	3.6	4.2	3.8	3.7
females	3.5	4.0	3.7	3.5
50% of median equivalent income	8.7	11.0	9.5	9.1
males	8.8	11.0	9.5	9.1
females	8.7	11.1	9.6	9.1
60% of median equivalent income	15.9	20.1	16.9	16.8
males	15.1	19.4	15.9	16.0
females	16.7	20.7	17.8	17.5
70% of median equivalent income	23.4	28.6	24.9	24.6
males	22.3	27.3	23.6	23.4
females	24.5	29.7	26.2	25.8

Notes: Computed for individuals according to their household disposable income (HDI) equivalized by the modified OECD equivalence scale. HDI are calculated as the sum of all income sources of all household members net of income tax and social insurance contributions. Poverty thresholds are kept constant at the baseline levels (see Table A14).

Source: Own calculation using EUROMOD version D25.

Table A9: Slovenia: poverty rates under the alternative scenarios by age and gender groups, 2005

	SI 2005	Flat1	Flat2	Flat3
Population	15.9	20.1	16.9	16.8
0-15	14.3	20.4	14.2	15.7
16-29	14.8	20.1	15.4	15.9
30-44	14.0	18.8	14.2	14.9
45-64	14.2	17.4	15.3	14.9
65-	25.3	26.5	28.6	25.3
Men	15.1	19.4	15.9	16.0
Women	16.7	20.7	17.8	17.5

Notes: Poverty threshold: 60% of the baseline median (i.e. constant across scenarios).

Source: Own calculation using EUROMOD version D25.

Table A10: Slovenia: percentage of winners and losers in comparison to baseline scenario

percentage of individuals by deciles	Flat1		Flat2		Flat3	
	winners	losers	winners	losers	winners	losers
1	3.8	35.3	8.0	26.3	4.8	22.7
2	1.0	71.5	15.1	67.1	5.5	59.6
3	0.5	83.8	19.8	73.5	4.6	73.3
4	0.8	86.6	20.6	78.4	9.5	74.9
5	1.2	87.7	15.7	84.3	10.4	77.6
6	0.9	90.7	29.5	70.5	18.1	76.5
7	3.3	90.7	38.9	61.1	28.7	68.9
8	10.2	85.9	50.6	49.4	48.5	51.0
9	30.3	68.5	63.0	37.0	77.2	22.4
10	87.8	12.2	85.8	14.2	93.0	7.0
Total	14.0	71.3	34.7	56.2	30.0	53.4

Notes: Winners are individuals with higher equivalized standard disposable income comparing to baseline scenario; losers are individuals with lower equivalized standard disposable income comparing to baseline scenario. Deciles refer to baseline scenario.

Source: Own calculation using EUROMOD version D25.

Table A11: Estonia: Income inequality under various policy scenarios

	EE 2005	Flat1	Flat2	Flat3
Gini Coefficient	0.323	0.334	0.332	0.332
Income quintile share ratio (S80/S20)	5.21	5.45	5.49	5.45
Average equivalized income per decile per individual (EUR PPP), monthly				
1	165	158	164	166
2	254	242	249	257
3	314	298	310	321
4	367	348	364	376
5	420	400	418	432
6	485	462	490	504
7	565	540	572	589
8	668	644	680	699
9	822	803	839	863
10	1,364	1,368	1,404	1,444
Mean income (equivalized)	542	526	549	565
Mean income (unequivalized)	365	355	368	379
Median income (equivalized)	450	430	453	467
Median income (unequivalized)	279	270	262	279

Notes: Computed for individuals according to their household disposable income (HDI) equivalized by the modified OECD equivalence scale. HDI are calculated as the sum of all income sources of all household members net of income tax and social insurance contributions.

Eurostat EUR PPP exchange rates (for 2005): 1 EEK = 1 / 9.23625 EUR PPP, 1 HUF = 1 / 151.922 EUR PPP, 1 SIT = 1 / 175.829 EUR PPP.

Source: Own calculation using EUROMOD version D25.

Table A12: Hungary: Income inequality under various policy scenarios

	HU 2005	Flat1	Flat2	Flat3
Gini Coefficient	0.274	0.316	0.302	0.309
Income quintile ratio (S80/S20)	4.03	4.85	4.46	4.65
Average equivalized income per decile per individual (EUR PPP), monthly				
1	203	183	203	200
2	299	269	293	290
3	361	324	351	348
4	413	377	397	400
5	469	427	446	453
6	524	483	499	512
7	584	543	562	576
8	665	627	648	664
9	781	771	788	812
10	1,242	1,377	1,393	1,435
Mean income (equivalized)	554	538	558	569
Mean income (unequivalized)	376	367	377	386
Median income (equivalized)	496	451	469	481
Median income (unequivalized)	350	313	322	332

Notes: See Table A11.

Source: Own calculation using EUROMOD version D25.

Table A13: Slovenia: Income inequality under various policy scenarios

	SI 2005	Flat1	Flat2	Flat3
Gini Coefficient	0.270	0.300	0.292	0.296
Income quintile ratio (S80/S20)	3.99	4.46	4.36	4.41
Average equivalized income per decile per individual (EUR PPP), monthly				
1	390	379	386	387
2	542	503	530	532
3	667	610	651	648
4	776	709	756	754
5	872	806	844	851
6	973	903	950	955
7	1,090	1,023	1,067	1,079
8	1,229	1,175	1,214	1,233
9	1,456	1,437	1,470	1,497
10	2,272	2,470	2,504	2,553
Mean income (equivalized)	1,026	1,001	1,037	1,049
Mean income (unequivalized)	660	646	664	675
Median income (equivalized)	922	854	890	900
Median income (unequivalized)	602	562	572	598

Notes: See Table A11.

Source: Own calculation using EUROMOD version D25.

Table A14: Constant poverty lines, in EUR PPP (monthly)

% of median income	EE	HU	SI
40%	180	198	369
50%	225	248	461
60%	270	298	553
70%	315	347	645

Note: Eurostat EUR PPP exchange rates (for 2005): 1 EEK = 1 / 9.23625 EUR PPP, 1 HUF = 1 / 151.922 EUR PPP, 1 SIT = 1 / 175.829 EUR PPP.

Table A15: Estonia: Fiscal cost and change of total tax burden 2005

	EE 2005		Flat1		Flat2		Flat3	
	EUR PPP	Ratio	1000 EUR PPP	Ratio	1000 EUR PPP	Ratio	1000 EUR PPP	Ratio
Surplus/deficit for the budget (thousands)	-53,522		-39,735		-57,616		-72,896	
Compared to the baseline			13,787		-4,094		-19,374	
Total **monthly income** tax burden by income decile								
1	212		1,158	5.46	368	1.73	151	0.71
2	682		1,741	2.55	1,343	1.97	387	0.57
3	1 536		2,895	1.88	2,217	1.44	984	0.64
4	2 412		3,986	1.65	2,892	1.20	1,647	0.68
5	3 216		4,828	1.50	3,584	1.11	2,190	0.68
6	5 465		7,542	1.38	5,267	0.96	3,941	0.72
7	7 187		9,319	1.30	6,669	0.93	5,222	0.73
8	10 289		12,387	1.20	9,318	0.91	7,637	0.74
9	13 820		15,482	1.12	12,493	0.90	10,339	0.75
10	28 478		28,069	0.99	25,113	0.88	21,436	0.75
All taxes	**73 299**		**87 409**	**1.19**	**69,264**	**0.94**	**53,934**	**0.74**

Note: Eurostat EUR PPP exchange rates (for 2005): 1 EEK = 1 / 9.23625 EUR PPP, 1 HUF = 1 / 151.922 EUR PPP, 1 SIT = 1 / 175.829 EUR PPP.

Source: Own calculation using EUROMOD version D25.

Table A16: Hungary: Fiscal cost and change of total tax burden 2005

	HU 2005		Flat1		Flat2		Flat3	
	EUR PPP	Ratio	1000 EUR PPP	Ratio	1000 EUR PPP	Ratio	1000 EUR PPP	Ratio
Surplus/deficit for the budget (thousands)	-869,976		-778,242		-878,157		-976,173	
Compared to the baseline			91,734		-8,181		-106,197	
Total **monthly income** tax burden by income decile								
1	7,345		21,831	2.97	6,959	0.95	8,770	1.19
2	8,924		31,728	3.56	13,973	1.57	16,687	1.87
3	15,438		40,546	2.63	23,215	1.50	23,908	1.55
4	14,822		37,770	2.55	27,501	1.86	22,868	1.54
5	19,281		46,120	2.39	36,711	1.90	28,660	1.49
6	26,448		52,550	1.99	45,770	1.73	34,116	1.29
7	38,969		65,322	1.68	56,618	1.45	44,005	1.13
8	59,156		82,012	1.39	72,449	1.22	58,632	0.99
9	104,731		110,788	1.06	103,209	0.99	84,754	0.81
10	328,322		237,103	0.72	229,250	0.70	199,225	0.61
All taxes	623,435		725,771	1.16	615,656	0.99	521,625	0.84

Note: Eurostat EUR PPP exchange rates (for 2005): 1 EEK = 1 / 9.23625 EUR PPP, 1 HUF = 1 / 151.922 EUR PPP, 1 SIT = 1 / 175.829 EUR PPP.

Source: Own calculation using EUROMOD version D25.

Table A17: Slovenia: Fiscal cost and change of total tax burden 2005

	SI 2005		Flat1		Flat2		Flat3	
	1000 EUR	Ratio	1000 EUR	Ratio	1000 EUR	Ratio	1000 EUR	Ratio
Surplus/deficit for the budget (thousands)	-263,460		-235,798		-272,636		-293,438	
Compared to the baseline			27,661		-9,177		-29,979	
Total **tax burden** by income decile								
1	364	-	3,127	8.58	1,125	3.09	764	2.10
2	1,412	-	6,560	4.65	3,568	2.53	2,691	1.91
3	2,948	-	9,960	3.38	5,539	1.88	5,187	1.76
4	4,909	-	12,759	2.60	7,881	1.61	7,466	1.52
5	6,698	-	14,546	2.17	10,819	1.62	9,058	1.35
6	10,358	-	18,688	1.80	13,773	1.33	12,460	1.20
7	14,184	-	22,149	1.56	17,417	1.23	15,300	1.08
8	19,530	-	25,928	1.33	21,844	1.12	18,991	0.97
9	31,445	-	33,485	1.06	30,143	0.96	26,185	0.83
10	92,978	-	67,221	0.72	63,862	0.69	57,050	0.61
All taxes	184,827	-	214,422	1.16	175,971	0.95	155,152	0.84

Note: Eurostat EUR PPP exchange rates (for 2005): 1 EEK = 1 / 9.23625 EUR PPP, 1 HUF = 1 / 151.922 EUR PPP, 1 SIT = 1 / 175.829 EUR PPP.

Source: Own calculation using EUROMOD version D25.

Chapter 6

Alternative Tax-benefit Strategies to Support Children in Poland[1]

Horacio Levy / Leszek Morawski / Michał Myck

1 Introduction

A non-refundable child credit was introduced in Poland in 2006 for the 2007 tax year. Initially announced at the value of €31.90 per year per child at its introduction the tax credit was raised to €306.40 which took the cost of this reform to between €1.73 and €1.89 billion per year or between 0.58% and 0.63% of the GDP.[2] In the light of the total value of social spending on family benefits (€2.18 billion per year) and social assistance (€0.4 billion per year) this represents a significant shift of resources to families with children.[3]

The early extension of the generosity of the credit, the full value of which could be claimed for 2007, coincided with the early parliamentary elections in fall of that year. It seemed like a rushed decision with little thought given to the consequences of the policy and little analysis of potential other options of supporting families with children. The coalition government at the time (with Jarosław Kaczyński as the prime minister)

1 We are grateful for useful comments on a previous version of this analysis to participants at the conference "Tax-benefit Microsimulation in the Enlarged Europe: Results from the I-CUE Project and Perspectives for the Future", particularly Isabelle Engstedt-Maquet and Manos Matsaganis. This chapter uses EUROMOD version D15 and data from the Polish Household Budget Survey (HBS) made available by the Polish Central Statistical Office and prepared by the Economic Department of Warsaw University. Data providers do not bear any responsibility for the analysis or interpretation of the data reported here. Any errors and the views expressed in this chapter are the authors' responsibility. In particular, the chapter does not represent the views of the institutions to which the authors are affiliated. A version of this chapter in Polish was published as an article in the "Bank i Kredyt" journal, 2009 (see: www.nbp.pl).

2 Information from the Ministry of Finance (converted using the exchange rate from 30.06.2007, €1=3.7658PLN).

3 Value for the cost of Family Allowance from Statistical Yearbook of Poland; value for the cost of Social Assistance from the Ministry of Labour and Social Policy (questionnaire MPiPS-03).

provided little justification for the policy beyond the claim that it was in line with its agenda of "supporting the family", and the policy attracted little scrutiny (and even less criticism) from the opposition parties. The election campaign certainly contributed to the unwillingness of opposing a major tax hand-out, but the policy could have actually appealed to the major opposition party at the time, the Civic Platform (PO). Not only did the policy represent a tax cut but also, as we shall show in this chapter, its benefits have gone largely to better-off families representing a significant proportion of the PO's electorate. The policy (together with some other tax cuts introduced by the Kaczyński government) was taken on board by the new government formed by Donald Tusk and there has been no discussion since of scaling it back.

To the best of our knowledge distributional effects of the reform have not been investigated in detail and not much is known about potential effects of the reform on child poverty, and more generally on the incomes of households with children. All this despite the very high rate of child poverty in Poland. According to the European Commission document "Child Poverty and Well-being in the EU" (European Commission, 2008) the at-risk-of-poverty rate among families with children in Poland was equal to 29% in 2005 and was the highest among all EU-25 countries. Significantly lower poverty rates were observed in the Czech Republic – 18%, Hungary – 20% and Estonia – 21%. This suggests that historical reasons (50 years of centrally planned economy) and low level of economic development do not present fully satisfactory explanations of the situation of families with children in Poland.

Poverty among families with children has been identified as a key challenge for social policy in Poland. An official document approved by the government entitled "National Report on Strategies for Social Protection and Social Inclusion" (Ministry of Labour and Social Policy, 2006) declared that "*comprehensive policy for families with children is the most essential priority for social integration*". The government agenda includes changes in the system of family benefits as well as in housing benefit and personal income tax regulations, with the goal of changing the structure of social spending. It is estimated that prior to 2007 only about 4.7% of total social expenditure (0.8% of GDP) was spent on family and child benefits.

Such an agenda finds justification in empirical studies that have shown that countries with the lowest child poverty rates are the ones that allocate the highest proportions of their gross national product to child support (Adamson et al., 2000; Bradshaw and Finch, 2002). Also, it has been shown that appropriately designed and well-funded policies can have a considerable effect on family incomes and hence on reducing child poverty. Adamson et al. (2000) note that differences in tax and social expenditure policies can result in different rates of reduction of "market child poverty" ranging from a high of 20 percentage points to a low of 5 percentage points. Such differences in the effect of policies are also reported by Levy et al. (2007) who found that in a swap of policies between the UK and Spain, policies from the UK were more effective at reducing poverty levels in Spain even when expenditure levels were held constant.

Considering the government intention to reduce poverty among families with children in Poland it is important to consider the consequences of the introduction of the child tax credit together with possible alternative solutions. In this chapter we assess the effect of the recent introduction of the Polish reform and ask what the outcome would have been if instead of that child policies had been reformed in line with the systems of Austria, France and the United Kingdom. The choice of these three systems is guided by the fact that they represent different approaches in supporting families. The Austrian system gives emphasis to universal credits, the French to tax concessions and targeting large and lone parents families, while the system in the United Kingdom gives more emphasis to means-testing. The Polish and other systems described in the chapter are the ones in force in 2005. Results are obtained by using the European tax-benefit microsimulation model EUROMOD.

To the best of our knowledge it is the first study in which effects of alternative policy scenarios based on implementation of policy solutions from other countries are presented for Poland. Our main result is that the significant amount of resources spent on the introduction of the child tax credit in 2007 could have brought greater reductions in poverty rates among children had it been channelled differently to households with children. We show that by increasing the social expenditure by the same amount as with the child credit tax reform, the rates of poverty for children would have decreased significantly more under the French or the UK system. We demonstrate that better targeting of social spending explains the effectiveness of these policies.

The chapter is organized as follows. Section 2 presents a detailed description of poverty among families with children and social protection in Poland. Section 3 describes the policies to support families with children in Poland, Austria, France and the United Kingdom. Section 4 discusses the methodology used for the assessment of alternative child policy reforms in Poland. Section 5 shows the results. Section 6 concludes.

2 Child poverty and social protection: Poland in the European context

The at-risk-of-poverty rate for children in EU-25 countries in 2005 was 19%. The highest rate, 29%, was observed in Poland, where the rate was not only above the average level in the EU but also children had significantly higher risk of being in poverty than the overall population (21%). Lower poverty rates for children in the Czech Republic (18%), Hungary (20%) and Estonia (21%) suggest that other than historical reasons explain high levels of child poverty in Poland.

In comparison to other EU-25 Member States, the relative position of children living with lone parents in Poland is relatively better than in other household groups. The poverty rate of 46% is similar to those in Cyprus, Spain, Estonia and Greece, and lower than in the Czech Republic, Ireland, Malta and Lithuania. However, only 8% of poor children live in a lone parent type of household while the average for the EU-25 is 23%. Among large households (couples with 3 and more children) and complex households (more than one family) the child poverty risk in Poland is the largest and well above the EU average. While in Poland the poverty rate is 47% for "couples with 3 and more children" and 26% for "complex households with children", the EU-25 average is 25% and 20%, respectively. Consequently, the distribution of poor children by type of households in Poland is different from that in other EU-25 countries. A noticeable difference in Poland is the higher share of poor children living in households consisting of more than one family (25%). This proportion was similar to those in Latvia (21%) and Slovakia (20%) and significantly above the EU-25 average (11%) and countries such as the Czech Republic (11%) and Hungary (12%). Interestingly, while the rate of poverty for couples with 3 and more children in Poland (47%) is above the rates in France (20%), Austria (21%), and the UK (27%), the share of poor children living in such families in Poland (34%) is similar to the shares in France (33%) and Austria (34%), and larger than in the UK (26%). This might mean that policies implemented in other countries reduced poverty among families with three and more children more effectively than the benefit system that was in force in Poland in 2005.[4]

Having work is thought to be an effective protection against poverty. In Poland, however, in-work poverty remains a problem. For example, the at-risk-of-poverty rate among couples with 3 or more children where both

4 All poverty and expenditure statistics quoted in this section are taken from European Commission (2008).

parents work full-time is 30% (the EU-25 rate – 13%), while in families with one parent working full-time and the second part-time the rate rises to 41% (10% in the EU-25). This could be partially explained by the lack of in-work benefits in Poland in 2005. It may also mean that implementing systems that include such benefits and tax credits for children may improve the financial situation of working poor families with children.

The level of social spending and its structure are crucial when explaining child poverty rates. In Figure 6.1 we show the relationship between family-related spending (as a proportion of the GDP, and as a proportion of total social expenditure) and child poverty. There is a clear pattern in both relationships – higher overall spending on families and greater share of social expenditure allocated to families are generally associated with lower rates of child poverty. In 2005 the amount of social transfers in Poland was equal to 19.6% of GDP. Similar fractions were spent in Hungary, the Czech Republic and Slovakia. However, social spending in Poland has been characterized by large shares of expenditures related to old-age, sickness and disability pensions. Family and child care benefits accounted only for 0.8% of the GDP. The corresponding figure was 1.4% of the GDP in the Czech Republic and 2.5% in Hungary.

Figure 6.1: Spending on families and child at-risk-of-poverty rates in the EU

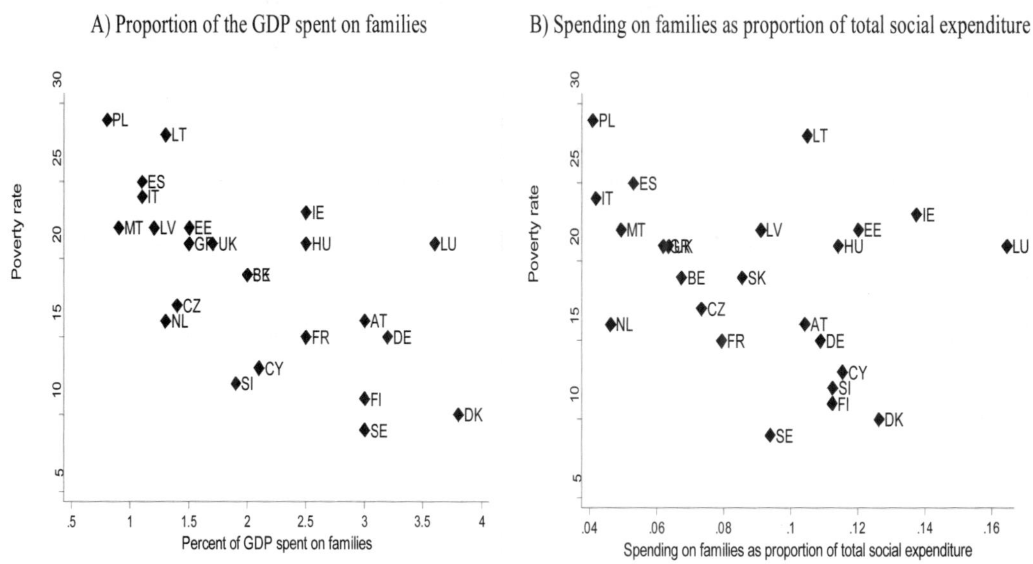

Note: Symbol overlaps: Figure 1A: SK and BE, Figure 1B: UK and GR.

Source: Based on statistics given in European Commission (2008).

The at-risk-of-poverty rate before transfers in Poland was lower than in the UK, Ireland and Hungary. However, the rate after transfers was the highest in the EU-25 (Figure 6.2). Overall social expenditure decreased the child at-risk-of-poverty rate by 26% – from 39% to 29% – in Poland. This was similar to the effects observed in Italy (23%) and Portugal (23%) and was larger than in Lithuania (20%), Spain (14%) and Greece (9%). In Hungary and the Czech Republic the at-risk-of-poverty rate fell by more than 50% as a consequence of social transfers.

Figure 6.2: Child at-risk-of-poverty rates – effects of family and non-family transfers in 2005

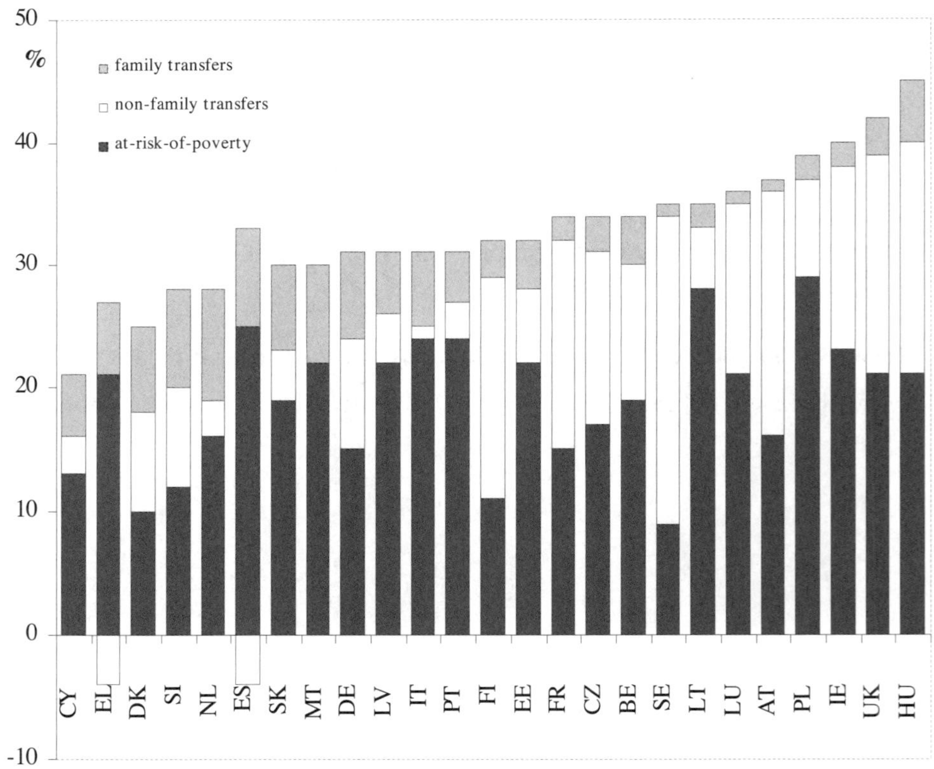

Source: European Commission, 2008.

Some explanation for the findings presented above may rest in a significant share of agricultural households with high values of own consumption and imputed rents. But even if this is true, child poverty rates are still very high in Poland. As we shall demonstrate below a significant reduction in the rate of child poverty in Poland could have been achieved with the level of spending implied by the introduced 2007 tax credit reform. Allocating the resources in the form of a non-refundable tax credit brought smaller reductions in child poverty compared to several alternative child support designs we consider.

3 Policy description

In the analysis which follows we describe in detail the cash benefits and direct personal taxes operating in 2005 which are specifically designed for the support of children and their families in Poland, Austria, France and the United Kingdom.

3.1 *Poland*

In 2005, support to families in Poland consisted mainly of two policies: joint taxation in personal income tax available for couples and lone parents, and an income-tested family allowance with supplements.[5]

- Joint taxation ("Łączne Opodatkowanie Dochodów"): personal income tax is individual but couples and single parents may fill in a joint tax return with their partners or children, respectively. In both cases and independently of the number of children, joint taxation doubles the amount of the universal tax credit and applies a splitting rule, by which only half of the family income is subject to the tax schedule and the resulting tax liability is then multiplied by two. The income tax schedule consists of three bands: 19% up to €9,167 per year, then 30% up to €18,334, and 40% beyond. Under income tax rules, dependent children are defined as (i) child aged 18 or below, (ii) child disabled regardless of age but entitled to nursing allowance (see below), or (iii) child aged 25 or below, in education and with income below a limit.
- Family Allowance ("Zasiłek Rodzinny"): beneficiaries are families with children whose monthly income in the previous year did not exceed €125 per capita. The monthly amount is €11 for the first and second child, €13 for the third and €16 for each consecutive one. The allowance is paid until the end of the child's education at school (usually

5 The nominal exchange rate used for the conversion of system values into euros is that of 30.06.2005, €1=4.0388PLN.

to the age of 18). In case the child continues education at school or university the allowance is paid until the age of 24. In 2005, about 5.2 million children (about 56-58% of children of age below 18) received the Family Allowance.

- Parental Leave Allowance ("Dodatek z Tytułu Opieki nad Dzieckiem w Okresie Urlopu Wychowawczego"): is a supplement to Family Allowance granted to a parent, factual or statutory guardian of a child, who takes parental leave to take care of at least one child aged 6 years or less. The amount is €99 per month.
- Supplement for Child Birth ("Dodatek z Tytułu Urodzenia Dziecka"): one time lump sum grant of €124 upon the birth of a child.
- Supplement for Starting the School Year ("Dodatek z Tytułu Rozpoczęcia Roku Szkolnego"): €22 per year, payment for each child in primary and secondary school.
- Supplement for Education of Disabled Child ('Dodatek z Tytułu Opieki i Edukacji Dziecka Niepełnosprawnego'): granted until the child reaches the age of 16 or 24 (if in education) and subject to moderate or severe degree of disability. The monthly amount is €12 per child under the age of 5 and €17 per child aged 5 to 24.
- Supplement for Lone Parents ("Dodatek z Tytułu Samotnego Wychowywania Dziecka"): granted to lone parents who are not receiving alimony because the child's father is dead or unknown. Eligibility is not granted if alimony is legally determined but father does not pay (in this case, the mother receives payments from the state alimony fund). The monthly amount is €42 per child and €62 per disabled child, with a maximum of €186 per family.
- Nursing Benefit ("Świadczenie Pielęgnacyjne"): granted to a parent (either in couple or single family) in case of resignation from employment to take care of a disabled child. There is no condition on the child age to qualify. The amount of the benefit is €104 per month.
- Nursing Allowance ("Zasiłek Pielegnacyjny"): a benefit granted to a handicapped child, a handicapped person over 16 years of age with a medical certificate confirming significant degree of disability or to a person who is over 75 years old. The benefit may also be granted to a person above 16 years of age with a medical certificate of moderate disability if disability occurred before reaching the age of 21. The allowance is paid monthly at €36 per month.

As was stated before, the non-refundable child tax credit introduced in 2007 is also considered in the analysis as a reform to the 2005 system. The amount of the tax credit in 2007 is twice the universal tax credit of €142, which is equivalent to €24 per month for every child.[6] The tax deduction is independent of the source of taxable income. However, self-employed whose income is not taxed in accordance with general income tax regulation with progressive tax rates are not eligible for the child tax credit.

Figure 6.3: Poland, 2005/07 policies for two family types

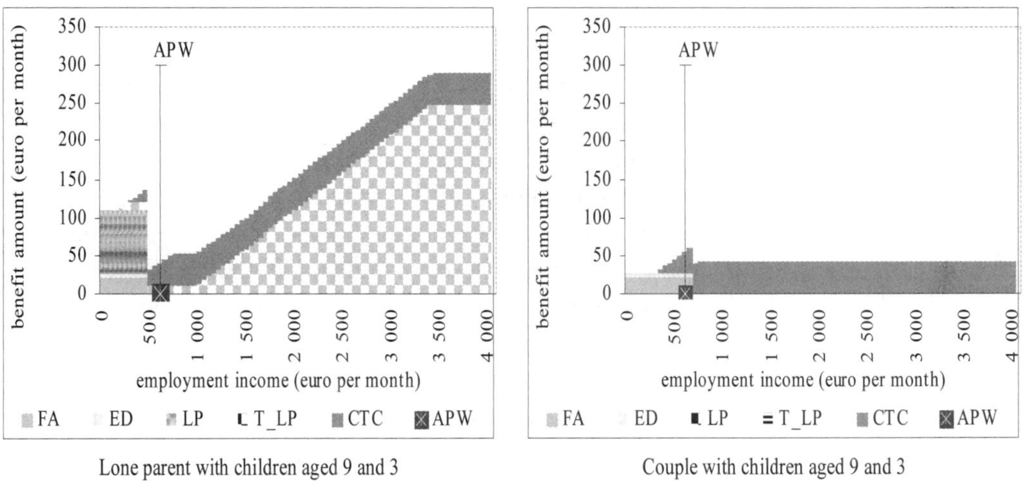

Notes: The first family type consists of a 41 year-old, employed single mother. The second family type consists of a couple with a 41 year-old employed husband and a 41 year-old non-working wife. In both cases, individual original income is computed as the product of multiplying a fixed hourly wage (11.54 per hour) times an increasing number of working hours. All families are assumed to be tenants paying a rent of €300 per month.

Acronyms: FA: family allowance; ED: supplement for starting the school year; LP: lone parent supplement; T_LP: tax relief due to joint taxation; and CTC: 2007 child tax credit (in 2005 prices); APW: Eurostat's gross earnings of a one-earner married couple, at 100% of average production worker, with two children.

Source: EUROMOD.

Figure 6.3 illustrates the structure of child protection in Poland using two synthetic family types: a lone parent and a one-earner couple with two children aged 9 and 3. This gives an indication of the relative size of each policy element and how it is targeted by parental income for these family

6 The value we simulate in the analysis relates to the value of the universal tax credit in 2005, which was €131. The maximum value of the child tax credit is then €262 per child per year.

types. Being contingent on the presence of a dependent child, we treat the advantage to lone parents of being taxed under joint taxation as a policy targeted to support children. Although couples can also take advantage of joint taxation this is not treated as a "child policy" as they could be taxed in this way whether or not they have children. Low-income lone parent families are also covered by the Supplement for Lone Parents. The figure also suggests that the introduction of the child tax credit has considerably increased the expenditure and extended the range of families covered.

3.2 Austria

Austria has one of the most generous child protection systems in Europe. According to Eurostat (2005), social expenditure on policies to support families with children accounts for 3% of the GDP, this figure is exceeded only by Denmark, Luxembourg and Germany. Child protection is provided mainly through universal benefits that are complemented, by central and regional governments, for groups with special needs or high vulnerability.[7] There is no standard definition of dependent children in the Austrian system. However, the most commonly used includes children up to the age of 17, and below 25 if in full-time education and with income below a given limit.

- Family Allowance ("Familienbeihilfe"): universal benefit paid per child. The basic amount is €105 per month and it increases with age, disability and number of children in the family. An additional €36 supplement for the third and following children is available for families with income below €3,630 per month.
- Child Tax Credit ("Kinderabsetzbetrag"): refundable tax credit paid per child. The amount is €51 per month.
- Lone Parent Tax Credit ("Alleinerzieherabsetzbetrag"): refundable tax credit for lone parents. The basic monthly amount is €30, plus €11 for the first child, €15 for the second and €18 for subsequent children.
- Child Care Benefit ("Kinderbetreuungsgeld"): paid to one of the parents of children aged up to 3 years whose income does not exceed €1,217 per month. The income test is applied at the individual level, i.e. the income of the other parent is not considered. The monthly amount of the benefit is €442.

---

7 For more details about the Austrian tax-benefit system and its recent reforms see Fuchs and Lietz (2007).

- Child Care Supplement ("Zuschuss zum Kinderbetreuungsgeld"): supplement of €184 per month for parents receiving the universal child care benefit and with family income below €433 per month.
- Family Bonus ("Familienzuschuss"): income-tested benefit provided by provincial governments. In Vienna, it is paid to families with children aged 1 or 2. The amount of benefit per child depends on the family income and family composition (e.g. a couple with a child and monthly income less than €769, would receive up to €153).

Figure 6.4 illustrates how Austrian child protection is dominated by universal policies and complemented by generous benefits to lower-income families. Of course the shape of the figure is contingent on family type used in the illustration and particularly on the age of children. Had the youngest child been aged 4 instead of 3, only the universal benefits would apply.

Figure 6.4: Austria, 2005 policies for two family types

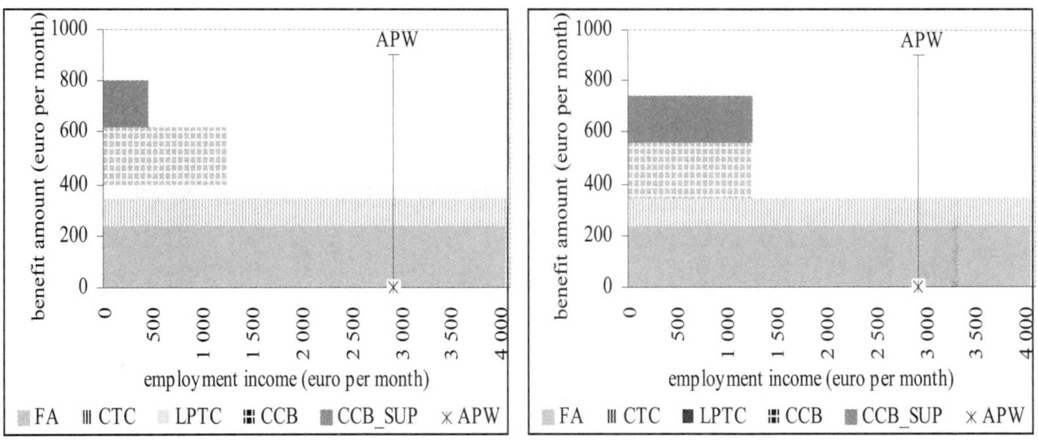

Lone parent with children aged 9 and 3

Couple with children aged 9 and 3

Notes: See notes to Figure 6.3.

Acronyms: FA: family allowance; CTC: child tax credit; LPTC: lone parent tax credit; CCB: child care benefit; CCB_SUP: child care supplement; APW: Eurostat's gross earnings of a one-earner married couple, at 100% of average production worker, with two children.

Source: EUROMOD.

3.3 *France*

Policies to support families with children are also quite generous in France, and are particularly supportive for families with two or more children. The

French system combines universal and income-tested benefits with non-refundable tax concessions.

- Joint taxation ("Quotient Familial"): this instrument is similar to the Polish income tax splitting system. However, the amount of the "splitting factor" (used to divide the tax base by and then to multiply the resulting tax liability) changes with family composition and increases with the number of children.
- Family Allowance ("Allocation Familial"): universal benefit for families with 2 children or more. The basic amount for a family with two children aged below 11 is €115 per month. The amount increases considerably with age and number of children in the family.
- Young Children Allowance ("Allocation pour Jeunes Enfants"): income-tested benefit for children aged less than 3. The benefit amount (€165 per month) is fixed independently of the number of children, but the income test varies with the type of family (lone parent or couple) and the number of earners and children.
- Family Complement ("Complement Familial"): income-tested benefit for families with 3 or more dependent children aged 3 or more. As in the Young Children Allowance, the benefit amount (€150 per month) is fixed independently of the number of children, but the income test varies with the type of family (lone parent or couple) and the number of earners and children.
- Education Related Benefit ("Allocation de Rentrée Scolaire"): income-tested benefit for children aged 6 to 17 to support expenses on school material. Again, the benefit amount (equivalent to €30 per month) is fixed independently of the number of children, but the income test varies with the type of family (lone parent or couple) and the number of earners and children.
- Lone Parent Benefit ("Allocation de Parent Isolé"): income-tested benefit for lone parent families. In 2005, the basic benefit amount was €720 per month. The amount increases with each additional child but it is reduced on a euro per euro basis with family income.

Figure 6.5 illustrates the structure of French child policies. It reflects the relatively higher generosity towards low-income lone parent families. In contrast to the Polish income tax, the French splitting factor ("Quotient Familial") is more generous for couples with children. However, the factor is considerably higher for the first child in a lone parent family.

Figure 6.5: France, 2005 policies for two family types

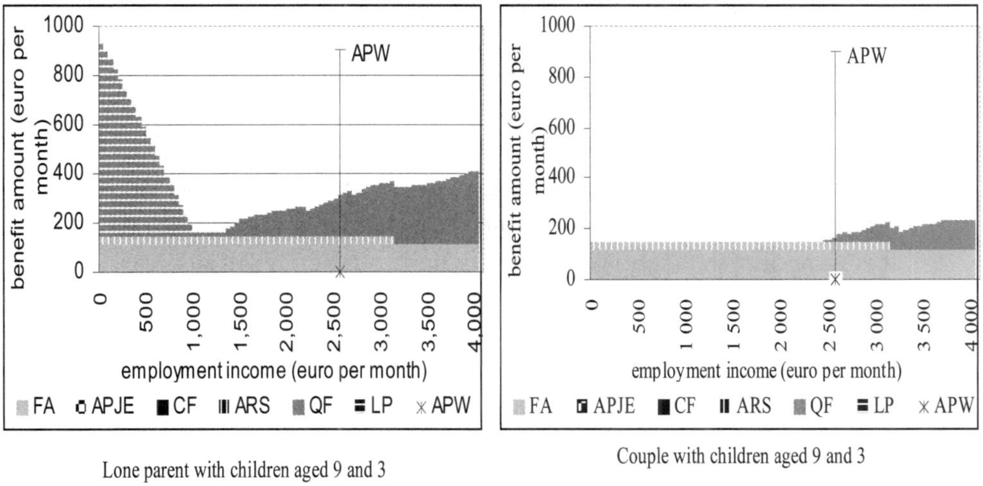

Notes: See notes to Figure 6.3.

Acronyms: FA: family allowance; APJE: young children allowance; CF: family complement; ARS: education-related benefit; QF: joint taxation (quotient familial); APW: Eurostat's gross earnings of a one-earner married couple, at 100% of average production worker, with two children.

Source: EUROMOD.

3.4 *United Kingdom*

Aiming to tackle high levels of child poverty, the UK government has considerably reinforced policies to support families with children over the last decade.[8] Although the system includes a universal Child Benefit, the main bulk of the protection is through means-tested benefits. The UK uses a single definition of dependent children in all benefits: children below the age of 16 or 19 if in full-time education.[9]

- Child Benefit: universal benefit paid per child. The benefit amount is €109 per month for the first child and €73 for the following children.
- Child Tax Credit: income-tested refundable tax credit divided in two elements. The family element is a fixed amount equivalent to €67 per month (it is doubled in the case of a newborn child) paid to all fami-

8 See, for example, Piachaud and Sutherland, 2001; Myck, 2000; and Brewer et al., 2006.

9 The nominal exchange rate used for the conversion of system values into euros is that of 30.06.2005, €1=£0.67473.

lies below an income limit equivalent to €6,175 per month and then reduced at the rate of 6.7% (of gross family income). The child element is equivalent to €209 per month per child and is withdrawn at the rate of 37% for families with gross income above €1,718 per month.

Other benefits that explicitly or implicitly also take into account the presence of dependent children are the Housing Benefit and the Working Tax Credit (an in-work benefit).[10] Figure 6.6 shows the generosity of the British system, mainly resulting from the family and child elements of the Child Tax Credit. It is very clear that relative to the Austrian and the French systems, family support in the UK is much more targeted on lower income families.

Figure 6.6: United Kingdom, 2005 policies for two family types

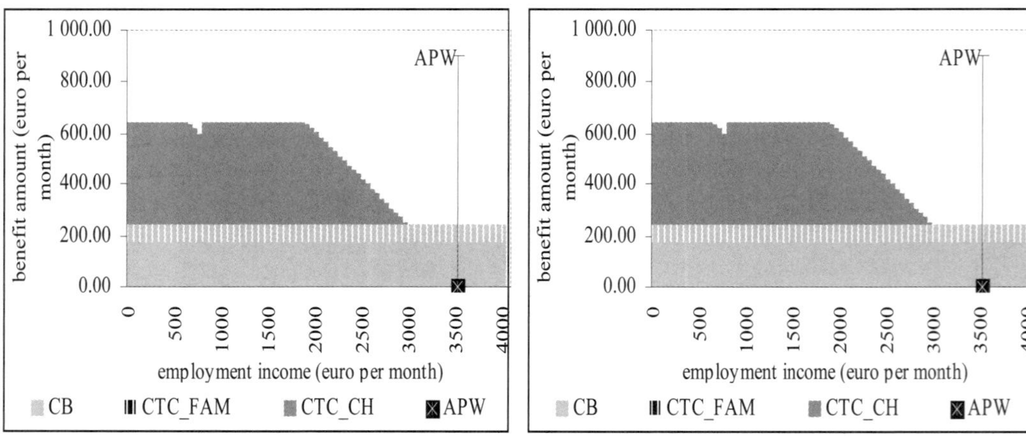

Lone parent with children aged 9 and 3 | Couple with children aged 9 and 3

Notes: See notes to Figure 6.3.

Acronyms: CB: child benefit; CTC_FAM: child tax credit, family element; CTC_CH: child tax credit, child element; APW: Eurostat's gross earnings of a one-earner married couple, at 100% of average production worker, with two children.

Source: EUROMOD.

10 The part of the Working Tax Credit which is child-related, i.e. for example the difference between the value of the WTC for a single person with and without children, is not included in the analysis as it could not be simulated in Poland due to lack of information on the hours of work in the BBGD data.

4 Methods

4.1 Model and data

The analysis presented in this chapter relies on the use of EUROMOD – a static tax-benefit microsimulation model that currently covers 19 Member States of the European Union (all 15 previous to 2004 and 2007 enlargements plus Estonia, Hungary, Poland and Slovenia).[11] EUROMOD facilitates comparability of outputs and transferability of policies across countries, therefore making it possible to analyse the effects of the application of policies from one country on the population of another.

The micro-data used in the microsimulation are derived from the 2005 Polish Household Budgets' Survey (Badanie Budżetów Gospodarstw Domowych – BBGD). The survey was the only large household survey with the combination of demographic and income information conducted in Poland until 2005 and until then all official poverty statistics were calculated using the BBGD data. Since 2005 the more recent poverty statistics have also been published based on the Polish SILC data, however the BBGD data has proved to be a very reliable source for the purpose of incomes analysis and microsimulation.

4.2 Simulation

In the following section, different policies to support families with children are simulated on the Polish BBGD database. These policy reforms consist of eliminating all 2005 Polish child policies simulated in EUROMOD (including lone parent joint taxation) and replacing them by the 2005 policies of Austria, France and the United Kingdom described in the previous section. Monetary amounts of policies "borrowed" from other countries have initially been scaled by GDP per capita ratio after applying the exchange rate.[12] Tax concessions are also scaled, but no adjustment is made to the tax schedule or the tax base. The child tax credit, implemented in Poland in 2007, is also simulated as a "reform" by adding it to the 2005 system after indexing its amount to 2005 prices.[13] We refer to this system as "PL-2007". Throughout

11 See Sutherland, 2001, Immervoll and O'Donoghue, 2001, and Lietz and Mantovani, 2007 for technical information on the EUROMOD framework.

12 According to Eurostat, in 2005 the GDP per capita was €6,405 in Poland, €29,797 in Austria, €27,348 in France and €29,968 in the United Kingdom.

13 According to Eurostat, inflation in Poland (measured by the HICP) between 2005 and 2007 was 4.1%.

we consider as if all policies (original and simulated) and incomes were as on 30 June 2005. No adjustment is made for changes in population composition or income across the year.

The budget effect of each policy (as well as its impact on household income) is measured as the difference between household disposable income including and excluding the analysed benefits and tax concessions. Policies or elements of policies that are not targeted at children, according to our common definition remain in place and interact with the reformed policies.

The simulations do not control for benefit-targeting failure, tax avoidance or evasion. Thus it is assumed that the legal rules apply and that the costs of compliance are zero. This can result in the over-estimation of taxes and benefits. More generally we make the strong assumption that individual behaviour such as benefit take-up, tax evasion and other relevant socio-economic decisions (e.g. labour supply or family formation) do not change as a result of the policy changes that are modelled.

4.3 *Measurement*

Following the United Nations Convention on the Rights of the Child, our definition of children is people aged under 18 (i.e. aged 0-17).[14] We generally assume that income is shared within the household such that household disposable income can be used to indicate the economic well-being of each individual within the household (the "within household" income incidence is not considered).

Household disposable income is defined as original income plus private transfers (e.g. alimony), replacement income (e.g. pensions and contributory benefits) and social benefits minus taxes and social contributions aggregated at the household level. Non-cash benefits are not included. Household disposable incomes are equivalized using the modified OECD equivalence scale, as recommended by Eurostat.[15]

Poverty is measured following the Laeken at-risk-of-poverty approach defined as those living in a household with equivalized household dispos-

14 Note that this diverges from the definition of a child used in the tax and transfer rules of our analysed countries (as would any common definition). Hence, our analysis does not consider part of the expenditure on these policies as support to children.

15 This assumes single person = 1; additional people aged 14+ = 0.5; additional people aged under 14 = 0.3.

able income below 60% of the median. The at-risk-of-poverty threshold, based on the EUROMOD ("baseline") simulation of the 2005 tax-benefit system is €141.53 per month (571.61 PLN) per equivalized person.[16] This threshold is maintained fixed in the assessment of all reform scenarios. Poverty incidence, intensity and severity are measured using FGT indexes α=0 to 2 (Foster et al., 1984).[17]

The efficiency of policies in alleviating poverty is measured through a set of indicators proposed by Beckerman (1979). These are graphically represented in Figure 6.7. Vertical Efficiency (VEE) measures the proportion of total transfers received by the poor. Poverty Reduction Efficiency (PRE) is the proportion of total transfers that effectively contributes to reduce the poverty gap. Spillover (S) is the amount of transfers paid to the poor that exceeds the poverty line, normalized by the amount of total transfers paid to the poor. The effectiveness or "horizontal efficiency" (Matsaganis et al., 2004) of policies in alleviating poverty can be measured using the Poverty Gap Reduction Efficiency (PGE) which computes the extent to which the transfers succeed in filling the aggregate poverty gap.

Figure 6.7: Target efficiency of social transfers

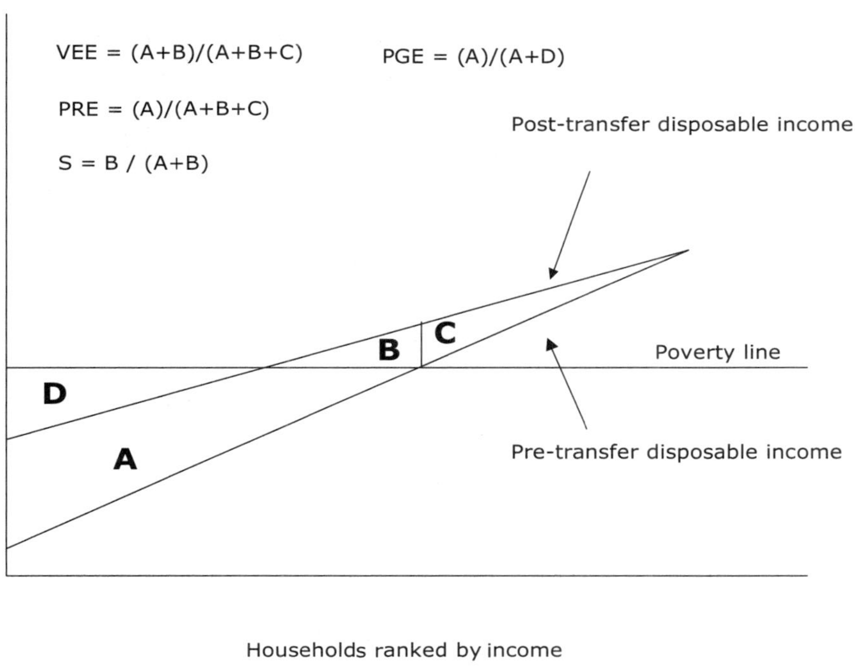

16 So, for example, for a household made up of two adults and two children this would be €297.213, while for a single adult with one child €183.989.

17 See Lambert, 2001, chapter 6 for a survey on poverty measurement.

5 The effects of alternative child policies in Poland

5.1 *Coverage and expenditure*

The spending and coverage levels of a policy are essential for achieving any significant distributional outcome. Estimates from EUROMOD depicted in Table 6.1 show that one third of Polish children are not covered by the 2005 child policies and that the monthly average spending is equivalent to about €16 per child. The introduction of the child tax credit (the simulated system "PL-2007") considerably increases the coverage and almost doubles the expenditure.

In spite of that, expenditure on child policies in Poland falls short if compared to those from Austria and the United Kingdom, even when controlling for differences in GDP per capita. If implemented in Poland, the UK and Austrian systems would imply monthly spending of about €50 per child. Interestingly, if we adjust the French system by the GDP per capita difference, the cost of implementing the French system in Poland would be lower than PL-2007. It is also remarkable that, analysing 2003 policies, Levy et al. (2007) find that when applied on their own countries the expenditure on child support in Austria (€220 per child) is considerably higher than in the UK (€174). This reflects the fact that the distribution of the characteristics of children and their households in Poland is quite different from these countries. In particular, in comparison to these countries there is a higher concentration of children in the bottom of the income distribution in Poland, thus increasing the cost of means-tested benefits.

Table 6.1: Coverage and expenditure

	Baseline 2005 system	PL-2007 system	Austrian system	French system	UK system
Coverage (% of children)	67.3%	97.34%	100.0%	81.3%	99.9%
Average spending per child (€ per month)*	15.9	30.2	47.7	29.2	49.0

Note: * Average spending is calculated over all children under the age of 18 independently of whether covered by the tax-benefit system or not.

Source: EUROMOD.

In order to analyse what would have happened if instead of introducing the 2007 child tax credit the Polish government had reformed the child protection system in line with the systems of Austria, France or the UK, the monetary amounts of the child policies from the three countries were adjusted by factors that made the overall social expenditure budget-neutral with respect to the Polish system after introducing the child tax credit, i.e. so that their cost with respect to the 2005 system corresponds to the PL-2007 system. The overall expenditure level depends on elements whose distribution is quite irregular, in particular the characteristics and circumstances of the children and their families and the interaction between child policies and the rest of the tax-benefit system. Thus, finding the factors that achieve budget neutrality cannot be obtained analytically but requires an iterative exercise. The factors derived from this exercise are presented in Table 6.2.

Table 6.2: Factors applied at monetary amounts of the Austrian, French and UK systems to make them GDP per capita or Budget neutral with respect to PL-2007

	Austrian system	French system	UK system
GDP per capita neutral	0.2150	0.2342	0.2137
Budget-neutral – with respect to PL-2007	0.1415	0.2407	0.1526

Source: EUROMOD.

Figure 6.8 shows the decomposition of total spending by each policy instrument. In the case of the Austrian system the family allowance makes up 58% of total spending, this is followed by the refundable Child Tax Credit (24%) and the Childcare Benefit (14%). The Childcare Supplement, Family Bonus and the Lone Parent Tax Credit are nearly negligible. Accounting for more than half of total expenditure, the Family Allowance is the most significant French instrument, followed by the Lone Parent Benefit (17%), the Young Children Allowance and the Education Related Benefit (9% each). As one would expect, the expenditure on the French joint taxation is larger than on the current Polish system. However, the relatively low spending level reflects the fact that the progressivity of the tax schedule (e.g. number of tax bands, thresholds and rates) in the Polish income tax is much lower than in the French system. As for the UK system, the universal Child Benefit contributes with the largest proportion (49%), which is followed by the means-tested child element of the Child Tax Credit (35%), and then by the "affluence tested" family part of the CTC.

Figure 6.8: Coverage and expenditure decomposition

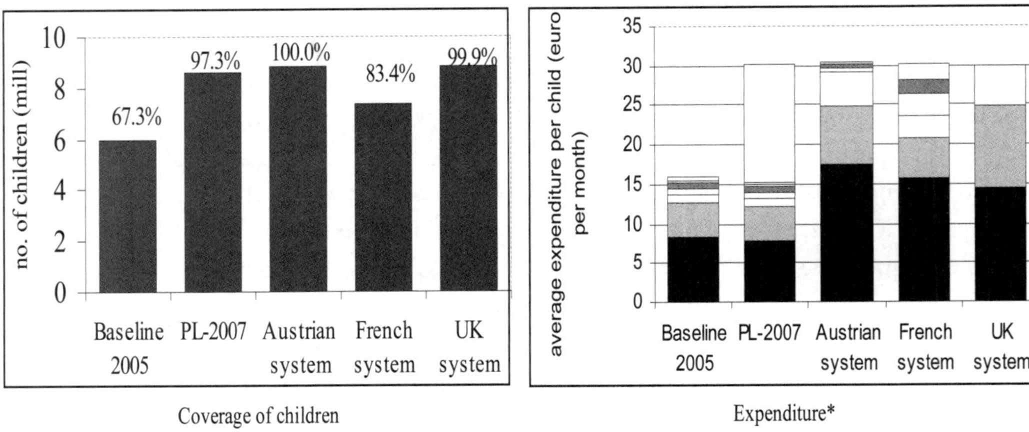

Notes: * List of policies per system in decreasing order of spending (from bottom to top in the figure):
Baseline-2005: family allowance, supplement for lone parents, nursing benefit, supplement for starting the school year, joint taxation, supplement for education of disabled child, supplement for child birth;
PL-2007: same as the Baseline-2005 system plus child tax credit;
Austrian system: family allowance, child tax credit, child care benefit, child care supplement, lone parent tax credit, family bonus;
French system: family allowance, lone parent benefit, young children allowance, education-related benefit, joint taxation (*quotient familial*), family complement;
UK system: child benefit, child tax credit: child element and family element.
The Austrian, French and UK systems adjusted to make the overall expenditure equivalent to the PL-2007 system when simulated on the Polish population (see Table 6.2 for conversion factors).

Source: EUROMOD.

Figure 6.9 shows the distribution of child policies by household income level in terms of the percentage of children covered and the average spending per child per decile of equivalized household disposable income. It reveals how coverage and average spending per child of Polish policies decrease with income in the 2005 system. This is clearly altered with the introduction of the 2007 child tax credit.

As for the alternative reforms based on other countries, the Austrian system covers all children and the spending per child is somehow more evenly spread over the income distribution, although slightly higher at the bottom. As for the French system, coverage and spending fall with income with the exception of the last decile where both rise as families benefit from the "Quotient Familial". The UK system virtually covers all children under 18 and, as expected from a system largely based on means-testing, spending monotonically decreases with household income.

Figure 6.9: Coverage and expenditure per decile

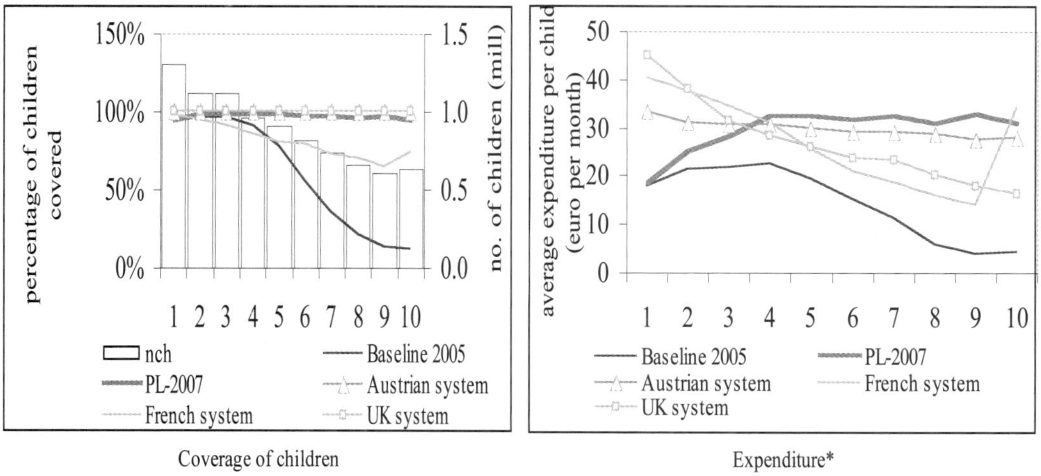

Notes: * Deciles of equivalized household disposable income. See notes on Figure 6.8.
Source: EUROMOD.

Looking at the distribution per household type (Figure 6.10), it is clear that children living with couples tend to be less covered by the 2005 Polish and French systems. This is especially the case for couples with one child. The average spending per child is substantially higher under almost all systems in lone parent households, but it is especially evident in the case of the 2005 Polish system. With the 2005 Polish system, a single child in a lone parent household received more than 5 times as much as a single child living with both parents, and for such couples the French and the 2005 Polish systems are evidently the least generous. In other systems children in lone parent households also get more than in couples, but the ratio is significantly lower. Interestingly the expenditure per child in the PL-2007 system does not vary much with the number of children. This is especially the case for couples but there is also little difference for lone parents. The Austrian and the UK systems contrast with the other in terms of lower variation of expenditure per child across household types. In contrast, in the French and the Polish 2005 systems an additional child increases spending per child substantially. In Poland, the presence of the second child increases spending per child, on average, by 36% in a lone parent household and by 49% in a couple. In France, such increases are 22 and 275%, respectively.

Figure 6.10: Coverage and expenditure per household type

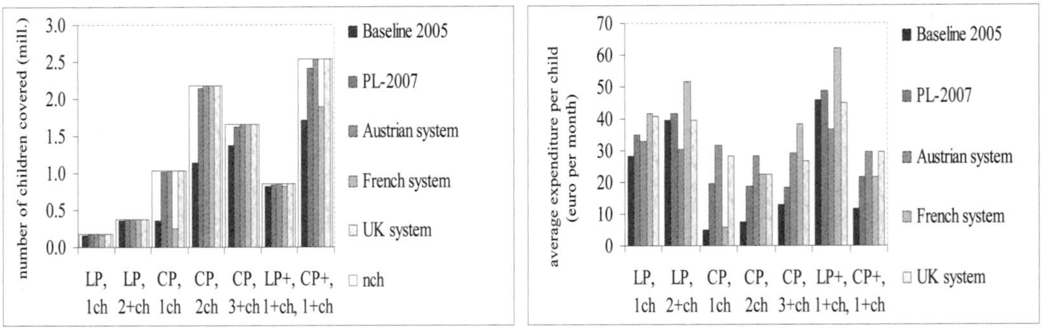

Coverage of children — Expenditure

See notes on Figure 6.8.
Source: EUROMOD.

5.2 *Poverty*

According to results presented in Figure 6.11, child policies considerably reduce the risk of falling into poverty. Measured by the headcount index (FGT with α=0), the at-risk-of-poverty rate is reduced by 6 percentage points (from 31.2 to 25.2%) due to the 2005 Polish child policies. Although almost doubling the expenditure, the introduction of the 2007 Child Tax Credit reduces the risk of poverty only by 1 percentage point (to 24.2%). At the same expenditure level, further reductions could be achieved by implementing the structure of the Austrian (to 22.5%), French (to 19.8%) or UK (to 19.7%) systems.

In relative terms these results are even stronger as one focuses on measures sensitive to the size of the poverty gap. Compared to the PL-2007 system, the normalized poverty gap (FGT with α=1) is 19% lower with the Austrian, 33% with the French and 37% with the UK system. When we attach a greater weight to incomes at the bottom of the distribution (FGT with α=2), the reduction is by 25, 37 and 44%, respectively.

The effect of policies on child poverty risk by household type is shown in Figure 6.12. The introduction of the 2007 child tax credit seems to bring highest poverty reduction among couple households. Whereas under the Austrian system child poverty in Poland *increases* among children living in lone parent households, under the French system this group would experience a substantial reduction.

Figure 6.11: Child poverty risk (FGT indices)

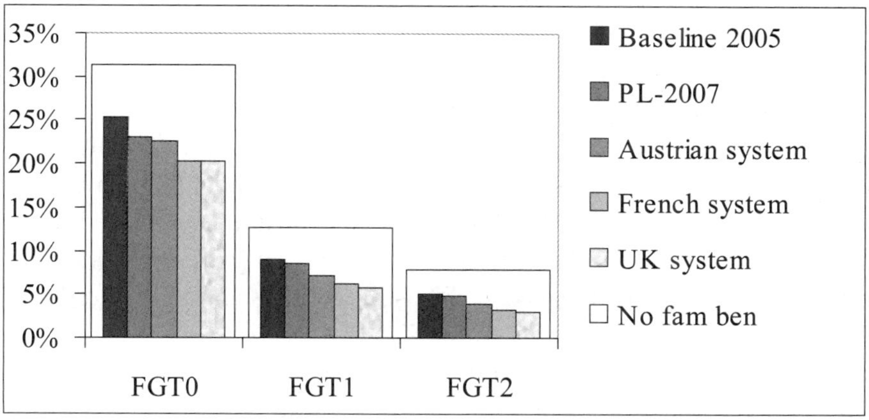

See notes on Figure 6.8.
Source: EUROMOD.

Figure 6.12: Child poverty risk per household type (FGT with α=0)

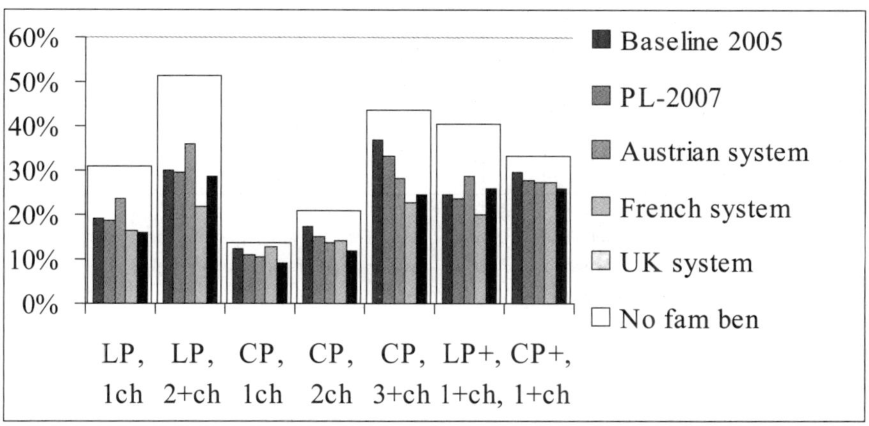

See notes on Figure 6.8.
Source: EUROMOD.

5.3 *Targeting efficiency*

As the VEE index in Table 6.3 indicates, a significant part of the 2005 Polish child policies are targeted to poor children (47% of total expenditure). As one would expect, the targeting level falls considerably (to about 26%) with the introduction of the 2007 child tax credit (PL-2007 system). This would be higher if replaced by the Austrian (34%), French (44%) or UK (46%) system in the budget-neutral fashion. The estimates of PRE and S measures confirm this general assessment.

Similar conclusions are drawn with regard to the effectiveness of child policies to reduce poverty as measured by the PGE index. The overall poverty gap falls by 21% with the Polish 2005 policies (22% including the child tax credit), 31 with the Austrian, 36 with the French and 40% with the UK system. Thus, while the 2007 child tax credit contributes to the reduction of poverty by increasing the horizontal target efficiency, it performs significantly worse relative to the systems of Austria, France and the UK introduced at the same cost.

The PL-2007 system therefore performs worse on all targeting measures relative to the Austrian and UK systems, and on three out of four measures relative to the French (with higher spillover) and the baseline system (PGE).

Table 6.3: Target efficiency

	Baseline 2005 system	PL-2007 system	Austrian system	French system	UK system
VEE	0.4711	0.2644	0.3397	0.4395	0.4569
PRE	0.3901	0.2131	0.2834	0.3306	0.3818
PGE	0.2076	0.2205	0.3070	0.3551	0.3966
S	0.1719	0.1937	0.1658	0.2478	0.1644

Note: For indices definitions see Figure 6.8. The Austrian, French and UK systems adjusted to make the overall expenditure equivalent to the PL-2007 system when simulated on the Polish population (see Table 6.2 for conversion factors).

Source: EUROMOD.

6 Conclusions

In 2005 the relative financial situation of families with children in Poland was worse than in any other of the EU-25 countries. As we show in the analysis presented above while the preferential tax treatment of those with children (the simulated PL-2007 system) improves the situation of many households, it is unlikely to have a very significant effect on the proportion of children in poverty. Significant changes have taken place since 2005 with improved economic conditions and increasing employment levels likely to ameliorate the conditions of many Polish families with children. Financial circumstances of some families may also have improved as a result of the recent wave of emigration out of Poland and frequent arrangements of one parent working abroad and the other staying in Poland and taking care of children. It would be at least questionable though to claim that the latter solution would be the most desirable way of helping children out of poverty.

With the recent deterioration of the economic climate any significant improvements in the situation of families with children resulting from the general economic growth are unlikely to come about in the foreseeable future. Facing a tighter budget the Polish government may need to re-consider the efficiency of the current system of family support if it still aims at reducing child poverty.

In the analysis we demonstrated the potential effects of alternative approaches to targeting resources on families with children, by importing three different European tax and benefit systems and replacing the Polish child-related policies. These three are characterized by very different emphasis, the Austrian on universal credits, the French on tax concessions and targeting large and lone parent families, and the UK's on means-testing. We have "imported" the three systems in static microsimulations in such a way so as to keep the level of expenditure in the range of the Polish system extended for the child tax credit introduced in 2007. This means that the analysed scenarios show the static effects that could have been achieved at the same cost in the hypothetical scenarios of implementing child-related policies of each of the three countries. Naturally, importing entire segments of tax and benefit systems is an unrealistic approach to reforms. However, the diverse nature of the three systems we considered allows us to relate the effects of the recent Polish reform to potential approaches that can be taken to child-related policies.

It is notable that in the case of all three systems the level of expenditure in the bottom three deciles of the income distribution is higher than under the PL-2007 system. This is reflected also on the pattern of spending by family type, with lone parents benefiting more under the French system, while couples are being treated more generously under the universal Austrian system and the means-tested British design. The systems of France and the UK reduce the poverty risk in almost all types of households relative to the PL-2007 system, and when the poverty figures are aggregated then all three analysed systems prove more effective in lowering child poverty relative to the introduced policies, as they are more precisely targeted on the poorest households relative to the PL-2007 system. The targeting efficiency of the latter is lower even compared to the tax-focused French design and unsurprisingly falls well short of the means-tested British system.

As always, the policies affecting household incomes should not be entirely separated from the potential effects they may have on the financial incentives to work. As recently demonstrated by Haan et al. (2008), the flip side of the low level of child-related benefits in Poland is relatively strong financial incentives on the labour market. Naturally each of the considered systems of support for families would produce a different set of changes to employment incentives. If governments aim to target the combined goal of reduced poverty and increased levels of employment, then the effects that future policies have on the financial incentives to work will have to be considered in combination with the way they influence family incomes and change the poverty rate.

However, the static analysis we presented demonstrates how different the design of the Polish system was in 2005 compared to the systems of Austria, France and the UK. The very limited generosity of the system towards families with children sheds some light on the reasons behind the position of Poland in the EU-25 child poverty table. Our results are also illustrative of the likely consequences of the introduction of the child tax credit in Poland in 2007 for changes in the level of child poverty, and set these effects in the light of important alternative policies that could have been considered. We showed that the introduction of the child tax credit will have a rather limited effect on poverty among children. If the government takes the priority of a *"comprehensive policy for families with children"* seriously, then further policies to address child poverty in Poland will be required. The three systems "imported" in our exercise may serve as reference points for any future considerations.

References

Adamson, P. / Micklewright, J. / Wright, A. (2000) *A League Figure of Child Poverty in Rich Nations*. Innocenti Report Card, Issue No. 1.

Beckerman, W. (1979) 'The Impact of Income Maintenance Payments on Poverty in Britain 1975', *The Economic Journal* 89: 261-279.

Bradshaw, J. / Finch, N. (2002) 'A Comparison of Child Benefit Packages in 22 Countries', Department for Work and Pensions Research Report, No. 174. Leeds: Corporate Document Services.

Brewer, M. / Duncan, A. / Shephard, A. / Suarez, M-J. (2006) 'Did Working Families' Tax Credit Work? The Impact of In-Work Support on Labour Supply in Great Britain', *Labour Economics* 13: 699-720.

European Commission (2008) *Child Poverty and Well-Being in the EU. Current Status and Way Forward*. Directorate-General for Employment, Social Affairs and Equal Opportunities.

Eurostat (2005) *European Social Statistics, Social Protection, Expenditure and Receipts*. Luxembourg: European Communities.

Foster, J.E. / Greer, J. Y. / Thorbecke, E. (1984) 'A Class of Decomposable Poverty Measures', *Econometrica* 52: 761-766.

Fuchs, M. / Lietz, C. (2007) 'Effects of Changes in Tax-Benefit Policies in Austria', EUROMOD Working Paper EM3/07, ISER. Colchester: University of Essex.

Haan, P. / Morawski, L. / Myck, M. (2008) 'Taxes, Benefits and Financial Incentives to Work. Britain, Germany and Poland Compared', *Bank i Kredyt* 1: 5-33.

Immervoll, H. / O'Donoghue, C. (2001) 'Towards a Multi-Purpose Framework for Tax-Benefit Microsimulation', EUROMOD Working Paper EM2/01, ISER. Colchester: University of Essex.

Lambert, P. (2001) *The Distribution and Redistribution of Income*, Third Edition. Manchester: Manchester University Press.

Levy, H. / Lietz, C. / Sutherland, H. (2007) 'Swapping Policies: Alternative Tax-Benefit Strategies to Support Children in Austria, Spain and the UK', *Journal of Social Policy* 36 (4).

Lietz, C. / Mantovani, M. (2007) 'A Short Introduction to EUROMOD: An Integrated European Tax-Benefit Model', pp. 1-26 in: O. Bargain (ed.), *Micro-simulation in Action: Policy Analysis in Europe using EUROMOD*, Research in Labor Economics 25. Elsevier Ltd.

Matsaganis, M. / O'Donoghue, C. / Levy, H. / Coromaldi, M. / Mercader-Prats, M. / Farinha Rodrigues, M. / Toso, S. / Tsakloglou, P. (2004) 'Child Poverty and Family Transfers in Southern Europe', EUROMOD Working Paper EM2/04, ISER. Colchester: University of Essex.

Ministry of Labour and Social Policy (2006) *National Report on Strategies for Social Protection and Social Inclusion*.

Myck, M. (2000) 'Fiscal Reforms Since 1997', Institute for Fiscal Studies Briefing Note 14, http://www.ifs.org.uk/bns/bn14.pdf.

Piachaud, D. / Sutherland, H. (2001) 'Child poverty in Britain and the New Labour Government', *Journal of Social Policy* 30 (1): 95-118.

Sutherland, H. (2001) 'EUROMOD: An Integrated European Benefit-tax Model, Final Report', EUROMOD Working Paper EM9/01, ISER. Colchester: University of Essex.

Part III: Evidence Based on Emerging National Models

Chapter 7

Reforming Child Allowances in Lithuania: What Does Microsimulation Tell Us?

Lina Salanauskaite / Gerlinde Verbist

Introduction

In July 2004 the new *Law on Allowances to Children* came into force in Lithuania (Republic of Lithuania, 2004a). Consequently, the state increased spending on benefits to families with children by 23% (20 million euros) in 2005, while spending on cash social assistance to low-income families dropped by 24% (14 million euros). Overall, this reform entails a shift from means-tested benefits to a more universal system. This chapter aims to fill in the lack of knowledge on the distributional income changes following from this shift. Given the specific anti-poverty objectives of Lithuanian family policy, this study focuses on the reform impacts on the most vulnerable household types, such as large and single-parent households, and rural households. Additionally to poverty implications, this chapter discusses changes in income inequality in order to capture income effects for the entire income distribution.

As the reform was introduced gradually, we look at the effects of the initial (1 July 2004) and final implementation (1 January 2008). Hence, we highlight both immediate and long-run estimations of poverty and inequality effects. Family policy can be defined as a set of social policy measures targeted at families to have an influence on their resources, and ultimately structure (Hantrais, 1999). Thereby, various policy instruments, such as child care services, tax allowances or transfer benefits, could be referred to as part of the family policy domain. Within this domain, we focus on benefits specifically designed as state financial support for raising children, which are further on referred to as *family benefits*.

As the 2004 family policy reform affects household income, it might also have an impact on other benefits, and more specifically on social assistance benefits. This chapter, therefore, systematically evaluates linkages of family and social assistance benefits in Lithuania. It then assesses direct (only reform-affected family benefits) and indirect (reform-affected family benefits plus social assistance) monetary impacts of the 2004 reform. Given the multifaceted nature of this study's objectives, it specifically focuses on the analysis of:

- the direct reform impact on poverty and inequality in the country, as well as within and between different household types;
- the indirect reform impact on households' eligibility to social assistance benefits.

In order to define the potential mechanisms of the direct and indirect impacts of the reform, this study first reviews legislative regulations of the Lithuanian family benefit and social assistance system before and after 1 July 2004. Secondly, it provides the methodological framework for the simulation of those benefits and assesses the EU-SILC micro-dataset in terms of its simulation potential of Lithuanian family policy measures. This study uses a static microsimulation approach in order to determine each household's entitlement to family and social assistance benefits before and after the reform. Finally, the chapter analyses and discusses direct and indirect distributional impacts of the reform using a range of standard inequality and poverty measures.

1 Combating child poverty: a European and a Lithuanian concern

A recent synthesis report on child poverty in the EU Member States (Frazer and Marlier, 2007) notes that children are at greater risk of poverty than the rest of the population in all countries, except for the Nordic countries, Cyprus, Greece and Slovenia. Furthermore, the difference between overall and child poverty is considerably large in most of the new Member States, such as the Czech Republic, Poland, Bulgaria, Hungary, Romania or Lithuania (Frazer and Marlier, 2007). The report also highlights that poverty severity is most acute in the three Baltic States, Poland and Southern Member

States, such as Italy, Spain and Portugal. Generally, child poverty rates in the EU are getting to such disturbing heights, the EU identifies the situation as "calling for urgent integrated actions across a wide range of social, economic and cultural policies"[1].

Despite growing concerns over long-term implications of an increasing number of children being raised in extreme poverty conditions, public policy responses to tackle the situation are rather limited and lagged. Heikkilä et al. (2006) claim that many EU countries do not have specific anti-poverty programmes but often address issues of poverty and social exclusion within the scope of broader public programmes. They also show that the EU (before 2004) countries with above average post-transfer national and child poverty rates, particularly Mediterranean countries, have less efficient poverty reduction measures.

A study of Matsaganis et al. (2007) on child poverty in Southern Europe identifies that observed inefficiency in poverty reduction is highly due to eligibility restrictions for income support (as is the case in Greece and in Italy) and low benefit levels of existing transfer schemes (as in Spain and to some extent in Portugal). The latter finding is confirmed by a number of other studies which indicate that lower child poverty rates are attributed to more generous child benefit programmes (i.e. Bradshaw and Finch, 2003; Notten and Gassman, 2008). However, impact of transfers on the poverty rates is also highly dependent on initial inequality of market incomes, as well as on the overall tax-benefit structure in the country. Thereby, Atkinson et al. (1995) find that for example Norway has both a low poverty rate and a low level of transfers, whereas the UK and Ireland have the opposite.

The debate on the effective design of anti-poverty programmes also relates to the issue of universal versus selective policy measures. Cross-national empirical evidence suggests a more mixed pattern of the redistributive effects of means-tested benefits compared to non-means-tested entitlements (Nelson, 2007). These findings vary based on the levels and design of the benefits offered (Notten and Gassman, 2008; Hölsch and Kraus, 2002). The results are also highly dependent on the institutional settings of selected countries, the initial distribution of market income, and the balance of means- versus non-means-tested benefits. Nelson (2007) finds for instance that the high degree of poverty reduction in Sweden and Germany is achieved by non-means-tested benefits, while means-tested benefits achieve a greater alleviation of poverty in the United Kingdom.

1 http://ec.europa.eu/employment_social/spsi/child_poverty_en.htm (accessed on 01.10.2008)

Of the new Member States in the EU (after the 2004 enlargement), Lithuania, Poland and Slovenia are the only countries that adopted distinct anti-poverty programmes (Heikkilä et al., 2006). *The Lithuanian Poverty Reduction Strategy*, approved in 2000, highlighted that one of the major national goals is to reduce the poverty level for large and single-parent families. Nonetheless, the current at-risk-of-poverty rate for single parents and for couples with three or more children remains more than 40% and is the highest in the country. This is twice the total poverty rate.[2]

Based on a 2002 qualitative study of policy-making elites, Aidukaite (2006) argues that policies to combat poverty among Lithuanian families with children were specifically designed along selective lines by using means-tested family benefits. However, since 2004, the Lithuanian family benefit system has shifted towards a more universal provision. The *Law on Allowances to Children* (Republic of Lithuania, 2004a), which became effective since 1 July 2004, is the main trigger of these systematic changes *(further on referred to as the "reform")*. This law aimed to redesign existing family benefits and to ensure their compatibility with the rest of the social security system, which was reformed intensely during the last decade. The new law abolished four existing family benefits, introduced two new benefits and redefined amounts and eligibility conditions of some other transfers to families with children.

Corresponding to the reform-induced changes, the total state spending on family benefits increased from 253 million Lt[3] in 2003 to 363 million Lt in 2005. This was mainly due to the introduction of a universal child benefit, commonly known as "child money". As the law established a gradual implementation of this child benefit, full reform implications were delayed until 2008. The introduction of this universal child benefit was explicitly aimed at combating child poverty, especially for large families (NAP, 2004; National Report on Strategies of Lithuania for Social Protection and Social Inclusion 2006-2008, 2006).

Despite embedded anti-poverty objectives of the family benefit system, the distributional effects of the newly introduced benefits are not straightforward. As the *National Report on Strategies of Lithuania for Social Protection and Social Inclusion 2006-2008* (2006) indicates, the largest number of children in poverty is found among children from three to five years old. In 2005[4], these families were mainly entitled to the universal child benefit and social

2 EUROSTAT (At-risk-of-poverty rate after social transfers, by household type: accessed on 10.07.2008) and Statistics Lithuania data (http://www.stat.gov.lt/en/pages/view/?id=2246) for 2005 and 2006.

3 3.4528 LT = 1 EUR.

4 The reference year of the conducted analysis.

assistance benefits. Alternatively, families with children under three years old experienced lower impoverishment. This was partially explained by a larger (in terms of benefit size and types) state support available to this age group.

Some indirect support for the anti-poverty effects of the newly designed family benefit system might stem from observed changes in state expenses: a year after the introduction of *the Law on Allowances to Children*, the state spending on transfers to families with children increased, while spending on social assistance decreased (see Table 7.1). This might indicate an increase in household income because of new family benefits, which simultaneously moved some households out of social assistance dependence. However, the diminishing role of Lithuanian social assistance programmes might also be linked to a cumulative effect of an increase in wages and pensions, changes in the evaluation procedures of income-testing and a stagnating state-supported income (SSI) level, which is used for the purpose of granting a right to social assistance (The Ministry of Social Security and Labour, 2006). No research has yet tested the plausibility and the extent of these hypotheses.

2 The Lithuanian family policy reform of 2004

Family policy in this chapter includes direct cash measures that are specifically targeted at families with children. Table 7.1 gives an overview of family policy measures in Lithuania around the reform year 2004. As Table 7.1 shows, the total budget of family benefits increased considerably from 2003 (253 million Lt) to 2005 (363 million Lt), mainly due to the reform. The amount is expected to increase further, as the reform comes into full swing from 2008 onwards. This is already indicated by 2007 data: the closest available data before the final implementation of the reform. We briefly discuss the specific pre- and post-reform measures here.[5] But before we do this, we must mention two important parameters of Lithuanian social policy: the "minimum standard of living" (MSL) and the "state supported income" level (SSI).[6] MSL was equal to 125 Lt (36.2 EUR) per person per month during the entire period of 2004, and the SSI to 135 Lt (39.10 EUR) (Statistics Lithuania, 2008).

5 More specific details on these and other benefits can be found in Annex 1 or on: www.socmin.lt

6 The MSL refers to a specified income level aimed at the satisfaction of basic needs. The SSI is the Government-approved personal income level after taxes and contributions, but before transfers of cash social assistance. Both measures are used as administrative tools for benefit calculation rather than tools for poverty monitoring,

2.1 *Main strands of the reform: direct effects*

Direct effects measure cumulative change in household disposable income due to change in eligibility and (or) size of benefits due to the new *Law on Allowances to Children.*[7] Specifically we focus on changes brought by the *abolishment* of the following monthly benefits:

1. *The family allowance* – a categorical benefit, i.e. non-means-tested and non-contributory cash *benefit* (for a detailed description of this benefit and the following ones, see Annex 1).
2. *The benefit for families raising three or more children* – a (partially) means-tested benefit.
3. *The orphan's stipend* – a categorical benefit.
4. *The maternity benefit for studying women* – a categorical benefit.

In 2003, these four measures accounted for around 70% of the total budget of family benefits (see Table 7.1). Additionally, on 1 July 2004, two benefits, which were partial adaptations of some of the abolished benefits, were *introduced*:

1. *The child benefit* – a monthly categorical benefit.
2. *The pregnancy grant* – a lump-sum benefit.

In 2005 these two measures took up around 72% of the total budget, which corresponds approximately to the share of the abolished benefits in the pre-reform period. We expect this share to increase, though, as the reform will only come into full effect in 2008. Some benefits were *not or only minimally affected* by the 2004 reform. These are:

1. *The birth grant* – a lump-sum benefit.
2. *The benefit to a conscript's child* – a monthly categorical benefit.
3. *The guardianship benefit* – a monthly categorical benefit.
4. *The grant for housing* – a lump-sum benefit.

---

7 Apart from the hereby described family benefits, two more measures belong to the family policy domain: baby diapers and municipal support. These benefits are defined outside the scope of *the Law on Allowances to Children*, and were not affected by the reform.

Table 7.1: State spending on non-contributory family policy measures

		Beneficiaries[1], 1000 of people				Budget expenditure, million Lt				Share within total, %			
		2003	**2004**	**2005**	**2007**	**2003**	**2004**	**2005**	**2007**	**2003**	**2004**	**2005**	**2007**
FAMILY BENEFITS													
1	Birth grant	29.85	29.56	29.52	29.76	22.39	22.30	28.52	30.09	8.85	7.60	7.85	6.61
2	Maternity benefit for studying women*	0.21	0.20	-	-	0.05	0.04	-	-	0.02	0.01	-	-
3	Pregnancy grant**	-	3.79	8.15	6.67	-	0.95	2.04	1.72	-	0.32	0.56	0.38
4	Family benefit*	76.56	74.7	-	-	82.88	47.32	-	-	32.77	16.12	-	-
5	Child benefit**	-	268.22	323.04	320.58	-	102.40	260.73	350.66	-	34.88	71.81	77.06
6	Benefit to conscript's child	0.07	0.04	0.02	0.01	0.12	0.07	0.04	0.02	0.05	0.02	0.01	-
7	Benefit for families raising 3 and more children*	43.54	41.27	-	-	78.59	44.21	-	-	31.07	15.06	-	-
8	Guardianship benefit	9.13	9.49	11.33	11.73	48.58	51.07	62.18	70.00	19.21	17.39	17.12	15.38
9	Orphan's stipend*	2.48	3.00	-	-	14.88	15.6	-		5.88	5.31	-	-
10	Grant for housing	1.30	1.66	2.24	3.09	5.43	5.43	7.50	2.56	2.15	1.85	2.07	0.56
11	Subsidy for baby diapers***	-	29.30	10.80	-	-	5.08	2.11	-	-	1.73	0.58	-
Total transfers		-	-	-	-	**252.92**	**293.6**	**363.1**	**455.05**	**100.00**	**100.00**	**100.00**	**100.00**
SOCIAL ASSISTANCE													
1	Social benefit	119.45	83.46	54.15	36.62	94.31	69.60	52.82	52.13	49.45	41.78	33.93	32.77
2	Compensation for housing utilities	428.34	n.a.	n.a.	n.a.	105.1	64.4	30.93	33.66	16.22	18.16	21.62	21.16
3	Municipal support	56.39	50.70	49.86	n.a.	4.31	4.70	6.50	9.7	2.26	2.82	4.18	6.10
4	Free meals for pupils	158.00	141.00	115.28	83.00	60.98	61.04	60.68	54.70	31.97	36.64	38.98	34.38
5	Free school supplies	21.00	40.00	56.00	57.00	0.20	1.00	2.00	8.90	0.10	0.60	1.28	5.59
Total social assistance		-	-	-	-	**264.92**	**200.70**	**152.93**	**159.09**	**100.00**	**100.00**	**100.00**	**100.00**

Notes: 1 Within this table, the term beneficiaries for all benefits, except of free meals to pupils and free school supplies, refers to families. Hereby the term "family" is used in the administrative context and means spouses or persons living together, or one of the parents, as well as their own and adopted children under 18 years of age (see Republic of Lithuania, 2004a). It also includes persons between the ages of 18 and 24 who are unmarried and not cohabitating: full-time pupils and students of general education schools or other institutions of formal education. Beneficiaries of free meals to pupils and free school supplies mean the number of beneficiaries receiving these entitlements.

* - Benefit erased since July 1, 2004; ** - Benefit introduced on July 1, 2004; *** - Temporary benefit.

Source: The primary source of data is Statistics Lithuania www.stat.gov.lt [accessed on April 30, 2008]; the secondary source of data is the Ministry of Social Security and Labour http://www.socmin.lt [accessed on November 15, 2008]

2.2 *Indirect effects*

Change in household income due to direct reform effects may alter eligibility and size of other income maintenance transfers, most notably social assistance. Thereby, we define indirect reform effects as changes in household disposable income because of recalculation of social assistance benefits. This is mainly due to the fact that family benefits are included in the calculation and testing of family income for the purpose of granting social assistance.

Modelling indirect effects will show to what extent a change in family benefits is counteracted by a likewise loss (or gain) in social assistance.

The Lithuanian social assistance system provides three major monthly cash and in-kind transfers to low-income families and single persons:[8]

1. *Social benefit* – a benefit.
2. *Compensation for heating, hot and cold water costs* – a reimbursement of the utility costs.
3. *Free meals to pupils* – an in-kind benefit to schoolchildren.

3 Methodology

This chapter uses a static microsimulation approach in order to determine each household's entitlement to family policy measures before and after the reform. A static microsimulation enables to evaluate distributional impacts of a certain tax-benefit policy system on a selected point in time (e.g. Spadaro, 2007). The static approach implies analysis of short-term effects for a given population. Due to data shortage, as well as numerous and rapid reforms in Lithuania, behavioural responses are not estimated in this study. Generally, these reasons, as Cok et al. (2008) point out, explain the low prevalence of microsimulation models in most of transition economies.

Lithuania did not have a functional tax-benefit microsimulation model (MSM) to test distributional impacts of such a reform (Immervoll et al., 1999; Lelkes, 2007). Hence, we have developed an MSM using the statistical software STATA. This chapter employs the EU-SILC (*Survey on Income and Living Conditions*) 2005 UDB version for Lithuania as the underlying database for the MSM.

8 Additionally to these three benefits, *provision of free school supplies*, such as exercise books, calculators or school apparel, is provided to low-income families with children. However, in 2004, the rules of provisions were not defined by any particular law, but based on the availability of the state-assigned budget.

3.1 *EU-SILC capacity to simulate non-contributory family policy measures*

EU-SILC collects comparable cross-sectional and longitudinal multidimensional micro-data on income poverty and social exclusion in European countries (EUROSTAT, 2007b). It provides information on a number of household attributes, such as income, social exclusion, housing, health, education and participation in the labour market.

Since 2005, the dataset contains information on income and living conditions of Lithuanian people. The Lithuanian part of the database is collected via a survey of 12,117 individuals, coming from 4,441 households. EU-SILC 2005 information on Lithuania refers to demographic information for 2005, but to income information of 2004. For the purpose of this analysis, we use EU-SILC demographic variables at the end of an income reference period (2004) in order to better align with income information.

The detailed overview on EU-SILC contained variables and their potential to carry simulation of Lithuanian family benefits is presented in Annex 1. The relative weight of the four family benefits which are simulated, constitutes around 73% of the state budget for all family benefits in 2003 and 2004. This share increased to 80% and 83% in 2005 and 2007 respectively. In 2004, social benefits consumed around 35% of the state budget on means of social assistance.

3.2 *Simulation framework*

Due to family benefits' interaction via income testing, the sequence of benefit simulation is conducted in a predefined order, which is indicated by numbers in parentheses (see Figure 7.1). Because of gradual implementation of the child benefit, this study simulates two reform scenarios: the initial schedule, effective as of 1 July 2004, and the final schedule, which became effective on 1 January 2008. Other policies, as well as the socio-economic and demographic structure of the population are held constant. We use the administrative rather than EU-SILC database definition of a child for the purpose of simulation.[9]

9 More details on the EU-SILC used child definition can be found in EUROSTAT (2007a).

Figure 7.1: The simulation framework

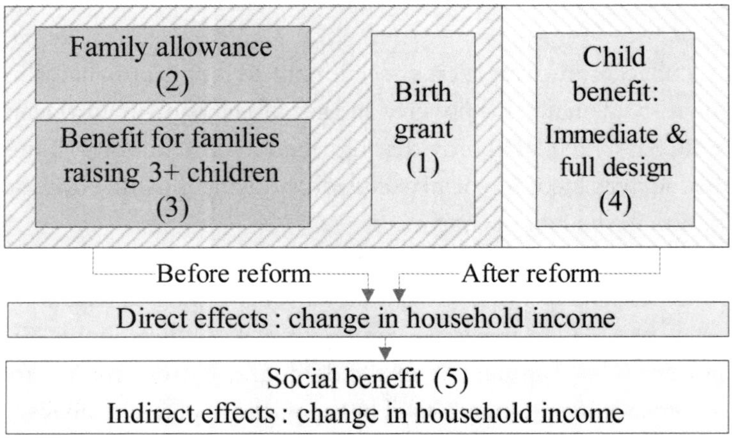

Note: Numbers in parentheses indicate the sequence of simulation.

3.3 *Measuring distributional impacts*

There are a number of ways to measure distributional impacts; this chapter focuses on a selection of commonly accepted inequality and poverty indices:[10]

- The *Laeken* indicators: the Gini coefficient, S80/S20 income quintile share ratio, and at-risk-of-poverty rate;
- Foster-Greer-Thorbecke (FGT) indicators (Foster et al., 1984): poverty gap index and poverty severity;
- GE class measures for inequality aversion parameter *a* of values [-1; 2].

Indicators are calculated before and after (immediate and full design scenarios of) the reform, and both direct and indirect reform effects are taken into account. Welfare measures are based on household disposable income, equivalized with the modified OECD scale.[11] A change in income due to the

10 GE indexes and Gini coefficient are obtained through the application of the STATA module "ineqdeco" (Jenkins, 1999). The FGT family of poverty measures are estimated using STATA module "sepov" (Jollife and Semykina, 1999). We use a bootstrap simulation method in order to estimate standard errors for both poverty and inequality indexes.

11 Household disposable income is established as the sum of all monetary income received from any source by each member of the household (including income from work, investments and social benefits) net of taxes and social contributions paid and certain unavoidable expenditures (EUROSTAT, 2008). The modified OECD equivalence scale assigns a weight of 1.0 to the first household member aged 14 or over; 0.5 to each additional member aged 14 or more and 0.3 to each member aged less than 14 years old.

reform is estimated by adding the difference between simulated transfers after the reform (child benefit and birth grant) and simulated benefits before the reform (birth grant, family benefit and benefit to families raising three or more children).

Results are calculated, as well as broken down for household types depending on household configuration, age of the children and place of residence. In order to better capture reform effects, this chapter also presents between- and within-group inequality measures.

4 Distributional impacts of family and child benefits reform

4.1 *Benefit simulation results*

The simulated number of beneficiaries for most of the benefits, as well as their intermediate estimation values, match administrative data within the interval of (±)10% (see Table 7.2). In-between simulation results are presented in order to identify potential sources of observed differences. As Table 7.4 indicates, the largest deviations from external estimates are found in a benefit for families raising three or more children, child benefit and social assistance, while birth grant and family benefit reveal a rather precise estimation. Generally, differences in simulations are larger if more diverse causes of possible deviations accrue:

- Influences of underlying demographic differences (i.e. over-representation of newborn children, as in birth grant, or under-representation of children, aged 17 to 23, as in child benefit);
- Identification of eligible population requires use of more socio-economic proxy variables to recreate a "nuclear" family category, defined as parents or guardians and children only (i.e. EU-SILC contains no information on foster care and contains limited information to identify the full-time studying status of potentially eligible children).
- Simulation of benefit requires means-testing. This might be affected by systematic income underreporting due to a long recollection period, high non-response rates among top-income households or other survey-related income reporting issues,[12] which could inflate a number of simulated social assistance beneficiaries.

12 For example, see Milanovic (1999) for more details on income underreporting in transition countries.

Table 7.2: Family benefits weights adjusted: simulation versus administrative data

	Av. yearly benefit per beneficiary, Lt[1]	Benefi-ciaries, EU-SILC data	Beneficiar-ies, exter-nal data	Δ, %
Total population, beginning of 2005	-	3391098	3425324	1
Average family size		2.65	3.18	-17
Transfers to families with children before reform:				
Birth grant	770 (122)	30729	29600	4
- children born in 2004	750 (0)	31560	30419	4
Family benefit	1217 (309)	73409	74703	-2
- eligible children	1125 (0)	79403	n.a.	n.a.
- children aged 0 to 2, beginning of 2005	-	89816	90302	-1
Benefit for families raising 3 or more children	1668 (351)	54332	41274	32
- eligible children	330 (36)	183263	n.a.	n.a.
- children aged 0 to 15, beginning of 2005	-	629125	637431	-1
- children aged 16 to 23, beginning of 2005	-	419068	426712	-2
- families with 3 or more children until age 18	-	46855	49613[2]	-6
- persons in families with 3 or more children until age 18	-	300969	278487[3]	8
Transfers to families with children after reform:				
Child benefit (immediate implementation)	1341 (832)	206320	266000	-22
- children aged 0 to 2, beginning of 2005	1777 (1114)	89816	90302	-1
- children aged 3 to 6, beginning of 2005	600(0)	130042	135762	-4
- eligible children aged 7 to 23, raised in 3 or more children families	600 (0)	148585	n.a.	n.a.
- all eligible children	751 (284)	368443	n.a.	n.a.
- eligible children receiving 0.4 MSL	600 (0)	278627	320000[4]	-13
Child benefit (full design)	1069 (633)	499714	n.a.	n.a.
- children aged 0 to 17, beginning of 2005	-	743684	746274	0
- children ages 18 to 23, beginning of 2005	-	304507	317869	-4
- families with children under 18	-	473404	509973[5]	-7
- eligible children	-	802954	700000[6]	15
Social assistance before reform				
Social benefit	1629 (1167)	97403	83 463	17
Social assistance after reform				
Social benefit, immediately after reform	1601 (1112)	95001	54100	76
Social benefit, given full design of reform	1519 (1035)	89933	n.a.	n.a.

Notes: 1 Positive values only
2 http://www.stat.gov.lt/lt/pages/view/?id=1696 (2001 Population census)
3 http://www.stat.gov.lt/lt/pages/view/?id=1696 (2001 Population census)
4 Figure refers to an estimate by Social Security and Labour Ministry on an average number of eligible children per month: http://www.bernardinai.lt/index.php?url=articles/52805
5 http://www.stat.gov.lt/lt/pages/view/?id=1696 (2001 Population census)
6 Figure refers to an estimate by Social Security and Labour Ministry on an average expected number of eligible children per month: http://www.vtv.lt/naujienos/socialiniai-reikalai/vaiko-pinigai-skiriami-visiems-vaikams.html

Source: Own calculation (standard errors reported in parentheses).

In addition to simulation deficiencies due to household survey design, differences in estimated and reported number of beneficiaries could occur because of actual benefit take-up or targeting performance being lower than 100% (i.e. stigma, administrative complexity or targeting leakage-related reasons)[13]. Comparison of simulated and actual number of beneficiaries is also rather cumbersome due to shortage of administrative data. For example, we use the latest available 2001 Population Census data to verify distribution of benefits for large families, even though the representation of this data for the population in 2004 is weakened by relatively rapid changes in fertility rates and current migration processes.[14] In addition to this, administrative information might contain possible erroneous accounting of beneficiaries due to complexities of family identification, when merging quarterly collected regional data into the pooled annual central administrative social security database.[15]

A note should also be made that selected external data in Table 7.2 also refer to expected rather than observed number of beneficiaries (i.e. eligible children receiving 0.4 MSL, children receiving child benefit after the full implementation of reform). These data help to assess the potential accuracy of ex-ante simulations.

4.2 Disposable household income before and after the reform

4.2.1 Direct effects

According to the EU-SILC data allowances to families and children constituted around 4% of average household income in 2004. 16% of Lithuanian households received transfers to families, which on average amounted to 14% of their equivalized disposable income. Allowances to families play an especially significant role among poor households: more than 25% of the first income decile households receive these transfers. Their average weight within the household budget reaches 34%.

---

13 More details on targeting and take-up rates of social benefits in Lithuania can be found at: http://siteresources.worldbank.org/SAFETYNETSANDTRANSFERS/Resources/281945-1131468287118/1876750-1138736077420/Lithuania_Brief.pdf

14 More details on fertility rates and international migration in Lithuania can be found at: http://www.stat.gov.lt/en/pages/view/?id=1383

15 Based on personal communication with Social Security and Labour Ministry, 21 May 2008.

The average *simulated* weight of transfers to families within household income before the reform constituted 16% of recipient households' income. Around 10% of all Lithuanian households receive these types of state transfers.

With the initial implementation of the reform, annual transfers to families raising children increased by around 78 Lt per household (see Figure 7.2). Full implementation of the reform would have raised household income by an additional 221 Lt per year, revealing a large impact of the reform still to be realized. Reform-induced income gains are highly diverse for different types of households. Households raising three or more children gain mostly from the initial part of the reform. On the other hand, full implementation of the reform brings relatively higher gains to single-parent families and families raising one or two children, as before the reform most of these households were not eligible for existing benefits.

The performed simulation also suggests that despite significantly lower income levels, rural households have on average gained less than urban households during the initial reform implementation stage. This is largely due to the fact that rural households are larger, but poorer than urban households, and therefore had a higher incidence of family benefit receipt before the reform implementation. Furthermore, a breakdown of household by children's age indicates that households with at least one child under age three are found at completely opposite sides of the distribution if residence is taken into account: rural households' annual income is more than 5000 Lt lower compared to their urban counterparts. In contrast, urban households with children aged seven or more are the poorest household type within this group. All rural households with children above age 3 have a comparably similar mean income, which is significantly higher than the income of households with very small children.

Additionally, Figure 7.2 demonstrates that on average the income ranking of the analysed household types with or without children did not change due to the direct budgetary impacts of the reform. This finding particularly implies that direct income gains are not sufficiently large to significantly raise well-being of the most vulnerable household types: large families with children, single-parent households or certain rural households with children. Thereby, poverty and particularly inequality implications of the reform are expected to be limited.

Figure 7.2: Average yearly equivalized household income by household types, Lt

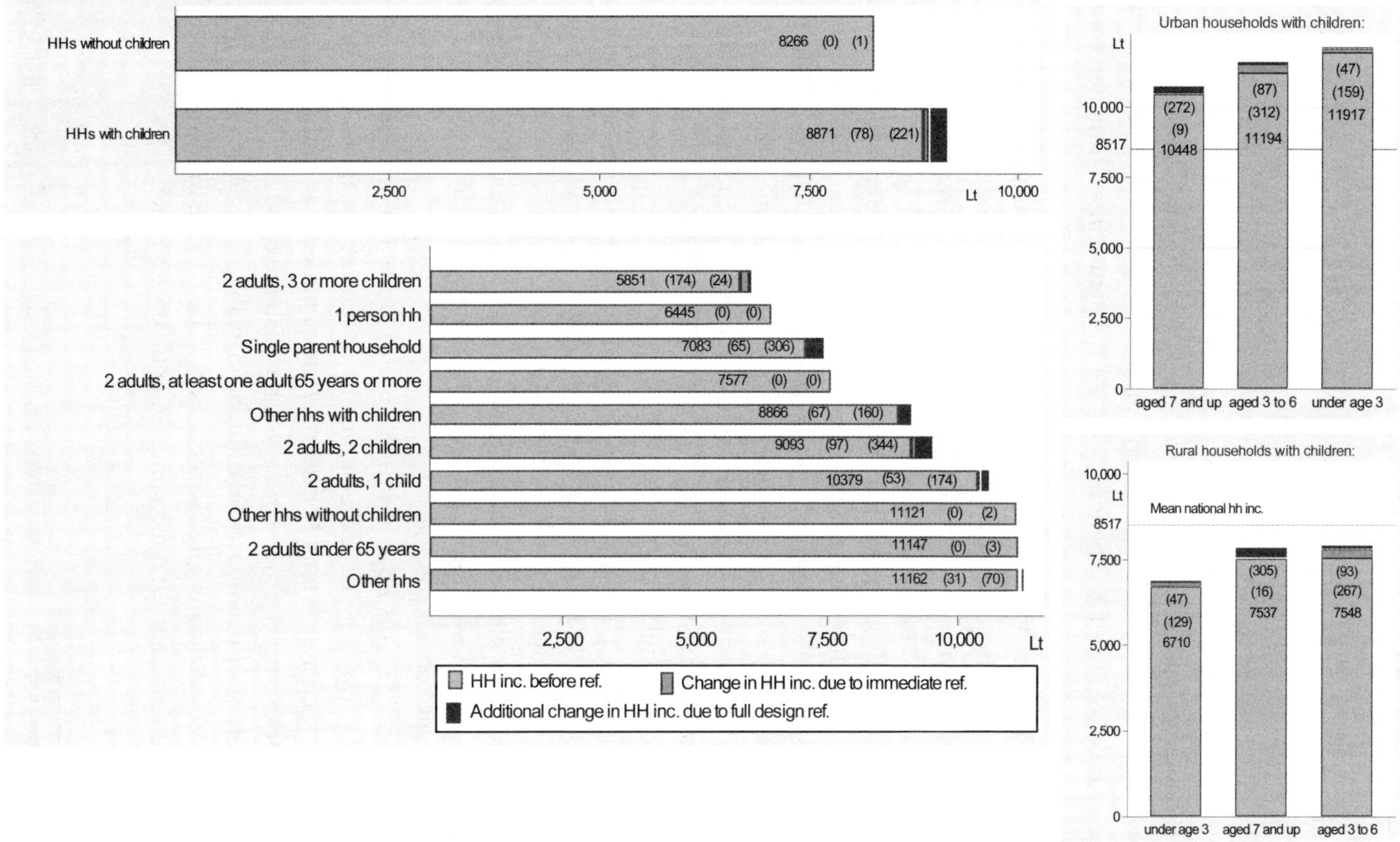

Notes: 1 Values inside bars show income before reform and income changes (in parentheses) due to immediate or full design reform.
2 Household types are ranked based on the group's average pre-reform equivalized household disposable income (ascending).
3 Households with children in several age categories are assigned to a group based on the age of the youngest child.

Source: Own calculation, based on the Lithuanian tax-benefit model.

4.2.2 Indirect effects

As mentioned before, indirect effects measure change in household disposable income if change in eligibility and size of the cash social assistance benefit is considered.[16] Adding the simulated value of this benefit increases the average weight of before-reform transfers to families from 16% to 45% of recipient households' income. Approximately 15% of all households receive these types of state transfers, which points to a 5 percentage point rise in the number of simulated beneficiaries. At the same time, simulated total yearly equivalized transfers increase from 684 Lt to 859 Lt.

Nevertheless, Figure 7.3 reveals that income of households with children shrinks slightly from 78 Lt to 72 Lt if recalculation of social benefits is considered. The drop is even larger if the full design of the reform is considered: then income gains on average decline from 221 Lt to 206 Lt. This finding proves that analysis of indirect effects is vital in order to comprehend the full reform effect on household income.

A significant loss in reform-related gains is especially observed for households eligible for social assistance, but with income close to the set threshold. Larger drops in income gains due to recalculation of social benefit amounts are observed for e.g. rural families with children aged seven or more or with children aged three to six. Alternatively, the poorest rural households, which tend to raise children under three, are less affected by the change in eligibility for social benefit. As their income falls greatly below the given social assistance threshold compared to the other two household types, the probability of moving out of social assistance due to family benefits is much lower. Other primary losers of the reform are found to be single-parent households.

Generally, Figure 7.3 confirms that more affluent households are less or not affected by reform-associated influences on social assistance. Therefore, their income change is mainly driven by direct rather than indirect reform effects. For example, urban households, which tend to have higher than average national income, are less influenced by indirect reform effects. This is demonstrated by a negligible reduction or no change in income due to both immediate and full reform implementation scenarios.

16 The effect might be even larger when changes in entitlements to free meals for pupils, as well as their monetary values, would be taken into account.

Figure 7.3: Average yearly equivalized household income change due to direct and indirect effects (by household types), Lt

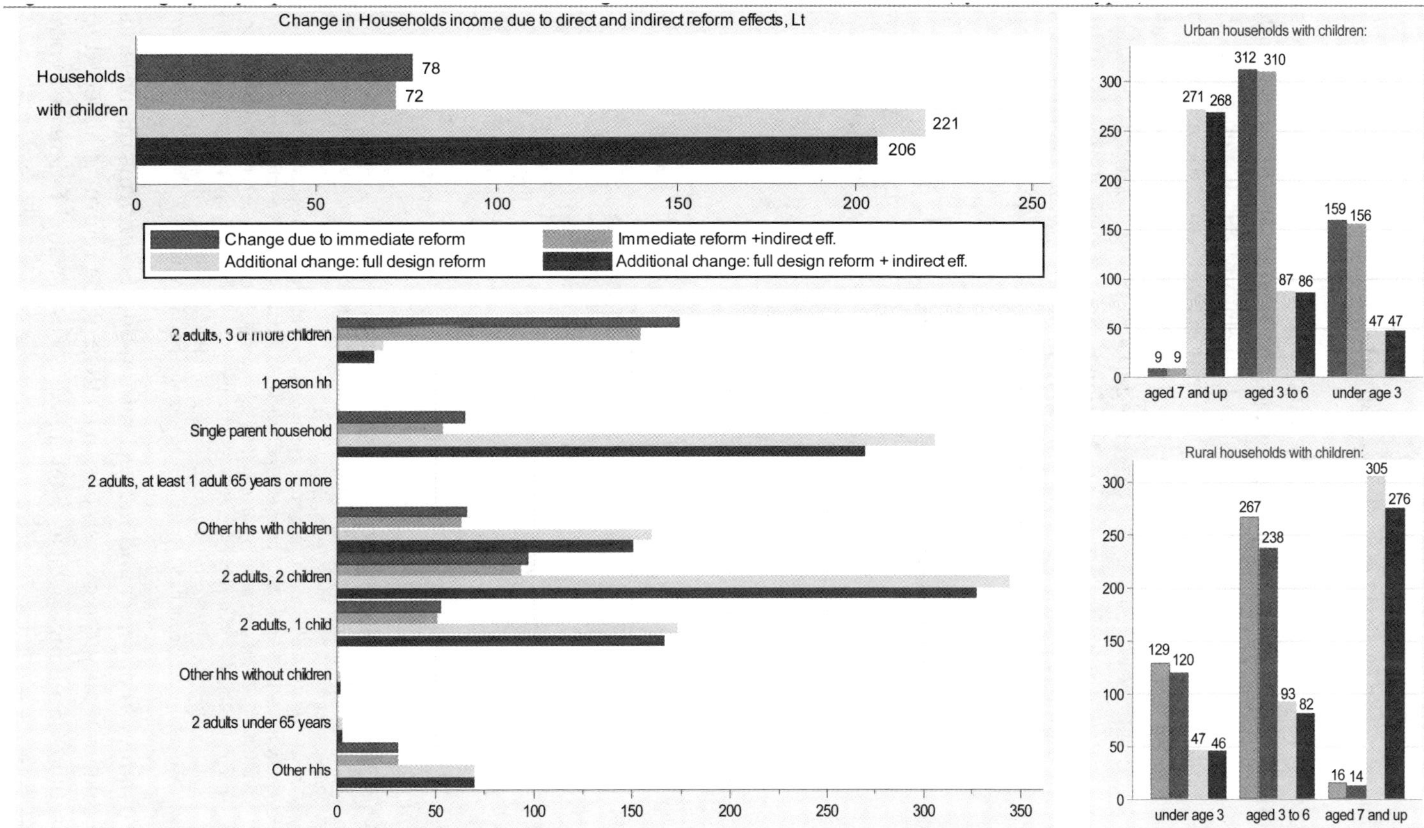

Notes: 1 Household types are ranked based on the group's average pre-reform equivalized household disposable income (ascending).
2 Households with children in several age categories are assigned to a group based on the age of the youngest child.

Source: Own calculation, based on the Lithuanian tax-benefit model.

4.3 *Poverty and inequality before and after the reform*

4.3.1 Direct and indirect effects: total population

Before the reform, 20.25% of the Lithuanian population were poor.[17] Due to the initial part of the reform quite a few poor households in Lithuania would be lifted just above the poverty threshold (see Figure 7.4). Given relatively small child benefit amounts and rather minor changes in the amounts of other family benefits, a 0.5 percentage point decrease in the poverty rate and a simultaneous relief in the poverty gap and poverty severity could be considered as a positive poverty reduction action. If the full design of the reform would be implemented, the poverty alleviation would become even more significant: the at-risk-of-poverty rate would drop by approximately 1.5 percentage points.

Figure 7.4: Poverty changes: implications for total population[1]

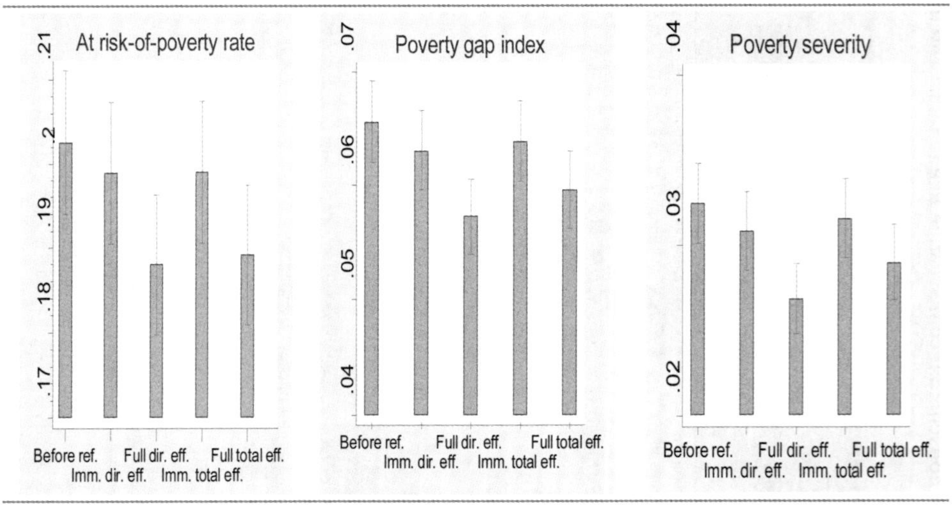

Notes: 1) The income ranking for poverty measures is based on the pre-reform income distribution, while the income ranking for inequality measures reflects income distribution in pre- and post-reform environments.
The *at-risk-of-poverty* rate is the percentage of persons, over the total population, with an income below the "at-risk-of-poverty threshold (poverty line)", set at 60% of the national median income (EUROSTAT, 2005). The *poverty gap* measures the average difference between the income of poor people (people with income below the at-risk-of poverty threshold) and the poverty line. The *poverty severity index* is defined as the squared poverty gap index.

Source: Own calculation ("error bars" represent a 95% confidence interval).

The evaluation of direct and indirect reform effects confirms the observation that, in reality, the overall positive effect of the reform is lessened for households receiving social assistance. We observe a slight increase in pov-

17 EUROSTAT's (http://epp.eurostat.ec.europa.eu) estimate for total Lithuanian at-risk-of-poverty rate after social transfers in 2005 is 21% (Date of extraction: October 15, 2008).

erty measures displaying direct versus total reform effects. Remarkably, this difference is not that significant as shown by the 95% confidence interval.

Inequality measures provide a similar picture of income mobility before and after the reform: overall inequality slightly falls during both the initial and final phases of the reform. It is worth pointing out that these changes are only significant if the full reform design is taken into account. Full reform implementation would lead to greater equality, especially when comparing bottom and top income quintiles. For example, with full reform design, the s80/s20 income quintile ratio would fall by more than 0.3 percentage points.

Figure 7.5 also depicts that the overall magnitude of inequality reduction is mitigated by relatively lower income gains for households at the threshold of receiving social assistance. This is captured by a slight increase in inequality measures if in addition to direct effects, indirect effects are also considered. On the other hand, inequality measures, portraying changes in the upper part of the income distribution (i.e. GE [2]), point out to almost no significant changes in inequality. This finding goes in line with previous observations that higher-income households are relatively less affected by the monetary impacts of the reform.

Figure 7.5: Inequality changes: implications for total population

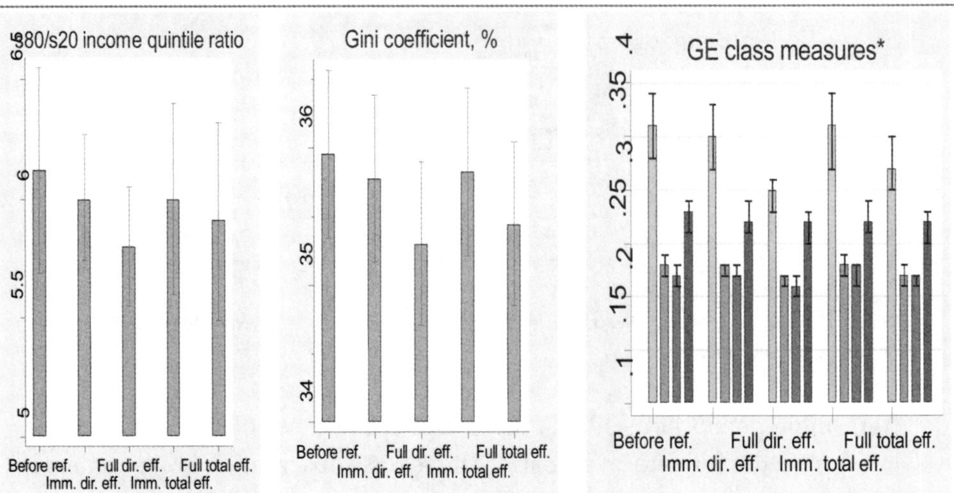

Notes: * GE(α), for α [-1; 0, 1, 2] measures are ranked in α ascending order.
The *S80/S20 income quintile ratio* is the ratio of the sum of income received by the 20% of the country's population with the highest income to that received by the 20% of the country's population with the lowest income (EUROSTAT, 2005). The *Gini coefficient* is defined as the relationship of cumulative shares of the population arranged according to the level of income, to the cumulative share of the total income received by them. The *GE class measures* for parameter α of values [-1; 2], where α is an income difference sensitivity parameter, describe income distribution with the emphasis on higher or lower ends of the distribution.

Source: Own calculation ("error bars" represent a 95% confidence interval).

4.3.2 Direct and indirect effects: decomposition by household groups

Figure 7.6 displays initial poverty indices before the reform, as well as their respective changes due to initial reform set-up and additional change if the full design reform is carried out.[18] It reveals that all households raising children, except urban households with children, are more likely to be poor compared to the average poverty rate in the country. All households with children also experience poverty alleviation either in one or the other stage of the reform.

Figure 7.6: Poverty changes (%): implications for selected household groups

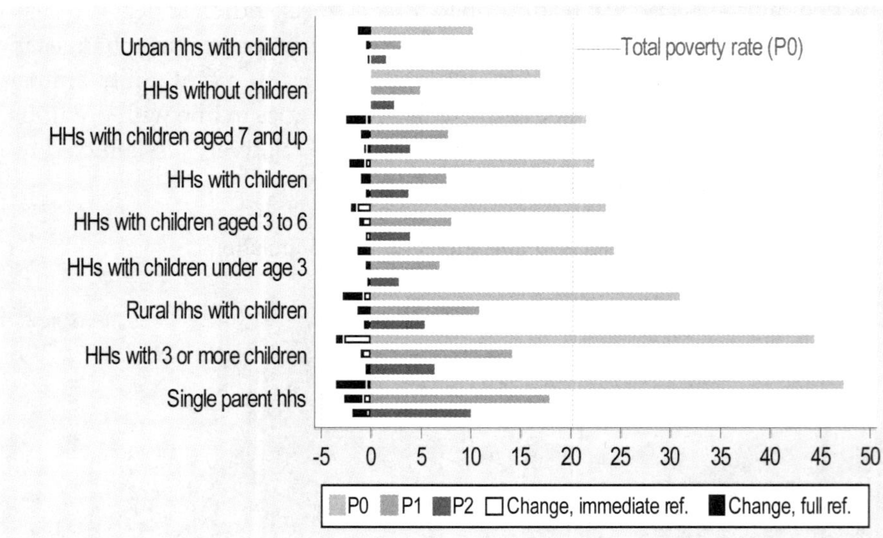

Note: Household types are not exclusive and ranked based on the group's poverty rate before the reform.
Source: Own calculation.

Yet, single-parent households, the most deprived population group, gain most from the full reform scenario. The reverse observation holds for large households: they gain most from the initial reform scenario. The graph also displays that poverty intensity would be first and foremost addressed among single-parent households. Actually, poverty gap and poverty severity indices reveal that this group is the most disadvantaged on all poverty dimensions, and that the full reform scenario brings largest gains to it.

18 Precise indices and associated standard errors are presented in Annex 2.

Rural households with children are among the primary gainers, mainly due to the initial reform implementation. The rules of gradual extension of eligibility to child benefit, based on number of children and their ages, are reflected in moderate immediate poverty alleviation among households with children aged seven and up.

In addition to poverty decomposition, we analyse changes in inequality. For this purpose we form four broad household groups among dimensions of: living in a household with children, children's age, rural or urban residence place and income vulnerability.

Figure 7.7[19] reveals that the most widespread income inequality is observed among single-parent households. This group is much more heterogeneous compared to the next most vulnerable household group: large families with three or more children. If pooling these two household types into group II, as displayed in Figure 7.7, we identify diverse inequality changes during different reform stages. All GE(α) measures, and particularly the ones focused on lower incomes, point to a sharp decrease in inequality among single-parent households due to full reform implementation. On the other hand, inequality among households with three or more children does not display any significant reduction, but rather points to a marginal rise of inequality among these families. If taken into account within-group II inequality reduction, we note that opposing inequality movements led to narrowing income dispersion immediately after the reform. This indicates that broadening income dispersion among large families significantly reduced overall dispersion within the group II after the initial reform.

Overall, GE(α) measures focusing on higher incomes point to a marginal increase in inequality within group III (composed of all households raising children). As this group includes households with children, separated by different age categories, we conclude that despite slight inequality reduction among specific age groups, full reform implementation brings a small inequality increase within households with children.

The breakdown by residence place displays the largest within-group inequality increase after the full reform implementation. As already observed in Figure 7.2, these two household groups have contrasting income profiles.

19 Precise indices and associated standard errors are presented in Annex 2. Inequality between different household types is negligible; therefore, this data is not included in Figure 7.7. Within groups, the inequality measure is sensitive to a group's composition. As presented in Annex 2, the total inequality index GE(α) is composed of each group's within and between inequality indexes: GE_within(α) + GE_between(α), Jenkins (2006).

Therefore, the aggregate effect of tightening income dispersion among both rural and urban households, indicates an increasing income gap among households with children, if place of residence is considered.

Figure 7.7: Inequality changes (%): implications for selected household groups

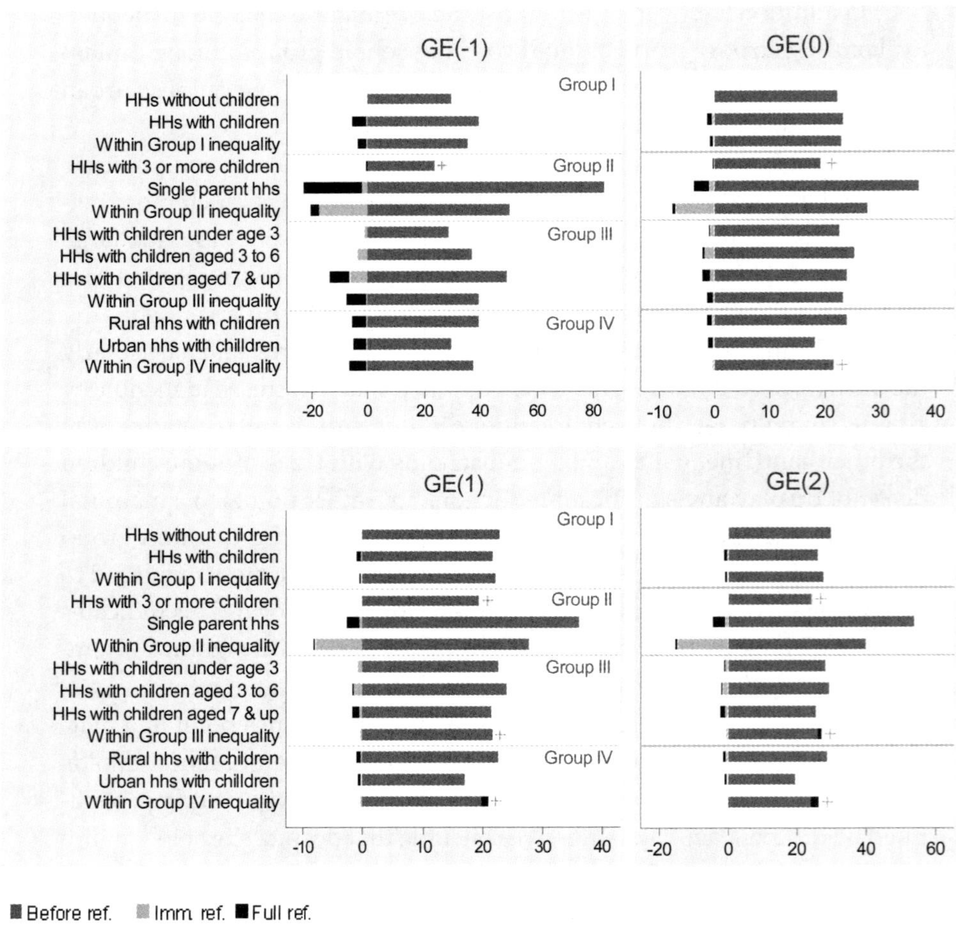

Notes: • Groups [I-IV] are composed of mutually exclusive household types, as indicated on the y-axis.
• "+" indicates observation of an increase in inequality measure.

Source: Own calculation.

In sum, the reform has contributed towards narrowing income dispersion for all selected household groups (Figure 7.7). This principally holds for the lower part of the income distribution. However, significant inequality reduction is also expected for overall income distribution, especially if looking at income movements among the poorest household types: large and single-parent families. This analysis proves that single-parent households are primary beneficiaries of the full design of the reform, while large families have received relatively more income gains with initial implementation of the reform.

5 Conclusions

This chapter is one of the first attempts to use a microsimulation method for the evaluation of public policy effectiveness in Lithuania. EU-SILC data enable simulation of four family benefits, which together constitute around 73% of the state budget for all family benefits in 2004. The simulated social benefit accounts for around 35% of the state budget on social assistance in 2004.

We find that the shift from a means-tested to a universal family benefit system raised average population income without causing income losses for eligible households. Analysis of direct (only reformed family benefits) and indirect (with changes in social assistance) reform effects also suggests that total poverty and inequality declined in the country. From this point of view, the reform could be seen as effective in terms of reaching its overall anti-poverty goals, even though its capacity to alleviate poverty is very limited: we estimate a 0.5 poverty headcount reduction due to initial and a 1.5 percentage points reduction due to full design reform implementation. This would bring the Lithuanian total poverty rate to around 19%: a level that is around three percentage points above the overall EU at-risk-of-poverty rate.[20]

The magnitude of income changes associated with the reform is small, which is also reflected in a small decrease in the number of social assistance recipients. We estimate that around 2% and 7% of Lithuanian families would be lifted out of dependence on social assistance respectively due to initial and full reform implementation. If take-up problems associated with pre-reform means-tested family benefits are taken into account, actual gains are expected to be higher.

20 In 2005, the total EU at-risk-of-poverty rate after social transfers was at 16% (http://epp.eurostat.ec.europa.eu)

There are two main types of social implications of our results: one is related to the gradual implementation of the reform, which means temporary poverty or income loss for certain groups, the other highlights a change in the situation of groups after the full implementation of the reform. From a policy point of view, the latter is perhaps of greater relevance.

Due to gradual implementation of this reform, eligibility to universal child benefit was initially restricted to families raising less than three children if children were above the age of six. Because of that, we find that poverty reduction among these households is much larger in the case of the full reform implementation.

Our analysis also points to delayed income gains for one of the poorest population groups: single-parent households. Actually, there are almost twice as many single-parent households (5.8% of all households) compared to households raising three or more children (3.3% of al households), and both of these groups are recognized as primary anti-poverty targets. Nevertheless, our research reveals that single-parent households would obtain income gains comparable to those of large families only when the full design reform scenario is implemented. If considering indirect effects, their relative gains become even smaller.

The full implementation of the reform would reduce poverty among rural households with children: one more vulnerable population group, especially if not only place of residence, but also household composition and age of children are considered. Actually, our analysis points out that high poverty prevalence among households with children under age three is mainly due to extreme impoverishment of rural households. Taking into account a potential increase in inequality between rural and urban households with children after the full reform implementation, additional policy measures targeted at improving the income situation of rural households seem appropriate.

This chapter also shows the importance of distributional analysis, given a rapidly changing policy context. We hope to have highlighted that this kind of evaluation research by using a microsimulation model can be a feasible and useful exercise for a country in transition such as Lithuania, both for ex ante and ex post monitoring of policy reforms. There is wide scope of potential research in this area. An important issue to tackle is how to handle the rapidly changing demographic and socio-economic environment in a transition country. Another route for future research is to integrate the simulation framework presented here in a tool like the EU-wide tax-benefit microsimulation model EUROMOD (Immervoll et al., 1999); this would open up the perspective of comparing Lithuanian tax-benefit policies more easily with those used in other countries.

Annex 1: Rules of family benefits and EU-SILC capacity to simulate them

- Beneficiaries of specific family and child benefits are not identified in EU-SILC. The database only contains an aggregate on family / children related allowances, which is defined as financial support to households raising children or taking care of relatives other than children (EUROSTAT, 2007a). Due to the aggregate nature of this variable, it cannot be used for the identification of receipt of specific transfers.
- EU-SILC does contain individual demographic information, as well as descriptions of personal socio-economic characteristics, which enable full or partial simulation of 9 out of 15 family policy measures.
- Due to the lack of EU-SILC information, orphan's stipend, guardianship benefit, grant for housing, compensation for housing utilities and funeral grant could not be simulated.
- A few benefits are not simulated due to their low representation within the dataset. For example, the benefit to conscript's child could not be simulated as EU-SILC identifies only 9 persons in compulsory military service. The maternity benefit for studying women and the pregnancy grant are not simulated for similar reasons: there are only 12 women eligible to receive these benefits.
- Other benefits are excluded from simulation due to ambiguous rules or timing of implementation. For example, municipal support is not simulated due to lack of clear eligibility rules. A subsidy for baby diapers is excluded from the further analysis, as it was only a temporary policy measure (not applicable at the timing of our simulation). Eligibility to free meals could be simulated; however the monetary value of this benefit is defined as a subsidy to meal providers.

	Benefit type	Benefit rules	Data limitations in EU-SILC	Simulation
1	Family allowance	A monthly benefit for families raising a child up to the age of three. Its monthly amount equalled 0.75 MSL per eligible child. The benefit was paid only if a family did not receive a corresponding maternity (paternity) social insurance. The reform integrated this allowance into the *child benefit*.	No information on maternity (paternity) social insurance; this is estimated by working status.	Yes
2	Benefit for families raising 3+ children	A monthly 1.0 MSL benefit for the 3rd child; the amount for the 4th and each additional child was increased by 0.3 MSL. Income testing[1] was not applied for families raising more than 3 children. From July 1, 2004, this benefit was integrated into the *child benefit*. The reform also provided an income security measure for large families: if the calculated *child benefit* would be lower than the previously received *benefit for families raising three or more children*, a family should continue receiving the latter benefit until a change in entitlement rights occurs.	Approximate reconstruction of income list, as indicated by the law.	Yes
3	Orphan's stipend	A monthly benefit paid to unemployed full-time students until the age of 24 if both parents have passed away. The amount of the benefit was equal to 4 MSL. The reform has transformed it into the *guardianship benefit*	Lack of information on the loss of parents	No
4	Maternity benefit for studying women	A monthly benefit given to pregnant women in full-time education who have no right to receive a maternity benefit under the Law on Sickness and Maternity Social Insurance. The benefit level equalled to 0.75 MSL per month and was paid for the 70 days preceding delivery. Since 1 July 2004, this benefit was replaced by a *pregnancy grant.*	Lack of information on receipt of maternity (paternity) social insurance; too few cases in EU-SILC	No
5	Child benefit	A monthly benefit for children up to the majority age of 18 or older, if they continue in full-time secondary education. Full-time students from families with 3 children or more, who continue in secondary or higher education, are eligible for the benefit until age 24. The benefit size is determined by the child's age and the size of the family: Child under age 3 / 3 to 6 / 7 to 18 / 19 to 24, if in full-time education 1 or 2 children 0.75 MSL / 0.4 MSL / 0.4 MSL* / 0.4 MSL[2]* 3 or more ch. 1.1 MSL / 0.4 MSL / 0.4 MSL / 0.4 MSL * *Entitlement available only since January, 2008*	Birth data: EU-SILC indicates the quarter of a birth	Yes
6	Pregnancy grant	A lump-sum benefit to a pregnant unemployed woman who, under *the Law on Sickness and Maternity Social Insurance*, is not eligible to receive a maternity leave benefit. The grant totals to 2 MSL and is given upon the 28th week of pregnancy (70 calendar days before a baby is due).	No information on receipt of maternity (paternity) social insurance; too few cases in EU-SILC	No
7	Birth grant	A universal lump-sum benefit paid upon the birth of a child to one of the parents or a guardian. This benefit amounts to 6 MSL per child. The grant is not paid for a child who is maintained in an institution financed by the state or municipality, or if a child has died before the moment of application.	Birth data: EU-SILC indicates the quarter of a birth	Yes

	Benefit type	Benefit rules	Data limitations in EU-SILC	Simu-lation
8	Benefit to conscript's child	A monthly benefit paid for each child during the military service of the father. The level of the benefit is equal to 1.5 MSL. The recipient of this benefit also has the right to receive a monthly child benefit as described above.	Approx. information on the duration of compulsory military service; too few cases in EU-SILC	No
9	Guardi-anship benefit	A monthly benefit for a child placed in a family or non-governmental institution during the period of the guardianship. Its amount equals to 4 MSL per month. In some cases the benefit can be paid until the child reaches the age of 24.	Lack of infor-mation to deter-mine adoptive parents	No
10	Grant for housing	A lump-sum benefit, given to a child upon the expira-tion of guardianship. The benefit is given to purchase a dwelling or to cover accommodation-related expenses. The entitled benefit amounts to 50 MSL. It cannot be paid in cash, unless the unused part of the grant is less than 1 MSL.	Lack of infor-mation to deter-mine adoptive parents	No
11	Social benefit	A means-tested benefit, which depends on the one hand on the value of the family or person's assets, and on the other on the level of per capita family income. The size of the social benefit is equal to 90% of the difference between the amount of SSI per family (single resident) and the average monthly income per family (single resident).	Lack of in-formation on the household assets	Yes/ par-tial
12	Compen-sation for housing utilities	A means-tested benefit, which depends on the actual cost of heating, sewage and hot and cold water used. The granted compensation is equal to the part of expenses that exceeds the thresholds set under the benefit means conditions.	Lack of infor-mation on the household as-sets and house-hold expenses on utilities	No
13	Free school meals	A free provision of school meals at the primary, basic, sec-ondary or special education institutions during the academic year. It consists of: lunch; lunch and breakfast for pupils from extremely low-income families[3]; free meals during summer holidays at summer day camps organized in schools. The benefit is granted if the monthly per capita family income is lower than 1.5 of SSI or if the family receives a social benefit[4].	Lack of infor-mation on the attendance of summer camps	Yes/ par-tial
14	A subsidy for baby diapers	Only a temporary measure (introduced in September, 2004 and abolished in 2005)		No
15	Municipal support	Lack of information on benefit eligibility rules		No

Notes:

1 The income test condition is to have per capita family income less than 3 SSI levels. The income list includes income from work, agricultural and commercial activities, property rent, dividends, aliments, pensions, scholarship, social support and incomes of other types of activities.

2 Only if in secondary education.

3 The meaning of the "extremely low-income" families was not explicitly defined until 2006, when the Law on Social Assistance to Pupils came into force. Since then, children growing up in the families, which have per capita household income lower than 1 SSI, were given a right to both free lunch and breakfast.

4 This benefit could also be granted if special circumstances, such as parents becoming severely sick or unemployed due to disability, occur.

Annex 2: Decomposition of poverty and inequality measures by household groups

	%, of all households	Before reform			After immediate reform, direct + indirect effects			After full reform, direct + indirect effects		
POVERTY		P0, %	P1, %	P2, %	P0, %	P1, %	P2, %	P0, %	P1, %	P2, %
Total	**100.00**	**20.25**	**6.57**	**3.24**	**19.90**	**6.96**	**3.15**	**18.92**	**5.96**	**2.90**
		(0.43)	**(0.18)**	**(0.12**	**(0.43)**	**(0.18)**	**(0.12)**	**(0.42)**	**(0.17)**	**(0.11)**
Households, without children	57.47	16.91	4.91	2.36	16.91	4.91	2.36	16.90	4.90	2.36
		(0.66)	(0.26)	(0.17)	(0.66)	(0.26)	(0.17)	(0.66)	(0.26)	(0.17)
Households with children	42.53	22.40	7.63	3.81	21.81	7.35	3.66	20.21	6.65	3.24
		(0.57)	(0.25)	(0.16)	(0.57)	(0.24)	(0.16)	(0.55)	(0.23)	(0.15)
Households with 3 or more children	3.33	44.47	14.24	6.38	41.77	13.47	6.04	40.92	13.24	5.85
		(1.99)	(0.82)	(0.47)	(1.97)	(0.81)	(0.46)	(1.97)	(0.79)	(0.44)
Single parent households	5.82	47.40	17.92	10.07	46.99	17.17	9.62	43.87	15.24	8.28
		(2.15)	(1.14)	(0.87)	(2.15)	(1.12)	(0.84)	(2.13)	(1.07)	(0.78)
Households with children under age 3	6.25	24.36	6.85	2.83	24.05	6.55	2.66	23.03	6.29	2.53
		(1.51)	(0.50)	(0.26)	(1.51)	(0.48)	(0.25)	(1.48)	(0.47)	(0.24)
Households with children aged 3 to 6	6.99	23.53	8.08	4.05	22.11	7.23	3.58	21.48	6.94	3.46
		(1.45)	(0.63)	(0.42)	(1.42)	(0.60)	(0.38)	(1.41)	(0.60)	(0.38)
Households with children aged 7 and up	29.28	21.59	7.70	3.99	21.16	7.58	3.58	19.14	6.65	3.36
		(0.68)	(0.31)	(0.21)	(0.67)	(0.31)	(0.38)	(0.65)	(0.29)	(0.19)
Rural households with children	24.13	30.93	10.86	5.44	30.17	10.50	5.25	28.18	9.57	4.68
		(0.83)	(0.38)	(0.25)	(0.82)	(0.37)	(0.25)	(0.81)	(0.35)	(0.23)
Urban households with children	18.39	10.29	3.04	1.49	9.95	2.88	1.41	8.90	2.50	1.20
		(0.62)	(0.23)	(0.15)	(0.61)	(0.22)	(0.15)	(0.56)	(0.21)	(0.14)

INEQUALITY	Before reform				After immediate reform, direct + indirect effects				After full reform, direct + indirect effects			
	GE(-1)	**GE(0)**	**GE(1)**	**GE(2)**	**GE(-1)**	**GE(0)**	**GE(1)**	**GE(2)**	**GE(-1)**	**GE(0)**	**GE(1)**	**GE(2)**
Total	**0.36**	**0.23**	**0.22**	**0.28**	**0.36**	**0.23**	**0.22**	**0.27**	**0.32**	**0.22**	**0.21**	**0.27**
	(0.01)	**(0.00)**	**(0.00)**	**(0.01)**	**(0.01)**	**(0.00)**	**(0.00)**	**(0.01)**	**(0.01)**	**(0.00)**	**(0.00)**	**(0.01)**
Households without children	0.30	0.22	0.23	0.30	0.30	0.22	0.23	0.30	0.30	0.22	0.23	0.30
	(0.01)	(0.00)	(0.01)	(0.01)	(0.01)	(0.00)	(0.01)	(0.01)	(0.01)	(0.00)	(0.01)	(0.01)
Households with children	0.40	0.23	0.22	0.26	0.39	0.23	0.21	0.26	0.34	0.22	0.21	0.25
	(0.02)	(0.00)	(0.00)	(0.01)	(0.02)	(0.00)	(0.00)	(0.01)	(0.02)	(0.00)	(0.00)	(0.01)
- within group inequality	0.36	0.23	0.22	0.28	0.35	0.23	0.22	0.27	0.32	0.22	0.21	0.27
	(0.01)	(0.00)	(0.00)	(0.01)	(0.01)	(0.00)	(0.00)	(0.01)	(0.01)	(0.00)	(0.00)	(0.01)
- between group inequality	0.00	0.00	0.00	0.00	0.00	0.00	0.00	0.00	0.00	0.00	0.00	0.00
	(0.00)	(0.00)	(0.00)	(0.00)	(0.00)	(0.00)	(0.00)	(0.00)	(0.00)	(0.00)	(0.00)	(0.00)
Households with 3 or more children	0.24	0.19	0.20	0.24	0.24	0.19	0.20	0.24	0.23	0.19	0.20	0.24
	(0.02)	(0.01)	(0.01)	(0.02)	(0.02)	(0.01)	(0.01)	(0.02)	(0.02)	(0.01)	(0.01)	(0.02)
Single parent households	0.84	0.37	0.36	0.54	0.82	0.36	0.35	0.53	0.61	0.33	0.33	0.49
	(0.12)	(0.02)	(0.03)	(0.08)	(0.12)	(0.02)	(0.03)	(0.07)	(0.07)	(0.02)	(0.03)	(0.07)
- within group inequality	0.50	0.28	0.28	0.40	0.33	0.21	0.20	0.25	0.30	0.20	0.19	0.25
	(0.05)	(0.01)	(0.02)	(0.04)	(0.05)	(0.01)	(0.02)	(0.04)	(0.03)	(0.01)	(0.01)	(0.04)
- between group inequality	0.00	0.00	0.00	0.00	0.02	0.02	0.02	0.02	0.02	0.02	0.02	0.02
	(0.00)	(0.00)	(0.00)	(0.00)	(0.00)	(0.00)	(0.00)	(0.00)	(0.00)	(0.00)	(0.00)	(0.00)

INEQUALITY	Before reform				After immediate reform, direct + indirect effects				After full reform, direct + indirect effects			
	GE(-1)	GE(0)	GE(1)	GE(2)	GE(-1)	GE(0)	GE(1)	GE(2)	GE(-1)	GE(0)	GE(1)	GE(2)
Households with children under age 3	0.29	0.23	0.23	0.28	0.27	0.22	0.22	0.27	0.27	0.22	0.22	0.27
	(0.01)	(0.01)	(0.01)	(0.02)	(0.01)	(0.01)	(0.01)	(0.01)	(0.01)	(0.01)	(0.01)	(0.01)
Households with children aged 3 to 6	0.37	0.25	0.24	0.29	0.33	0.24	0.23	0.28	0.33	0.23	0.22	0.27
	(0.02)	(0.01)	(0.01)	(0.02)	(0.01)	(0.01)	(0.01)	(0.01)	(0.02)	(0.01)	(0.01)	(0.01)
Households with children aged 7 and up	0.50	0.24	0.22	0.25	0.44	0.23	0.21	0.25	0.36	0.22	0.20	0.23
	(0.03)	(0.01)	(0.01)	(0.01)	(0.03)	(0.01)	(0.01)	(0.01)	(0.02)	(0.01)	(0.01)	(0.01)
- within group inequality	0.40	0.23	0.22	0.26	0.39	0.23	0.21	0.26	0.32	0.22	0.21	0.27
	(0.02)	(0.00)	(0.00)	(0.01)	(0.02)	(0.00)	(0.00)	(0.01)	(0.01)	(0.00)	(0.00)	(0.01)
- between group inequality	0.00	0.00	0.00	0.00	0.00	0.00	0.00	0.00	0.00	0.00	0.00	0.00
	(0.00)	(0.00)	(0.00)	(0.00)	(0.00)	(0.00)	(0.00)	(0.00)	(0.00)	(0.00)	(0.00)	(0.00)
Rural households with children	0.40	0.24	0.23	0.29	0.39	0.24	0.22	0.28	0.34	0.23	0.22	0.27
	(0.03)	(0.01)	(0.01)	(0.01)	(0.03)	(0.01)	(0.01)	(0.01)	(0.02)	(0.01)	(0.01)	(0.01)
Urban households with children	0.30	0.18	0.17	0.20	0.29	0.18	0.17	0.19	0.25	0.17	0.16	0.19
	(0.03)	(0.01)	(0.00)	(0.01)	(0.03)	(0.01)	(0.00)	(0.01)	(0.01)	(0.00)	(0.00)	(0.01)
- within group inequality	0.38	0.22	0.20	0.24	0.37	0.21	0.20	0.24	0.32	0.21	0.21	0.26
	(0.02)	(0.00)	(0.00)	(0.01)	(0.01)	(0.02)	(0.00)	(0.00)	(0.01)	(0.00)	(0.00)	(0.01)
- between group inequality	0.02	0.02	0.02	0.02	0.02	0.02	0.02	0.02	0.01	0.01	0.01	0.01
	(0.00)	(0.00)	(0.00)	(0.00)	(0.00)	(0.00)	(0.00)	(0.00)	(0.00)	(0.00)	(0.00)	(0.00)

Source: Own calculation (standard errors provided in parentheses).

References

Aidukaite, J. (2006) 'Reforming Family Policy in the Baltic States: The Views of the Elites', *Communist and Post-Communist Studies* 39 (2006): 1-23.

Atkinson, A. B. / Rainwater, L. / Smeeding, T. M. (1995) 'Income Distribution in OECD Countries: Evidence from the Luxembourg Income Study (LIS)', *Social Policy Studies* 18. Paris: Organization for Economic Cooperation and Development.

Biewen, M. / Jenkins, S. P. (2006) 'Variance Estimation for Generalized Entropy and Atkinson Inequality Indices: the Complex Survey Data Case', *Oxford Bulletin of Economics and Statistics*, Department of Economics, University of Oxford, 68 (3): 371-383.

Bradshaw, J. / Finch, N. (2003) 'Child Benefit Packages in 22 Countries', *4th International Research Conference on Social Security*, Antwerp, Belgium, May 5-7, 2003.

Čok, M. / Majcen, B. / Verbič, M. / Kosak, M. (2008) 'Use of Simulation Models for the Tax Reform in Slovenia', *Financial Theory and Practice* 32 (1): 29-43.

Davidson, R. / Flachaire, R. (2007) 'Asymptotic and Bootstrap Inference for Inequality and Poverty Measures', *Journal of Econometrics* 141 (1): 141-166.

EUROSTAT (2005) Continuity of indicators between end-ECHP and start-SILC: algorithms to compute cross-sectional indicators of poverty and social inclusion adopted under the open method of coordination. Retrieved March 30 2008 from the World Wide Web:http://www.insee.fr/en/insee-statistique-publique/colloques/pauvrete/pdf/Eurostat_social_indicators_EN.pdf

EUROSTAT (2007a) Description of SILC User Database Variables: Cross-sectional and Longitudinal (Version 2005.1 from 01-06-07).

EUROSTAT (2007b) EU-SILC User Database Description (Version 2005-2 from 27-06-07).

EUROSTAT (2008) Social Cohesion: Living Conditions Structural Indicators; EUROSTAT Metadata in SDDS format: Base Page. Retrieved October 15 2008 from the World Wide Web: http://ec.europa.eu/eurostat

Foster, J. / Greer, J. / Thorbecke, E. (1984) 'A Class of Decomposable Poverty Measures', *Econometrica* 52: 761-766.

Frazer, H. / Marlier, E. (2007) *Tackling Child Poverty and Promoting the Social Inclusion of Children in the EU: Key Lessons,* European Commission 2007, available at http://www.peer-review-social-inclusion.net/policy-assessment-activities/reports/first-semester-2007/synthesis-report-2007-1/.

Hantrais, L. (1999) 'Comparing Family Policies in Europe', pp. 95-113 in: Clasen, J. (ed.), *Comparative Social Policy: Concepts, Theories and Methods*. Blackwell Publishers.

Heikkilä, M. / Moisio, P. / Ritakallio, V.M. / Bradshaw, J. / Kuivalainen, S. / Hellsten, K. / Kajanoja, J. (2006) *Poverty Policies, Structures and Outcomes in the EU-25.* Report for the Fifth European Round Table on Poverty and Social Exclusion, 16-17, October, 2006, Finland.

Hölsch, K. / Kraus, M. (2002) 'European Schemes of Social Assistance: An Empirical Analysis of Set-Ups and Distributive Impacts', *International Journal of Social Welfare* 15 (1): 50-62.

Immervoll, H. / O'Donoghue, C. / Sutherland, H. (1999) An Introduction to EUROMOD. Microsimulation Unit, Department of Applied Economics, Cambridge University.

Jenkins, S. P. (1999) 'Analysis of Income Distributions', *STATA Technical Bulletin* 48: 4-18.

Jenkins, S.P. (2006) Estimation and Interpretation of Measures of Inequality, Poverty, and Social Welfare Using Stata. Presentation at North American Stata Users' Group Meetings 2006, Boston MA. Retrieved 15 October 2008 from the World Wide web: http://econpapers.repec.org/paper/bocasug06/16.htm

Jenkins, S. P. (2007) 'Inequality and the GB2 Income Distribution', *IZA Discussion Paper* 2831. Revised version forthcoming in *Review of Income and Wealth.*

Jolliffe, D. / Semykina, A. (1999) 'Robust Standard Errors for the Foster-Greer-Thorbecke Class of Poverty Indices: SEPOV', *Stata Technical Bulletin* 51: 34-36.

Lazutka, R. (2004) Poverty Reduction Action Plan and JIM in Lithuania. Conference Paper: *Aligning the European Union Social Inclusion Process and the Millennium Development Goals*, April 26-27, 2004, Vilnius, Lithuania.

Lelkes, O. (2007) 'Tax-Benefit Microsimulation Models In Eastern Europe', *International Journal of Microsimulation* 1 (1): 54-56.

Matsaganis, M. / Levy, H. / Mercader-Prats, M. / Toso, S. / O'Donoghue, C. / Coromaldi, M. / Rodrigues, C. F. / Tsakloglou, P. (2007) 'Child Poverty and Family Transfers in Southern Europe', pp 293-321 in: Spadaro, A. (ed.), *Microsimulation as a Tool for the Evaluation of Public Policies: Methods and Applications*. Bilbao: Fundación BBVA.

Milanovic, B. (1999) 'Explaining the Increase in Inequality During Transition', *The Economics of Transition* 7 (2): 299-341.

Ministry of Social Security and Labour (2006) *The Social Report 2005-2006*. Retrieved 20 January 2008 from the World Wide Web: http: / / www.socmin.lt / index.php?791115234.

National Report on Strategies of Lithuania for Social Protection and Social Inclusion 2006–2008 (2006). Retrieved 15 October 2008 from the Wolrd Wide Web: http: / / ec.europa.eu / health / ph_determinants / socio_economics / documents / lithuania_rd05_en.pdf

Nelson, K. (2007) 'Universalism versus Targeting: The Vulnerability of Social Insurance and Means-tested Minimum Income Protection in 18 Countries, 1990-2002', *International Social Security Review* 60 (1): 33-58.

Notten, G. / Gassmann, F. (2008) 'Size Matters: Targeting Efficiency and Poverty Reduction Effects of Means-tested and Universal Child Benefits in Russia', *Journal of European Social Policy* 18 (3): 260-274.

Republic of Lithuania (1999) *The Order on Provision of Free Meals in General Education Institutions for Pupils in Low-Income Families*, August 16, 1999. *Valstybes Zinios*, 1999-08-27 No. 72-2245.

Republic of Lithuania (2003) *The Law on Cash Social Assistance for Low-Income Families (Single Residents)*, July 1, 2003. *Valstybes Zinios*, 2003-07-23 Nr.73-3352.

Republic of Lithuania (2004a) *The Law Amending The Law On State Benefits To Families Raising Children*, May 18, 2004, Vilnius. *Valstybes Zinios*, 2004-06-03 Nr.88-3208.

Republic of Lithuania (2004b) *National Action Plan (NAP) Against Poverty And Social Exclusion in 2004-2006*. Retrieved 15 October 2008 from the World Wide web: http: / / ec.europa. eu / employment_social / social_inclusion / docs / nap_incl_2004_lt_en_version.pdf

Republic of Lithuania (2006) *The Law on Social Assistance for Pupils*, 13 June 2006, No. X-686, Vilnius. *Valstybes Zinios*, 2006-06-30 Nr.73-2755.

Spadaro, A. (eds.) (2007) *Microsimulation as a Tool for the Evaluation of Public Policies: Methods and Applications*. Madrid: FBBVA.

Statistics Lithuania (2007) *Income and Living Conditions: 2005*. Vilnius. Retrieved 15 October 2008 from the World Wide web: http: / / www.stat.gov.lt

Statistics Lithuania (2008) *Statistika (teminės lentelės), Gyventojai ir socialinė statistika, Darbo užmokestis, Minimalieji dydžiai 1995-2007 m*. Retrieved 20 January 2008 from the World Wide Web: http: / / www.stat.gov.lt

Chapter 8

Tax-free Income vs. In-work Tax Allowances: Effects on Labour Market Participation in Cyprus

Panos Pashardes / Alexandros Polycarpou

1 Introduction

The objective of this chapter is to investigate how in-work tax allowances linked to family size (dependent family members) compare with a revenue equivalent tax-free labour income in terms of their impact on labour market participation, especially among older workers.

The investigation of the relationship between the tax-benefit system and the labour force participation goes back to the 1950s (Break, 1957), but research on empirically measuring the effect of taxes on labour supply started in the 1970s, when statistical tools for dealing with the non-convexities in the budget set caused by taxation were developed (Burtless et al., 1978; Hausman, 1979; Heckman, 1979). Since then the impact of tax-benefit reforms on labour market participation and labour supply has been extensively investigated in the literature, in view of the importance of employment in realising the growth potential of the economy and reinforcing social cohesion.

In-work benefits (in the form of tax allowances, credits etc.) give strong incentives to individuals to take up gainful employment by lowering the net replacement rates of persons at minimum wage. Brewer et al. (2006) in their study of the replacement of the Family Credit (FC) with the Working Families Tax Credit (WFTC) system in the UK find that the introduction of WFTC has increased employment. Furthermore, Blundell and Hoynes (2004) find the impact of in-work benefits to be higher in the US than the UK in the 1990s because these benefits are not included in the calculation of income for establishing entitlement to means-tested benefits in the US, as they do in the UK. Blundell (2006) attributes the low impact of the introduction of the WFTC system in the UK to interactions of this system with other taxes and benefits and the rise in family allowance, which is not conditional on working.

This chapter is motivated by the heterogeneity of the tax reform effects on the labour market decisions of individuals. For example, Brewer et al. (2006) find that the introduction of WFTC has increased the employment rate by 5 percentage points for lone mothers and by only 1 percentage point for men with children. Furthermore, the employment rate of married women with children has decreased (Elissa et al., 2005). These results suggest that the overall impact of a tax-benefit reform on labour market participation can be sensitive to the distribution of gains and losses across individuals with different participation elasticity to wage change. Using numerical simulations Saez (2002) shows that exempting from taxation individuals with income below a threshold (as in the case of elderly, single mothers or secondary earners) can increase labour market participation because the labour market behaviour of these individuals is sensitive to wage changes. Thus, labour market participation can be raised by tax changes on labour income benefiting individuals that are relatively more responsive to net wage changes.

Following the argument above, this chapter investigates whether replacing in-work benefits (tax credits / allowances) linked to family dependants with a revenue equivalent tax-free labour income can increase the overall labour market participation. The idea here is that the beneficiaries of this tax reform are likely to be older individuals without dependent children and relatively high labour market participation elasticity to wage changes. Evidence of such high labour market participation elasticity among individuals without dependent children is found in Miniaci and Stancanelli (1998) and in Quinn et al. (1998). Furthermore, the hypothesis that older people have relatively high labour market participation elasticity to changes in net wage is supported by arguments in studies trying to explain the falling labour market participation rate of older people. That is, authors blame this phenomenon on the relaxation of the conditions for entitlement to unemployment and / or disability benefits for older people, which make these benefits act as retirement incentives to which older people appear to respond (Blöndal et al., 1999; Burtless et al., 2001; Blundell et al., 2002).

The structure of the chapter is as follows: the next section outlines the model used for estimation of the labour market participation decision and the results obtained from its empirical application; section 3 presents the results from simulating the labour market participation effects arising from replacing in-work benefits linked to family dependants with a revenue equivalent tax-free labour income; section 4 concludes the chapter.

2 Empirical model and estimation

The labour market participation decision is modelled using the structural form participation equation:

$$L_i = 1 \Leftrightarrow \gamma_1 \log\left(DI_i^1(y_i, a_i; \theta)\right) + \gamma_2 \log\left(DI_i^0(a_i; \theta)\right) + \beta X_{i1} + \varepsilon_{i1} \geq 0 \quad (1)$$

where: $L_i = 1$ if the individual i works and $L_i = 0$ if she/he does not work; $DI_i^1(y_i, a_i; \theta)$ and $DI_i^0(a_i; \theta)$ are the disposable income in case of employment and non employment, respectively; βX_{i1} captures the observed heterogeneity in preferences for leisure or in reservation income, where X_{i1} is a vector of demographic characteristics (age, gender, education, experience, marital and health status etc.); ε_{i1} captures random errors and the unobserved heterogeneity in the preferences for leisure or in reservation income. Disposable income from employment has a positive effect on participation decision, thus γ_1 is positive, while the opposite is true for disposable income from non employment, that is γ_2 is negative.

The disposable income for the two-activity statuses are given by

$$DI_i^0(a_i; \theta) = a_i + T_i^0(a_i; \theta) \text{ in case of non-employment, and} \quad (2)$$

$$DI_i^1(y_i, a_i; \theta) = y_i + a_i + T_i^1(y_i, a_i; \theta) \text{ in case of employment,} \quad (3)$$

where θ represents the characteristics of the tax-benefit system, α_i income other than labour or transfer income, y_i gross labour income (observed in the data only for employed individuals); T_i^0, T_i^1 are the amount of net public transfers (i.e. the public benefits minus direct taxes on income) to non-employed and employed individuals, respectively.

As is well known, equation (1) cannot be estimated from the observed data since DI_i^1 is not known for individuals not participating in the labour market. Here we follow the standard approach to solving this problem, i.e. use the maximum likelihood missing data procedure proposed by Griliches et al. (1978) to estimate the gross labour income of those not participating in the labour market. By allowing joint specification of the gross labour income and labour market participation decisions, this procedure eliminates potential bias in labour income.[1]

We define the gross labour income equation as

$$\log(y_i) = \delta_1 X_{i2} + u_{i1} \tag{4}$$

where X_{i2} is a list of explanatory variables that affect labour income (gender, experience, marital status, etc.) and u_{i1} the unexplained part of labour income (error term); and the (reduced-form) labour market participation equation as

$$L_i = 1 \Leftrightarrow \lambda_0 \log\left(DI_i^0(a_i;\theta)\right) + \lambda_1 X_{i1} + \xi_{i1} \geq 0 \tag{5}$$

The fitted values of gross labour income, y_i, are computed using equation (4), including the potential labour income of individuals who do not work. Then, the disposable income DI_i^1 is calculated for both working and not working individuals using equation (3) and the tax-benefit model[2]. The effect of DI_i^1 and DI_i^0 on employment is estimated using the structural form participation equation (1), in which demographic and other characteristics of policy interest are also included among the explanatory variables.

The dataset used for the regression analysis is the 2005 EU-SILC microdata prepared by the Statistical Service of the Member States on behalf of Eurostat. The dataset contains information on income (level and sources), demographic characteristics, employment status and other variables for each country in the EU25, plus Norway and Iceland, at household and personal level. For the estimations, data for individuals living in Cyprus between the age of 16 and 64 are used, forming a sample of 7585 individuals.[3]

1 An upward bias can arise, for example, when the relationship between the participation decision and labour income is ignored because individuals with potentially higher labour income are more likely to work, giving rise to correlation between the disturbance terms of the labour income and participation equations.

2 We use the tax-benefit model to simulate the tax liability of individuals based on the tax system of 2004.

3 Twenty one individuals were dropped from the sample because of lack of observations. This was due to their refusal to co-operate or their temporary absence.

Table 8.1 presents the results obtained from the estimation of the structural form equation, together with the results of the reduced form equation used in the first step of the Griliches et al. (1978) procedure. The results from the structural equation suggest that the probability of labour market participation increases for individuals between 25 to 54 years of age: among those in the 25 to 40 age group the high labour market participation probability is driven by women,[4] whereas for those in the 41 to 54 age group by both men and women. The labour market participation of women decreases with the number of dependent children and increases with the age of the youngest child, whereas the labour market participation of men does not appear to be affected by these family composition variables.

Education has a different effect on the labour market participation probability of men and women. Female college or university graduates have a significantly lower participation probability than lower-educated females, with a higher negative effect on participation among university graduates. Among men, those with up to secondary level of education (elementary, gymnasium, lyceum) have a higher probability of employment than higher educated or illiterate men. The health condition of individuals has also a significant effect on the labour market participation probability with this probability being, as expected, lower among individuals in fair or bad health. However, men and women behave differently in this respect as fair health lowers the labour market participation probability among women but not among men. Experience in the labour market (the number of years individuals have spent working) has a positive but decreasing effect on labour market participation probability, especially among women.

4 It may be worth noting here that we condition on the number of children and age of the youngest child. Therefore, it is not surprising for the coefficients of age variables to show higher labour market participation for women aged 25-40 without children than younger or older women.

Table 8.1: Labour market participation equation

Variables	Structural form			Reduced Form		
	Male	Female	All	Male	Female	All
Male			.018 (.064)			.659*** (.042)
Age 25-40	1.99 (2.13)	4.99*** (1.76)	3.27** (1.37)	-.043*** (.137)	.132*** (.088)	.122** (.069)
Age 41-54	5.02** (2.43)	4.60*** (1.76)	3.99*** (1.39)	-2.00*** (.430)	-.802*** (.123)	-.900*** (.116)
Age 55-64	2.44 (2.34)	1.47 (1.88)	1.56 (1.44)	-3.53*** (.491)	-1.68*** (.154)	-1.92*** (.147)
Number of dependent children	-1.31 (.946)	-2.33*** (.373)	-2.04*** (.319)	.132 (.086)	-.081* (.042)	-.015 (.035)
Age of youngest child less than 5	.150 (.264)	.264* (.164)	.298** (.135)	.396* (.236)	.030 (.119)	.193* (.100)
Age of youngest child between 6-12	.255 (.228)	.372** (.168)	.373*** (.135)	.170 (.219)	.168 (.120)	.246** (.103)
Age of youngest child between 13-18	.266 (.244)	.450*** (.146)	.442*** (.126)	.355 (.260)	.367*** (.120)	.438*** (.109)
Married	.214 (.183)	.015 (.093)	-.031 (.082)	.459*** (.143)	.069 (.071)	.120* (.064)
Elementary	.737*** (.285)	-.054 (.181)	.167 (.157)	.444* (.239)	.099 (.157)	.146 (.127)
Gymnasium	.726** (.324)	-.051 (.198)	.124 (.172)	-.348 (.255)	-.110 (.167)	-.337** (.134)
Lyceum	.675** (.306)	-.178 (.187)	-.007 (.164)	.327 (.252)	.180 (.159)	.110 (.130)
College	.371 (.441)	-.462* (.257)	-.255 (.227)	.021 (.350)	.156 (.408)	.010 (.177)
University	.251 (.324)	-.468** (.201)	-.367** (.173)	.721*** (.266)	.725*** (.164)	.530*** (.134)
Health condition: Fair	-.213 (.139)	-.195* (.102)	-.213*** (.083)	-.167*** (.131)	-.325*** (.086)	-.264*** (.071)
Health condition: Bad	-.612*** (.155)	-.411*** (.135)	-.512*** (.099)	-.937*** (.144)	-.414*** (.194)	-.749*** (.095)
Experience	-.028 (.022)	.076*** (.011)	.042*** (.009)	.243*** (.025)	.203*** (.009)	.199*** (.008)
Experience squared	-.001*** (.0003)	-.001*** (.0002)	-.0005** (.0002)	-.003*** (.0004)	-.003*** (.0002)	-.003*** (.0002)
$\log(DI^0)$	-.664*** (.092)	-.463*** (.095)	-.610*** (.069)	-.196*** (.013)	-.050*** (.009)	-.106*** (.007)
$\log(DI^0)$ x Dummy: age 25-40	.493*** (.097)	.306*** (.100)	.444*** (.072)			

table continues

Table 8.1: (continued)

log(DI^0) x Dummy: age 41-54	.447*** (.110)	.388*** (.098)	.502*** (.072)			
log(DI^0) x Dummy: age 55-64	.195 (.249)	.191* (.100)	.081*** (.077)			
log(DI^0) x number of dependent children	-.025 (.058)	-.008 (.024)	-.016 (.023)			
log(DI^1)	1.88*** (.310)	1.66*** (.260)	1.73*** (.220)			
log(DI^1) x Dummy: age 25-40	-.659* (.348)	-.874*** (.269)	-.785*** (.230)			
log(DI^1) x Dummy: age 41-54	-.999*** (.374)	-.937*** (.269)	-.953*** (.231)			
log(DI^1) x Dummy: age 55-64	-.643* (.380)	-.523* (.282)	-.610*** (.238)			
log(DI^1) x number of dependent children	.167* (.092)	.248*** (.043)	.227*** (.033)			
Constant	-11.55*** (1.86)	-10.48*** (1.67)	-10.08*** (1.29)	-.069 (.249)	-.873*** (.163)	-.634*** (.130)
Number of Obs	7585					

Notes: 1. standard errors in brackets
2. *, **, *** significant at 10%, 5%, 1% significance level, respectively.

As expected, the labour market participation probability is negatively related to disposable non-employment income and positively related to disposable employment income. In addition, in absolute terms, the magnitude of the effect of disposable employment or non-employment income on the labour market participation probability is larger for men than women, i.e. an increase in the disposable (non-)employment income of men (decrease) increases this probability more than a similar increase (decrease) in the disposable (non-)employment income of women.

Included in the structural form labour market participation equation, are also interaction terms between the disposable income (from each sources, employment and non-employment) and the age and number of children. These interaction terms show in the two employment states how the sensitivity of labour market participation to disposable income varies with the age and number of dependent children.

- As disposable income from non-employment increases, the labour market participation probability of individuals in all age groups decreases; but, it does less so among individuals in the 25-40 and 41-54 age groups. This suggests that a higher non-employment income makes individuals in the younger (16-24) and older (55-64) age groups more reluctant to participate in the labour market than it does for those in the 25 to 54 age group.

- Individuals in the younger (16-24) age group also appear to be more responsive to changes in income from employment, in the sense that as this income increases their labour market participation increases more than that of individuals in other age groups. The lowest response of labour market participation to changes in disposable income from employment occurs among individuals between 25 and 40 years old.
- How disposable income from non-employment affects the labour market participation probability of men and women does not appear to be significantly influenced by the number of dependent children. In contrast, the (positive) effect of disposable employment income on labour market participation increases significantly with the number of dependent children, especially among women.

An interesting result in the context of our investigation is that the magnitude of the effect of a change in income from employment (DI_i^1) on labour market participation is greater, in absolute terms, than the effect of an equal size change in non-employment income (DI_i^0). This suggests that an increase in disposable income from employment (as in the case of an increase in tax-free income examined later in this chapter) can be a more effective measure for increasing labour market participation than a measure adding the same amount to non-employment income, such as an increase of unemployment benefit.

Comparing the results obtained from the structural and reduced form equations, one can see that the change in magnitude and sign of variables that are highly correlated with labour income (e.g. education and experience) conforms to expectation, based on the fact that the first equation reflects direct, whereas the second equation can also reflect indirect (through labour income), effects on labour market participation. For example, while the structural form equation suggests that university graduates have a lower probability of labour market participation, the opposite is true in the reduced form equation. Also experience has a significant positive effect on the labour market participation of men in the reduced form but not in the structural equation. Although the effect of experience is significant in both equations for women, its size is about three times smaller in the structural than the reduced form equation.

Table 8.2 presents the parameter estimates obtained from the labour income equation, which are used for the estimation of the unobserved (reservation) labour income of individuals not participating in the labour market. In predicting this income gender, age, education and labour market experience are used as explanatory variables.

Individuals between the ages of 25 to 40 have, on average, 53.7% higher labour income compared to younger individuals (aged between 16 and 24). This difference decreases to 33.6 and 37.4% for individuals in the 41-54 and 55-64 age group, respectively. The effect of age on the wage rate is much higher among men than women. Also, other things being equal, men's labour income peaks between the ages of 25 to 40, whereas women's labour income does so between the ages of 55 to 64. It is also interesting to note that the labour income of both men and women decreases between the ages of 41 to 54 and increases afterwards.

Table 8.2: Labour income prediction equation

Variables	Male	Female	All
Male			.353*** (.020)
Age 25-40	.706*** (.066)	.161*** (.057)	.537*** (.046)
Age 41-54	.497*** (.088)	.122*** (.074)	.336*** (.057)
Age 55-64	.584*** (.102)	.336*** (.088)	.374*** (.065)
Elementary	-.124 (.089)	.296*** (.094)	.142** (.071)
Gymnasium	-.070 (.096)	.384*** (.101)	.207* (.075)
Lyceum	-.097 (.094)	.680*** (.095)	.296*** (.073)
College	.044 (.119)	.817*** (.172)	.554*** (.094)
University	.432*** (.096)	1.15*** (.097)	.869*** (.074)
Experience	.103*** (.005)	.036*** (.007)	.086*** (.004)
Experience squared	-.002*** (.0001)	-.0004*** (.0001)	-.001*** (.0001)
Constant	8.03*** (.104)	8.01*** (.111)	7.54*** (.086)
Number of Obs		7585	

Notes: 1. standard errors in brackets

2. *, **, *** significant at 10%, 5%, 1% significance level, respectively.

As one would expect, labour income also increases with education. For men this increase is not significant for education below university level. In the case of women, however, education at all levels adds to labour income. More precisely, women with elementary education have 29.6% higher labour income than women without education. Also, women with gymnasium, lyceum, college and university education have, respectively, 38.4, 68.0, 81.7 and 115% higher labour income than women with no education. Experience also adds to labour income, albeit at a declining rate.[5] Finally, the constant term suggests that men in the reference group (aged between 16 and 25, without education and work experience) have higher labour income than women with the same characteristics.

3 Simulation results

In this section we use the tax-benefit model for the Cyprus economy (Andreou et al., 2007) and the estimated structural employment equation to simulate the effects of two revenue equivalent tax scenarios on labour market participation, with emphasis on particular target groups like youngsters, older persons and women. The two tax scenarios are based on the Cypriot tax system of 2002, where income up to 15,380 EUR (9,000 CYP) was tax-free (zero tax rate), income over 15,380 EUR and up to 20,500 (12,000 CYP) was taxed at 30% and income over 20,500 EUR was taxed at 40%. Each household member is treated as an individual taxpayer and tax allowances are apportioned to the two spouses in proportion to their individual income. In the 2002 tax system there were tax allowances (up to 850 EUR (500 CYP)) for the spouse, for each dependent child under 16 and for each dependent child over 16 in secondary school or in military service. In addition, a tax allowance of 2,550 EUR (1,500 CYP) was given for each child in tertiary education. The tax scenarios for which the labour market participation effects are simulated are:

- the "tax-free income" where there are no tax allowances and the tax rates and bands are the same as the ones in the tax system of 2002; and
- the "tax allowance" where income tax rates and bands are as in the tax-free-income scenario, except for (i) income up to 15,380 EUR is taxed at a rate equal to 20% and (ii) tax allowances exist as in the 2002 tax

5 The average years of experience are 15.07, for men 17.98 and for women 12.25.

system but the amounts are scaled up to make this tax scenario revenue equivalent to the tax-free income one.[6]

Under each of the two scenarios above we compute the net disposable income for the 7,585 individuals in employment and non-employment in our sample. The labour market participation results from these tax scenarios are then compared with those obtained under a system with neither tax-free income nor tax allowances. In the discussion below this benchmark system is referred to as "reference system". The probability of labour market participation for each individual in the sample is estimated using the structural employment equation described in the previous section.

Table 8.3: Participation changes under the tax-allowances and tax-free income scenarios

Age	Men			Women			All		
	Tax allowances	Tax-free income	Difference	Tax allowances	Tax-free income	Difference	Tax allowances	Tax-free income	Difference
16-24	.017 (.008)	1.80 (.101)	1.78 (.101)	.199 (.042)	.958 (.082)	.760 (.069)	.099 (.020)	1.42 (.067)	1.32 (.065)
25-54	2.18 (.057)	2.73 (.065)	.555 (.058)	2.99 (.075)	4.43 (.086)	1.44 (.060)	2.60 (.048)	3.62 (.056)	1.02 (.042)
55-64	3.49 (.164)	4.26 (.164)	.769 (.130)	1.02 (.101)	3.01 (.156)	1.98 (.122)	2.21 (.101)	3.61 (.114)	1.40 (.090)
All	1.87 (.032)	2.75 (.054)	.887 (.048)	2.11 (.055)	3.51 (.039)	1.40 (.046)	1.99 (.036)	3.14 (.043)	1.15 (.033)

Note: Standard errors in brackets.

Table 8.3 shows the average participation changes by age under the tax-free income and the tax allowances scenarios, relative to the reference system; and the difference in the changes associated with the two scenarios.

- Among both men and women in all age groups the labour market participation is higher under the tax-free income compared to the tax allowances scenario, though the two scenarios differ *vis-à-vis* gender

6 Here we assume that tax allowances are available only to individuals who have income from employment and, in this sense, act as in-work benefits. This assumption is not unrealistic since taxable income is mainly income from work, while income from other sources (capital gains, dividends and interest receivable) is exempted from direct taxation as are the benefits, which are mostly means-tested. Family-related allowances are not means-tested, therefore are not withdrawn as income rises.

and age. The highest participation difference is observed among males in the 16-24 age group for whom the labour market participation is by 1.8 percentage points higher in the tax-free income than the tax-allowances scenario; whereas this difference is only 0.77 among males in the 55 to 64 age group and drops even more (to 0.56) among those in the 25-54 age group.

- As regards females, the highest participation difference between the two scenarios occurs among the 55 to 64 age group, where the participation rate is by 2 percentage points higher under the tax-free income than under the tax allowances scenario. For females in the 25-54 age group this difference is 1.4 and for those in the 16-24 age group 0.76 percentage points. Overall, having a high tax-free income rather than tax allowances system increases the participation rate by 1.32 percentage points among the 16-24, by 1 percentage point among the 25-54 and by 1.4 percentage points among the 55-64 age group. Notably, under both scenarios the increase in the labour market participation of women is higher than men's (1.4 vs. 0.89) *vis-à-vis* the reference system.

The main reason behind the labour market participation advantage of high tax-free income over tax allowances is that under the former regime, persons without dependent children are not in a disadvantage compared to those with dependent children. Although having children in the family, particularly young ones, is well-known to affect the income elasticity of demand for leisure, especially among spouses, the same elasticity seems to be also affected by age. Indeed, in the context of our analysis, income elasticity of demand for leisure appears to have a stronger association with age rather than children: as shown in Table 8.1, individuals in the 16-24 and 55-64 age groups (who tend to have no dependent children) are more likely to participate in the labour market when their disposable income from employment increases compared to individuals in the 25-54 age group. Therefore, tax allowances linked to dependent children and, thereby, biased against individuals in the 16-24 and 55-64 age groups, are associated with a lower labour market participation rate compared to a not so biased (revenue equivalent) increase in tax-free income.

To illustrate the argument in the previous paragraph, Table 8.4 presents the labour market participation differences between the two tax scenarios by age and number of dependent children. These differences are positive between individuals without dependent children in all age groups because these individuals benefit from high tax-free income but not from tax allowances. Negative differences, indicating an advantage of the tax allowances over the high tax-free income scenario, occur among individuals with dependent children. Yet, the labour market participation corresponding to this scenario is not as high as that corresponding to the high tax-free income scenario. This results in a net overall labour market participation advantage for the high tax-free income scenario.

Table 8.4: Participation differences between the tax-free and tax-allowances scenarios by age and number of children

Number of Children	Men			Women			All		
	16-24	25-54	55-64	16-24	25-54	55-64	16-24	25-54	55-64
0	**1.81** (.103)	**2.28** (.123)	**1.40** (.133)	**.816** (.075)	**3.36** (.137)	**2.11** (.127)	**1.37** (.068)	**2.84** (.093)	**1.79** (.093)
1	.0001 (.0001)	**-.360** (.133)	**-1.87** (.380)	**.177** (.055)	**1.05** (.092)	**.868** (.419)	**.135** (.043)	**.403** (.082)	**-.904** (.309)
2	.0000 (.0000)	**-.427** (.031)	**-1.65** (.353)	.0001 (.0001)	**.295** (.055)	.102 (.887)	.0000 (.0000)	-.048 (.034)	**-1.18** (.366)
3		**-.368** (.032)	**-1.70** (.626)	.015 (.015)	.008 (.042)	**-1.48** (.731)	.015 (.015)	**-.171** (.028)	**-1.65** (.494)
4 or more		**-.211** (.025)	-1.63 (1.62)		-.003 (.049)			**-.105** (.029)	-1.63 (1.62)
All	**1.78** (.101)	**.555** (.058)	**.769** (.130)	**.760** (.069)	**1.44** (.060)	**1.98** (.122)	**1.32** (.065)	**1.02** (.042)	**1.40** (.091)

Note: 1. Standard errors in brackets.
2. Figures in bold are significant at 5% significance level.

4 Conclusions

Countries throughout the world often resort to in-work benefits to encourage higher labour market participation. Empirical investigations, in general, find these measures to have a positive effect on labour market participation, even though this effect varies substantially between groups of individuals and between countries. This chapter investigates the labour market participation effect from linking in-work benefits to the number of dependent persons (spouse and children). According to our empirical findings (based on Cyprus data) such a linkage can result in an overall lower labour market participation rate than that achieved with a revenue equivalent universal increase in tax-free income from employment.

The analysis in the chapter is based on a model where the labour market participation of individuals is influenced by their personal and family characteristics as well as their disposable income from employment and non-employment. The parameter estimates obtained from this model are then used in a tax-benefit model to simulate the tax liability of individuals under two alternative revenue equivalent tax scenarios: one with a high tax-free income and no tax allowances for spouse and children; and one with tax allowances for children and spouse but no tax-free income.

The elasticity of demand for leisure of the beneficiaries is underlining the differences in labour market participation between alternative tax-benefit systems. In the context of our analysis, the labour market participation advantage of a high tax-free income over tax allowances linked to dependents is that the latter do not, in general, benefit individuals in the 16-24 and 55-64 age groups. Yet, according to our empirical findings, these individuals are the ones with the highest income elasticity of demand for leisure.

In interpreting the results above, one has to consider that the focus of the analysis in the chapter is labour market participation, so that the effects of alternative tax policies on the supply of hours are ignored. This may or may not be a serious limitation depending on how far one subscribes to the view that achieving higher labour market participation is of higher priority than increasing the labour supply of those already in employment. Nevertheless, excluding the effects on hours supplied means that the difference between the overall employment effect of the two tax approaches considered in the chapter is not known.

Another limitation of our analysis is that no attention is paid to distributional effects associated with alternative tax policies. For instance, while in-work benefits linked to dependents may not raise labour market participation as tax-free income, one may favour such benefits because they are more likely to reduce income inequality. For this reason the analysis needs to be extended to incorporate welfare considerations before one can conclude that one tax policy is preferable to another.

References

Andreou, M. / Nikolaidou, N. / Polykarpou, A. / Hadjispyrou, S. (2007) "Tax-benefit Microsimulation Model for the Cyprus Economy", Economic Policy Paper 12-07, Economics Research Centre, University of Cyprus.

Blöndal, S. / Scarpetta, S. (1999) 'The Retirement Decision in OECD Countries', OECD Economics Department Working Papers 202, OECD Publishing.

Blundell, R. / Meghir, C. / Smith, S. (2002) 'Pension Incentives and the Pattern of Early Retirement', *Economic Journal* 112 (478): 153-170.

Blundell, R. / Hoynes, H.W. (2004) 'Has "In-Work" Benefit Reform Helped the Labour Market?', pp. 411-460 in: Blundell, R. / Card, D. / Freeman, R. (eds.), *Seeking a Premier League Economy*. Chicago: University of Chicago Press.

Blundell, R. (2006) 'Earned Income Tax Credit Policies: Impact and Optimality, The Adam Smith Lecture 2005', *Labour Economics* 13 (4): 423-443

Break, G.F. (1957) 'Income Taxes and Incentives to Work: An Empirical Study', *American Economic Review* 47 (5): 529-549.

Brewer, M. / Duncan, A. / Shephard, A. / Suárez, M.J. (2006) 'Did Working Families' Tax Credit Work? The Impact of In-work Support on Labour Supply in Great Britain', *Labour Economics* 13 (6): 699-720.

Burtless, G. / Hausman, J. (1978) 'The Effect of Taxation on Labor Supply: Evaluating the Gary Negative Income Tax Experiment', *Journal of Political Economy* 86 (6): 1103-1130.

Burtless, G. / Quinn, J.F. (2001) 'Retirement Trends and Policies to Encourage Work Among Older Americans', Boston College Working Papers in Economics 436.

Eissa, N.O. / Hoynes, H.W. (2005) 'Behavioural Responses to Taxes: Lessons from the EITC and Labor Supply', NBER Working Paper No. W11729.

Griliches, Z. / Hall, B.H. / Hausman, J. A. (1978) 'Missing Data And Self-Selection in Large Panels', *Annales de L'INSEE* 30-31: 137-176.

Hausman, J.A. (1979) 'The Econometrics of Labour Supply on Convex Budget Sets', *Economic Letters* 3 (2): 171-174.

Heckman, J. (1979) 'Sample Bias as a Specification Error', *Econometrica*, 47(1): 153-161.

Miniaci, R. / Stancanelli, E. (1998) 'Microeconometric Analysis of the Retirement Decision: United Kingdom', OECD Economics Department Working Papers 206, OECD Publishing.

Quinn, J. / Burkhauser, R. / Cahill, K. / Weathers, R. (1998) 'Microeconometric Analysis of the Retirement Decision:n United States', OECD Economics Department Working Papers 203, OECD Publishing.

Saez, E. (2002) 'Optimal Income Transfer Programs: Intensive Versus Extensive Labour Supply Responses', *Quarterly Journal of Economics* 117 (3): 1039-1073.

Chapter 9

Looking Ahead: What Priorities for Tax-benefit Modelling?

Herwig Immervoll / Orsolya Lelkes

1 Tax-benefit models are powerful and informative – but often underutilized

The rich chapters in this book demonstrate that micro-analytical models provide important insights for policy-makers. In the EU, tax-benefit models now exist at the European level as well as for most "old" and "new" Member States (Table 9.1 provides an overview of national models in the latter group of countries). By complementing data on real families with accurate representations of social and fiscal policy rules they show who benefits from policy packages or individual measures, and who pays for them.

These distributional effects of "who gains" and "who loses" are central for understanding both policy effectiveness and the political process that leads to the success or failure of reform initiatives. And once a need for reform has been identified, tax-benefit models are again essential for creating realistic "what-if" scenarios that are used for designing policies, for evaluating the relative merits of alternative options and for clarifying the trade-offs between different policy objectives (such as distributional fairness, work incentives and budgetary cost).

While tax-benefit models are highly complex analytical tools, the results they create can be easily related to the very tangible circumstances faced by different population groups, such as the unemployed, pensioners or working families with children. This illustrative power brings to life debates about policies that may otherwise be conducted in a highly technical and abstract fashion. Simple, but provocative results can equally evoke further debates.

Could a politician still stand up for a flat-tax reform, when confronted with the evidence that it would increase inequality and poverty, with 80% of the population being worse off (Chapter 5, analysing flat tax proposals which appeared in political debates in Hungary and Slovenia)?

But does the way such models are currently used live up to this promise of informing the policy process and making policy debates more transparent and inclusive? There have been major advances in recent years, and several examples of important and immediate inputs of model results into the policy process. On a European level, EUROMOD is regularly used by the European Observatory on the Social Situation.[1] In some countries, such as the UK, policy evaluation and costing of policy options has become a standard practice and results are often in the public domain. (Although, as mentioned in Chapter 2, this does not necessarily mean that they are taken up by the UK media.) In Estonia, tax-benefit modelling was used recently to prepare the implementation of an ecological tax reform, and to show the impact of this reform on different regions and the minority groups concentrated there. In Slovenia, flat-tax reform proposals were not successful, in part because of their adverse distributional effects uncovered by microsimulation analysis (Čok and Majcen et al., 2008).

But in some areas, the impact of models as a source for policy-relevant evidence is held back by a number of factors. For instance in Hungary, although the first model was built already back in 1995, seven years passed before the model was utilized for policy analysis. Currently, tax policy alternatives are routinely analysed by civil servants, but this information is not shared and therefore absent from the public debate. There are several other EU countries where government models cannot be used for independent analyses.

The chapter by Tony Atkinson has already highlighted a number of important areas where the potential of tax-benefit models is not being exploited to the full. Like any other research area, the feasibility and impact of microsimulation depends on a number of important external factors, such as funding institutions, data availability, and the demand for evidence that is informative but frequently politically sensitive. More specifically, the demand for evidence-based policy-making is shaped by the political culture in countries and the degree of economic literacy of commentators

1 On behalf of the European Commission, the Observatory is tasked with monitoring social and demographic trends and with analysing the underlying factors. Annual reports and research notes of the Observatory are available on http://www.socialsituation.eu/ .

Table 9.1: Overview of tax-benefit microsimulation models

Country	Model name	Model type	Funder	Constructor	Purpose	Elements of the benefit/pension system omitted	Main data source	Data size (house-holds)	Users
Czech Republic	-	Dynamic	Nat. Bank	Kamil Galuščak – Nat. Bank	Incentive effects Redistributive effects	Indirect taxes Pensions Local taxes	Mikrocenzus	8,000	MFin Nat. Bank
Cyprus	-	Static	Research Promotion Foundation	Panos Pashardes – University of Cyprus (UCY)	Incentive effects Redistributive effects	Income tax Indirect taxes Benefits	HBS	12,102	Economics Research Centre – UCY
Estonia	ESTEEM	Static	Ministry of Environment, NUIG	Silja Kralik – Ministry of Environment	Incentive effects Redistributive effects Analyse environmental tax reform (incl. spatial analysis and behavioural impact)	Pensions Local taxes and benefits	HBS, Administrative data	3,000	Min of Environment
Estonia	ALAN	Static	PRAXIS MSo	Alari Paulus and Andres Võrk – PRAXIS	Incentive effects Redistributive effects Benefit and tax reforms	Pensions Local taxes and benefits	HBS 2000-2007	3,000	PRAXIS MFin MSoc
Hungary	TÁRSZIM	Static	Mfin, Msoc PrimeMinO Nat. Bank. MinEcon MinJustice	Péter Szivós – TARKI	Incentive effects Redistributive effects	Pensions Local taxes and benefits	Pooled: Income survey HBS Tax records	8,000	MFin TARKI
Lithuania	LITSIM Under construc-tion	Static (with dynamic population projection element)	IDARI, NUIG (PhD Program)	Tatjana Stirling NUIG/DWP	Incentive effects Cross country (LT/EE) analysis Redistributive effects (incl. indirect taxation)	Indirect taxes Pensions Personal taxes and family benefits	HBS, FFS (for dynamic population projection)	8,000	University
Lithuania	(Under construc-tion)	Static	Maastricht University	Lina Salanauskaite (Maastricht University)	Redistributive (family benefit) effects	Taxes and social contributions Local taxes and benefits	EU-SILC, UDB version	4,441	Uni. Maastricht, Uni. Antwerp
Poland	SIMPL	Dynamic (labour supply)	MFin MSoc MLab	Olivier Bargain, Leszek Morawski, Michał Myck – Uni. of Warsaw	Incentive effects Redistributive effects Prepare tax reform	Indirect taxes Pensions Local taxes and benefits	HBS	32,500	MFin, MSoc MLab University
Slovenia	-	Static	MFin NRF	Mitja Čok – Uni. of Ljubljana; Boris Majcen – IER	Redistributive effects Prepare tax reform	Indirect taxes Pensions Local taxes and benefits	Administrative data	38,000	University, Institute, MFin

Notes: There is no model in Bulgaria, Latvia, Malta, Romania, and Slovakia currently (2009) according to our knowledge. The information about each model was provided by the model constructor.

Abbreviations: MFin=Ministry of Finance; MSoc=Ministry of Social Affairs (actual name varies by country); MLab= Ministry of Labour; NRF=National Research Fund; IDARI: Integrated Development of Agricultural and Rural Institutions; DWP: Department for Work and Pensions, UK; NUIG: National University of Ireland, Galway; FFS: Family Fertility Survey; IER: Institute for Economic Research.

and policy-makers. But while it is easy to list factors that inhibit the use of valuable evidence, researchers have an important role in creating demand for good evidence. The way models are constructed and used is one of the main determinants of their success. In this chapter, we reflect on what the users and builders of such models could do in order to maximize the contribution of these tools towards a more evidence-driven policy process.

2 Making the most of costly infrastructure: casting the scope of models …

The broad thematic and geographical scope of the studies presented in this volume is a powerful evidence that the modelling community anticipates and actively responds to new directions that policy debates are taking. The extension of EUROMOD to several new Member States only a few years after they have joined the EU is a remarkable achievement, notably when considering the time and resources required for building even a single national microsimulation model. The absence of an analytical tool for comparing and analysing country policies in a consistent manner has so far presented a serious, and potentially costly, obstacle to a truly EU-wide policy dialogue. A key contribution of the "enlarged" EUROMOD and the emerging network of its users consists of facilitating the mutual understanding of policy challenges and solutions. There is much to be learned from policy experiences in both "old" and "new" Member States, and from hypothetical policy experiments such as introducing a specific measure from country A in another country B.[2] The newly extended EUROMOD model provides much-needed analytical capacity in this area, especially if it continues to be extended to Member States that are not yet covered (see Chapter 3 for details on the status quo and future plans for this model).

Equally important, one may expect growing analytical – if not political – interest in the EU as a single entity, and a corresponding interest in analytical tools that operate at the EU level. For instance, when analysing the distribution of resources and economic well-being, converging living standards will make it natural to compare the situation of EU citizens not only within, but also between countries (say, in relation to a single European poverty threshold). Likewise, even with the large majority of social and fiscal policies remaining national responsibilities, important questions about

2 For informative examples of such "policy swaps" see Paulus and Peichl (2008), Bargain and Orsini (2006) and Chapter 6 in this volume.

redistribution at the EU level as a whole nevertheless arise in a number of policy contexts. One example is environmental policy (e.g. in the form of emissions trading systems), which requires co-ordination between countries in order to be effective. Finally, on a global level, the mere role of the EU as one of the major discernible groups of countries will continue to strengthen interest in social and economic indicators for the EU as a whole, including on income distribution. For all these reasons, the continuing extension of EUROMOD to cover all of the EU is highly desirable.

Beyond geographical coverage, it is the types of analyses performed with tax-benefit models that determine whether they provide useful input into particular policy debates.

Much of this is a question of model capabilities. To be sure, there is no omnipotent model, which can answer all questions. In the science fiction novel of Douglas Adams, the *"Answer to Life, the Universe, and Everything"* from the supercomputer called Deep Thought took 7½ million years to compute and the result was disappointing.[3] Tax-benefit models tend to be customized to maximize their usability for a relatively limited number of common tasks, such as costing, incidence analysis and specifying alternative policy scenarios.

While it is easy to anticipate routine tasks, other model uses are less foreseeable. It is neither reasonable nor useful to expect model developers to prepare their models for every possible use: specific models require specific expertise and very large-scale models quickly become too complex and too demanding to use or maintain. But what *is* possible is to avoid model designs that are so rigidly tied to a small set of routine tasks that they preclude their use for less common purposes from the outset.

To make the most of the substantial investment into modelling infrastructure, considerable effort should be put into making the model architecture sufficiently open and flexible to link the models to other analytical tools, such as labour supply estimations, life-course analyses or macro-economic models. Such a modular concept can be realized using a simple tax-benefit model built around a core tax-benefit calculator that is customizable and scalable and provides well-defined interfaces for linking to external modules. EUROMOD is one example of a modular model architecture, which enables different model components to be used in different country and analytical contexts.

3 The Hitchhiker's Guide to the Galaxy.

3 ... and extending the scope of model uses

Even a powerful and flexible model, however, does not guarantee that its potential capabilities are exploited. One area where population-based micro-analytical models could have a big impact, but are currently little-used, is the interface between micro- and macro-economic policy evaluation and analysis. While it is clear on a theoretical level that micro- and macro-economic phenomena are fundamentally linked, the large majority of policy-oriented empirical analyses remain confined to the strict disciplinary boundaries between the two spheres. As pointed out in Chapter 2, this separation is particularly consequential for understanding the impact of inter-personal distribution policies for macro-economic outcomes, and vice versa. For instance, the results of micro-level incidence studies of redistribution policies, which are easily aggregated to provide population-based estimates, are rarely utilized for general equilibrium analysis – and therefore fail to account for relevant feedback effects on distributional outcomes (see Peichl, 2008, for a recent contribution combining microsimulation and Computable General Equilibrium models).

Similarly, macro-level changes that take place independently of redistribution policies can have very substantial effects on the distribution of resources at the household level. This is starkly evident following the severe global economic downturn which began in late 2008. From what is known about the financial and job losses six months later, it seems relatively safe to conclude that the resulting changes in earnings and capital income may cause some of the most sudden and significant changes in the distribution of household resources in several decades. This has governments around the world searching for appropriate policy responses in order to strengthen support for the most vulnerable groups in particular.

But while there is no shortage of projections of, say, national income or unemployment levels, studies about what is likely to happen to poverty or the income distribution more generally are missing almost entirely. The study of resource distribution, in short, is still largely backward-looking. Tax-benefit models, with their underlying rich data on the household population and their detailed representation of links between household circumstances and public policy, are well-placed to inform and support policy-making by contributing forward-looking income distribution scenarios. For instance, it is technically relatively straightforward to combine unemployment projections with micro-data and tax-benefit algorithms in order to estimate short-term and medium-term consequences of mounting joblessness for income inequality and poverty. In a second step, tax-benefit models could be used to evaluate the cost and distributional effectiveness of alternative policy responses, such as adjusting unemployment insurance systems or strengthening minimum safety-nets. (Such techniques do in fact have some tradition in analyses conducted at the World Bank and others engaged in empirical work on developing countries, where rapid changes in economic fundamentals are the rule rather than the exception – see Bourguignon and Spadaro, 2006).

Like projections of GDP or labour-market performance, forward-looking scenarios of changes in resource distributions would be subject to a considerable degree of uncertainty, especially during times of rapid economic change. It is therefore essential that the results of such projection exercises are communicated and used in a responsible way that highlights their purpose and limitations. The uncertainty of projections largely reflects the real economic uncertainty that households and policy-makers are facing, however. In the face of strong pressures to come up with timely policy responses, policy-makers cannot afford to ignore information about the links between sizable economic adjustments and the well-being of families. Tax-benefit models can, and should, provide such information.

4 Sharing methods and research tools: Securing access for experts in different areas

Microsimulation models are best seen as research infrastructure. They involve a very significant investment of resources for both construction and maintenance and they potentially have a large number of users with expertise in different fields. To maximize the pay-off of investments in model infrastructure, it is essential that they are accessible to as many interested researchers and analysts as possible. Yet, a recent informal survey of models used in New Member States found the number of individual users to be between 2 and 5, and even the most optimistic estimates do not go higher than 10 users (Lelkes, 2007). As model constructors in these countries tend to be researchers external to government (in contrast to Western Europe at large, where models are commonly constructed and maintained by civil servants), most of these models are not used routinely for impact assessment.

There are of course different strategies for organizing model access and there can be legitimate commercial interests in limiting or controlling accessibility. Likewise, publicly-funded model developers may often not have the resources required to run a truly open research infrastructure, and concerns over data confidentiality may lead data providers to stipulate restrictions on access to the underlying micro-data. It seems clear, however, that the public interest is served best if model access is available for any legitimate purpose in principle. As in the case of household micro-data, broad accessibility is a prerequisite for exploiting the many opportunities that tax-benefit models offer. It also leads to constant validation of these complex models, and hence to improvements in the models themselves.

Naturally, mechanisms need to be put in place to safeguard the interests of developers and other relevant parties, including funders, providers of micro-data and individuals whose information is recorded in these data. Yet, with reliable anonymization procedures in place, concerns of data providers can be addressed in principle. The rich administrative dataset provided by the Slovenian national statistical office is an excellent example of a successful and mutually beneficial cooperation between data providers and model developers.[4] Moreover, numerous examples from the open-access software industry demonstrate that it is possible to combine open access and decentralized software development in a way that ensures the quality of the evolving product and at the same time protects the interests of its contributors.

One factor that contributes to the broad accessibility and use of microsimulation models probably includes the provision of an institutional "home" for the model. The functions of such a home institution, which may itself be shared between different institutions, may include

- acting as a point of contact for model users,
- administering access to model and data resources,
- co-ordinating and consolidating decentralized model development activities,
- facilitating training of and networking between developers and model users, and
- maintaining a central repository or "knowledge-base" of model documentation, methods and results.[5]

4 The Slovenian data (as part of EUROMOD) are used in Chapters 4 and 5.

5 See for instance the EUROMOD Working Paper series, which covers all research based on EUROMOD as well as model documentation: www.iser.essex.ac.uk/research/euromod.

In addition to supporting current access, such an arrangement secures a minimum degree of institutional memory, which is critical for securing long-term survival of the model resources and for protecting past infrastructure investments.

Most importantly, sharing the results in an appropriate form is central to maximizing the benefits of the research infrastructure. Policy evaluation and model building need to be based on scientific rigour, yet the best results are of limited use for the policy debate if they can only be found in highly technical scientific articles. A generous dissemination strategy should be designed to connect the research community to policy circles and the public in order to create a virtuous circle where good evidence stimulates demand for further policy analysis.

References

Bargain, O./Orsini, K. (2006) 'Beans for Breakfast? How Exportable is the British Workfare Model?', *Research in Labour Economics* 25: 165-198.

Bourguignon, F./Spadaro, A. (2006) *Journal of Economic Inequality* 4: 77-106.

Čok, M./Majcen, B./Verbic, M./Kosak, M. (2008) 'Use of Simulation Models for the Tax Reform in Slovenia', *Financial Theory and Practice* 32 (1): 29-43.

Lelkes, O. (2007) 'Tax-benefit Microsimulation Models in Eastern Europe', *International Journal of Microsimulation* 1 (1): 54-56.

Peichl, A. (2008) 'The Benefits of Linking CGE and Microsimulation Models: Evidence from a Flat Tax Analysis', IZA Discussion Paper No. 3715. Bonn: Institute for the Study of Labor.

Paulus, A./Peichl, A. (2008) 'Effects of Flat Tax Reforms in Western Europe on Equity and Efficiency', ISER Working Paper Series 2008-06. University of Essex.

Sutherland, H./Figari, F./Lelkes, O./Levy, H./Lietz, C./Mantovani, D./Paulus, A. (2008) 'Improving the Capacity and Usability of EUROMOD – Final Report', Euromod Working Paper EM04/08.

List of Contributors

Anthony B. Atkinson, Senior Research Fellow at Nuffield College, Oxford, UK

Mitja Čok, Associate Professor at the Faculty of Economics, University of Ljubljana, Slovenia

Francesco Figari, Senior Research Officer at the Institute for Social & Economic Research (ISER), University of Essex, UK

Péter Hegedűs, Researcher at TÁRKI Social Research Institute, Budapest, Hungary

Herwig Immervoll, Head of Employment-oriented Social Policies at the OECD in the Directorate for Employment, Labour and Social Affairs. Research Affiliations at IZA (Bonn), ISER (University of Essex) and the European Centre for Social Welfare Policy and Research, Vienna

Silja Kralik, PhD student at the National University of Galway, Ireland

Nataša Kump, Researcher at the Institute for Economic Research in Ljubljana, Slovenia

Orsolya Lelkes, Research Fellow and Economic Policy Analyst at the European Centre for Social Welfare Policy and Research, Vienna

Horacio Levy, Institute for Social & Economic Research (ISER), University of Essex, UK, Research Affiliate at the European Centre for Social Welfare Policy and Research, Vienna

Christine Lietz, Research Assistant at the Institute for Advanced Studies, Vienna, Austria

Daniela Mantovani, Lecturer at the Universitá di Modena e Reggio Emilia, Italy

Leszek Morawski, Lecturer at the Department of Economics at the University of Warsaw, Poland, and Research Associate at the Centre for Economic Analysis (CenEA)

Michał Myck, Research Associate at the German Institute for Economic Research (DIW-Berlin), Board Member of the Centre for Economic Analysis (CenEA) and International Research Fellow at the Institute for Fiscal Studies (IFS)

Panos Pashardes, Economics Research Centre and Department of Economics, University of Cyprus

Alari Paulus, Senior Research Officer at the Institute for Social & Economic Research (ISER), University of Essex, UK

Alexandros Polycarpou, Economics Research Centre, University of Cyprus

Lina Salanauskaite, PhD Researcher at Maastricht Graduate School of Governance, Maastricht University, the Netherlands

Holly Sutherland, Research Professor in the Institute for Social and Economic Research (ISER) at the University of Essex, UK, and co-ordinator of EUROMOD projects

Péter Szivós, Managing Director of TÁRKI Social Research Institute, Budapest, Hungary

Gerlinde Verbist, Senior Researcher at the Centre for Social Policy, University of Antwerp, Belgium

Andres Võrk, Research Fellow at PRAXIS Center for Policy Studies, Tallinn, Estonia

Wohlfahrtspolitik und Sozialforschung
Herausgegeben vom Europäischen Zentrum Wien
mit dem Campus Verlag, Frankfurt am Main/New York

Band 15: HOLZMANN, R., PALMER, E. (HG.) (2007)
Revolution in der Alterssicherung.
Beitragskonten auf Umlagebasis
810 S., EUR 79,-

Band 14: WALDRAUCH, H., SOHLER, K. (2004)
Migrantenorganisationen in der Großstadt.
Entstehung, Strukturen und Aktivitäten am Beispiel Wien
708 S., EUR 59,90

Band 13: ZARTLER, U., WILK, L., KRÄNZL-NAGL, R. (Hg.) (2004)
Wenn Eltern sich trennen.
Wie Kinder, Frauen und Männer Scheidung erleben
500 S., EUR 45,-

Band 12: OECD (2003)
Behindertenpolitik zwischen Beschäftigung und Versorgung.
Ein internationaler Vergleich
408 S., EUR 34,90

Band 11: KRÄNZL-NAGL, R., MIERENDORFF, J., OLK, Th. (Hg.) (2003)
Kindheit im Wohlfahrtsstaat.
Gesellschaftliche und politische Herausforderungen
474 S., EUR 34,90

Band 10: MARIN, B. (2000)
Antisemitismus ohne Antisemiten.
Autoritäre Vorurteile und Feindbilder
880 S., EUR 51,-

Band 9.1: DAVY, U. (Hg.) (2001)
Die Integration von Einwanderern.
Rechtliche Regelungen im europäischen Vergleich
1056 S., EUR 69,-

Band 9.2: WALDRAUCH, H. (2001)
Die Integration von Einwanderern.
Ein Index der rechtlichen Diskriminierung
582 S., EUR 51,-

Campus Verlag, Postfach 90 02 63, D-60442 Frankfurt am Main
Tel: (069) 97 65 16-0; Fax: (069) 97 65 16
www.campus.de, info@campus.de, vertrieb@campus.de

Public Policy and Social Welfare
A Series Edited by the European Centre Vienna with
Ashgate, Aldershot, Brookfield USA, Singapore, Sydney